Page 19 - Tea Ceremony
Page 23 - "What larger needs can our gatherings address?
"Think what you want to be different because you gathered."

- Wendy Woon-

- 12th Century Monastery S. West France
Routes to Camino de Santiago

- Marina abramvic

THE ART OF
GATHERING

THE ART OF GATHERING

How We Meet and Why It Matters

PRIYA PARKER

RIVERHEAD BOOKS
New York
2018

RIVERHEAD BOOKS
An imprint of Penguin Random House LLC
375 Hudson Street
New York, New York 10014

Copyright © 2018 by Priya Parker
Penguin supports copyright. Copyright fuels creativity, encourages diverse voices,
promotes free speech, and creates a vibrant culture. Thank you for buying an authorized edition
of this book and for complying with copyright laws by not reproducing, scanning,
or distributing any part of it in any form without permission. You are
supporting writers and allowing Penguin to continue to
publish books for every reader.

Library of Congress Cataloging-in-Publication Data

Names: Parker, Priya, author.
Title: The art of gathering: how we meet and why it matters / Priya Parker.
Description: New York: Riverhead Books, 2018.
Identifiers: LCCN 2017058605| ISBN 9781594634925 (hardback) |
ISBN 9780698410879 (ebook)
Subjects: LCSH: Self-actualization (Psychology) | Interpersonal relations. |
BISAC: SELF-HELP / Personal Growth / General. | BUSINESS & ECONOMICS /
Leadership. | PSYCHOLOGY / Interpersonal Relations.
Classification: LCC BF637.S4 P357 2018 | DDC 302/.1—dc23
LC record available at https://lccn.loc.gov/2017058605

International edition ISBN: 9780525537373

Printed in the United States of America
1 3 5 7 9 10 8 6 4 2

Book design by Amanda Dewey

For my Anand,

who shows me daily the true meaning of awing and honoring

Contents

• • •

Introduction

.   .   .

The way we gather matters. Gatherings consume our days and help determine the kind of world we live in, in both our intimate and public realms. Gathering—the conscious bringing together of people for a reason—shapes the way we think, feel, and make sense of our world. Lawgivers have understood, perhaps as well as anyone, the power inherent in gatherings. In democracies, the freedom to assemble is one of the foundational rights granted to every individual. In countries descending into authoritarianism, one of the first things to go is the right to assemble. Why? Because of what can happen when people come together, exchange information, inspire one another, test out new ways of being together. And yet most of us spend very little time thinking about the actual ways in which we gather.

We spend our lives gathering—first in our families, then in neighborhoods and playgroups, schools and churches, and then in meetings, weddings, town halls, conferences, birthday parties, product launches, board meetings, class and family reunions, dinner parties, trade fairs, and funerals. And we spend much of that time in uninspiring, underwhelming moments that fail to capture us, change us in any way, or connect us to one another.

Any number of studies support a notion that's obvious to many of us: Much of the time we spend in gatherings with other people disappoints us. "With the occasional exception, my mood in conferences usually swings between boredom, despair, and rage," Duncan Green, a blogger and specialist in international development, confesses in the *Guardian*. Green's take isn't unique to conferences: The 2015 *State of Enterprise Work* survey found that "wasteful meetings" were employees' top obstacle to getting work done.

We don't even seem to be thrilled with the time we spend with our friends. A 2013 study, *The State of Friendship in America 2013: A Crisis of Confidence*, found that 75 percent of respondents were unsatisfied with those relationships. Meanwhile, in *How We Gather*, a recent report on the spiritual life of young people, Angie Thurston and Casper ter Kuile write, "As traditional religion struggles to attract young people, millennials are looking elsewhere with increasing urgency."

As much as our gatherings disappoint us, though, we tend to keep gathering in the same tired ways. Most of us remain on autopilot when we bring people together, following stale formulas, hoping that the chemistry of a good meeting, conference, or party will somehow take care of itself, that thrilling results will magically emerge from the usual staid inputs. It is almost always a vain hope.

When we do seek out gathering advice, we almost always turn to those who are focused on the mechanics of gathering: chefs, etiquette experts, floral artists, event planners. By doing so, we inadvertently shrink a human challenge down to a logistical one. We reduce the question of what to do with people to a question of what to do about things: PowerPoints, invitations, AV equipment, cutlery, refreshments. We are tempted to focus on the "stuff" of gatherings because we believe those are the only details we can control. I believe that's both shortsighted and a misunderstanding about what actually makes a group connect and a gathering matter.

I come to gatherings not as a chef or an event planner, but as someone trained in group dialogue and conflict resolution. I've spent much of the past fifteen years of my life studying, designing, and advising gatherings whose goals were to be transformative for the people involved and the communities they were trying to affect. Today I work as a professional facilitator. Though there are many of us around, you may have never heard of us. A facilitator is someone trained in the skill of shaping group dynamics and collective conversations. My job is to put the right people in a room and help them to collectively think, dream, argue, heal, envision, trust, and connect for a specific larger purpose. My lens on gathering—and the lens I want to share with you—places people and what happens between them at the center of every coming together.

In my work, I strive to help people experience a sense of belonging. This probably has something to do with the fact that I have spent my own life trying to figure out where and to whom *I* belong. I come on my mother's side from Indian cow worshippers in Varanasi, an ancient city known as the spiritual center of India, and on my father's side from American cow slaughterers in South Dakota. To cut a very long story short, my parents met in Iowa, fell in love, married, had me in Zimbabwe, worked in fishing villages across Africa and Asia, fell out of love, divorced in Virginia, and went their separate ways. Both of them went on to remarry, finding spouses more of their own world and worldview. After the divorce, I moved every two weeks between my mother's and father's households—toggling back and forth between a vegetarian, liberal, incense-filled, Buddhist-Hindu-New Age universe and a meat-eating, conservative, twice-a-week-churchgoing, evangelical Christian realm. So it was perhaps inevitable that I ended up in the field of conflict resolution.

I discovered that field in college when I became interested in, and anguished by, the state of race relations at the University of Virginia. Upon graduating, I worked in communities—in the United States and abroad—to train leaders in a group dialogue process called Sustained Dialogue. It is a gathering technique that aims to transform fractured relationships across racial, ethnic, and religious lines. Through that work, I became fascinated with what occurs when people attempt to come together across difference.

In the years since, I have applied the methods of conflict resolution in a variety of settings and to a great variety of problems. I've run meetings in five-star hotels, in public parks, on dirt floors, and in college dorm rooms. I've led sessions with villagers in western India grappling with how to rebuild their community after ethnic riots and with Zimbabwean activists fighting the threat of a government shutdown of their NGOs. I've worked on dialogues between Arab opposition leaders and their European and American counterparts to explore the relationship between Islam and democracy. I've designed gatherings for state and federal officials in the United States to figure out how to revitalize a national poverty program for a new generation. I've facilitated gatherings for technology companies, architecture firms, beauty brands, and financial institutions, helping them hold complicated, difficult discussions about their future.

I live in New York City, where people gather a lot. I am often a host and often a guest, and in both roles I am endlessly intrigued by the small and important interventions we can all make to help groups gel. Among my friends and relatives, I am the person people text or call with questions like "Should my work dinner have a guided conversation around a question, or should we just let people chat?" and "How should we handle the one blabbermouth church volunteer?" How, a half-Muslim, half-Christian immigrant friend asked me, might she come up with her own version of a Jewish shiva to mark the death of her father in Germany with friends in New York who never knew him?

In all my gatherings, whether a board meeting or a birthday party, I have come to believe that it is the *way* a group is gathered that determines what happens in it and how successful it is, the little design choices you can make to help your gathering soar. So *The Art of Gathering* is part journey and part guidebook. It is for anyone who has ever wondered how to take an ordinary moment with others and make it unforgettable—and meaningful.

My hope is that this book will help you *think* differently about your gatherings. I have organized the chapters to reflect the sequence that I walk my clients and friends through, and that I employ myself, when designing a meaningful event. Though there are certainly some principles that I believe apply to even the simplest of gatherings, you need not follow every suggestion or step in this book. You are the best person to decide what will be helpful for you and what makes sense in the context of your gatherings.

This book is based on my own experience and ideas, both what I know has worked and what I know hasn't. Yet because gathering is inherently a collective endeavor, I've also interviewed more than one hundred other gatherers to learn their secrets and test my own ideas. My conversations with conference organizers, event planners, circus choreographers, Quaker meeting clerks, camp counselors, funeral directors, DJs, auctioneers, competitive wingsuit flying-formation instructors, rabbis, coaches, choir conductors, performance artists, comedians, game designers, Japanese tea ceremony masters, TV directors, professional photographers, family wealth advisers, and fundraisers have all informed the ideas here. I intentionally draw from a wide variety of gatherings—museums, classrooms, partner meetings, birthday parties, summer camps, and even funerals—to illustrate the creativity that people use regardless of the context, and I hope it inspires you to do the same. All the stories that follow are true, though I have changed some identifying names, details, and locations of events and people for private gatherings. Among the variety of people I spoke with, they all shared one crucial trait: a fascination with what *happens* when people come together.

As I send you off into these pages, let me declare my bias up front:

I believe that everyone has the ability to gather well.

You don't have to be an extrovert. In fact, some of the best gatherers I know suffer from social anxiety.

You don't need to be a boss or a manager.

You don't need a fancy house.

The art of gathering, fortunately, doesn't rest on your charisma or the quality of your jokes. (I would be in trouble if it did.)

Gatherings crackle and flourish when real thought goes into them, when (often invisible) structure is baked into them, and when a host has the curiosity, willingness, and generosity of spirit to try.

Let's begin.

THE ART OF
GATHERING

One

Decide Why You're *Really* Gathering

• • •

Why do we gather?

We gather to solve problems we can't solve on our own. We gather to celebrate, to mourn, and to mark transitions. We gather to make decisions. We gather because we need one another. We gather to show strength. We gather to honor and acknowledge. We gather to build companies and schools and neighborhoods. We gather to welcome, and we gather to say goodbye.

But here is the great paradox of gathering: There are so many good reasons for coming together that often we don't know precisely why we are doing so. You are not alone if you skip the first step in convening people meaningfully: committing to a bold, sharp purpose.

When we skip this step, we often let old or faulty assumptions about why we gather dictate the form of our gatherings. We end up gathering in ways that don't serve us, or not connecting when we ought to.

In our offices, we spend our days in back-to-back meetings, many of which could be replaced with an email or a ten-minute stand-up meeting. In college, we stare at the floor in lecture halls, when the same facts would be better conveyed via video and the professor's time would be better spent coaching students on specific difficulties with the material. In the nonprofit world, it is customary to throw galas for causes because that is what nonprofits do, even if they don't raise much more than they cost.

And yet at moments when we could benefit from gathering—to determine how to make a neighborhood park safe again, to strategize with a friend and think through ways to help her struggling career, to rebuild focus after a particularly brutal sales cycle—we don't think to gather, or are too busy to, or, in the modern way, we don't want to ask people for their time. So widespread is this desire not to impose that a growing number of people report not wanting any funeral at all when they die.

In short, our thinking about gathering—when we gather and why—has become muddled. When we do gather, we too often use a template of gathering (what we assume a gathering should look like) to substitute for our thinking. The art of gathering begins with purpose: When should we gather? And why?

A CATEGORY IS NOT A PURPOSE

Think back to the last several gatherings you hosted or attended. A networking event. A book club. A volunteer training. If I were to ask you (or your host) the purpose behind each of those gatherings, I wouldn't be surprised to hear what I often do in my work: what you were supposed to *do* at the gathering.

That networking night, you might tell me, was intended to help people in similar fields meet one another.

The book club was organized to get us to read a book together.

The volunteer training was arranged to train the volunteers.

The purpose of your church's small group was to allow church members to meet in smaller groups.

This is the circular logic that guides the planning of many of our gatherings.

"What's wrong with that?" you might say. Isn't the purpose of a networking night to network? Yes, to a point. But if that's all it is, it will likely proceed like so many other networking nights: people wandering around and awkwardly passing out their business cards, practicing their elevator pitches on anyone with a pulse who'll listen. It will likely not dazzle anyone. It may even make some guests feel awkward or insecure—and swear off future networking nights.

When we don't examine the deeper assumptions behind *why* we gather, we end up skipping too quickly to replicating old, staid formats of gathering. And we forgo the possibility of creating something memorable, even transformative.

For example, in planning that networking night, what if the organizers paused to ask questions like these: Is our purpose for this gathering to help people find business partners or clients? Is the purpose to help guests sell their wares or to get advice on the weaker parts of their product? Is the purpose of the night to help as many people from different fields make as many new connections as possible, or to build a tribe that would want to meet again?

The answers to these questions should lead to very different formats of an evening.

When we gather, we often make the mistake of conflating category with purpose. We outsource our decisions and our assumptions about our gatherings to people, formats, and contexts that are not our own. We get lulled into the false belief that knowing the category of the gathering—the board meeting, workshop, birthday party, town hall—will be instructive to designing it. But we often choose the template—and the activities and structure that go along with it—before we're clear on our purpose. And we do this just as much for gatherings that are as low stakes as a networking night as for gatherings that are as high stakes as a court trial.

The Red Hook Community Justice Center, located in Brooklyn, New York, set out to reimagine one of the more intimidating gatherings in public life: the court proceeding. Founded in 2000, in the wake of a crisis, in a neighborhood struggling with poverty and crime, the center wanted to change the relationship between the community and law enforcement. Its founders wondered if it was possible to invent a new kind of justice system that would cure the ailments that a crime revealed instead of just locking up criminals.

The judge who would come to preside over Red Hook's experiment, Alex Calabrese, once described himself as having two options under the traditional justice system: "It was either prosecute or dismiss." Even judges who recognized the problems with the system didn't have much freedom to break out of this paradigm. And so a small group of organizers concluded that, in order to change how the justice system functioned in Red Hook, they would need to invent a new kind of gathering. To do so, they would have to ask themselves a basic question: What is the purpose of the justice system we want to see? And what would a court look like if it were built according to that purpose?

A traditional courtroom is adversarial. That is a design that derives from its own very worthy purpose: surfacing the truth by letting the parties haggle over it. But the organizers behind the Red Hook Community Justice Center were motivated by a different purpose. Would it be possible to use a courtroom to get everyone involved in a case—the accused, judges, lawyers, clerks, social workers, community members—to help improve behavior instead of merely punish it? "We take a problem-solving approach to the cases that come before us," said Amanda Berman, the Justice Center's project director and a former public defender in the Bronx. "When we're presented with a case—whether it's a housing-court case, a criminal-court case, or a family-court case—the question we are asking at the end of the day is, what is the problem, and how can we work together to come to a solution?"

This new purpose required the design of a new kind of courtroom. A traditional courtroom, built for surfacing the truth adversarially, was constructed to make the judge seem intimidating. It separated the prosecutors from the defense counsel. It featured grim-faced jailers and sympathetic social workers and psychologists. Everyone had their role. Even the décor reinforced the purpose. "Traditional courtrooms often utilize dark woods, conveying a message of gravity, judgment, and power," Berman said.

The experimental courtroom in Red Hook was created along very different lines. Set up in an abandoned parochial school in the heart of the neighborhood, the court has windows to let the sun in, light-colored wood, and an unusual judge's bench. "The planners chose to build the bench at eye level so that the judge could have these personal interactions with litigants coming before him, invite them up to the bench, which he loves to do, so that people could see that he is not looking down on them, both literally and figuratively," Berman said.

Calabrese is the judge. His experimental courtroom has jurisdiction over three police precincts that used to send cases to three different courts—civil court, family court, and criminal court—and now sends many to Calabrese. He personally presides over every case that comes in, taking the time to get to know its history and players. In many cases, a defendant is assigned a social worker, who does a full clinical assessment of the accused to figure out the bigger picture of his or her life. This holistic assessment—which can take place even prior to the initial court appearance—includes looking for substance abuse, mental health issues, trauma, domestic violence, and other factors. This assessment is then shared with the judge, the district attorney, and the defense. At the proceeding itself, Calabrese behaves more like a strict, caring uncle than a traditional judge. He verifies the details of the case and checks errors in front of the defendants. He takes the time to address each individual personally, often shaking their hand as they approach the bench. He explains their situation to them carefully: "The fine print says if you don't come through, they will come and evict you, and no one wants to see that happen, so I've written '12/30' in big numbers on the top of the page." You have the sense that the people here are rooting for defendants and litigants to get their lives in order. It's not uncommon for Calabrese to praise a defendant who has shown progress. "Obviously, this is a good result for you. It's also a great result for the community, and I'd like to give you a round of applause," he might say. And then you see everyone, even the police officers, applauding.

Under the rules of this special court, Judge Calabrese has available to him a diverse toolkit of possible interventions. In addition to traditional prison time, which he metes out when need be, he has the ability to evaluate each individual defendant and, based on both the clinical assessment and his own judgment of the situation, assign community service, drug treatment, mental health services, trauma counseling, family mediation, and so on. Still, sometimes he concludes that jail is the only option. "We give them every reasonable chance, plus two. So when I do have to send them to jail, it tends to be for twice as long as they might ordinarily get," Calabrese told *The New York Times*.

The Justice Center is starting to see some tangible results. According to independent evaluators, it reduced the recidivism rate of adult defendants by 10 percent and of juvenile defendants by 20 percent. Only 1 percent of the cases processed by the Justice Center result in jail at arraignment. "I have been in the justice system for twenty years," Calabrese says in a documentary film about the center, "and I finally feel that I have a chance to really get to the problem that causes the person to come in front of me." The Justice Center team has been able to do this because they figured out the larger purpose of why they wanted to gather: they wanted to solve the community's problems—together. And they built a proceeding around that.

Like all repeated gatherings, the Justice Center is a work in progress. The participants, Berman said, are constantly "making sure that we are remaining true to our mission. This is supposed to be a laboratory and a model. It's supposed to be a different way of doing things. And a better way of doing things."

Thinking of the place as a laboratory frees the people at the Justice Center to be great gatherers. "There are no lines in our head about how we should gather or what it needs to look like," Berman told me. "Every case and every client is looked at individually." This attitude allows them to separate their assumptions of what a court proceeding *should* look like from what a proceeding *could* look like. We can use the same mindset to begin reexamining our own purposes for gathering.

And it's not just in public gatherings like courtrooms where we follow traditional formats of gathering unquestioningly. A category can masquerade as a purpose just as easily, if not more so, in our personal gatherings, particularly those that have become ritualized over time. Thanks to ancient traditions and modern Pinterest boards, it's easy to overlook the step of choosing a vivid purpose for your personal gathering. Just as many of us assume we know what a trial is for, so we think we know what a birthday party is for, or what a wedding is for, or even what a dinner party is for. And so our personal gatherings tend not to serve the purposes that they could. When you skip asking yourself what the purpose of your birthday party is in *this* specific year, for where you are at this present moment in your life, for example, you forsake an opportunity for your gathering to be a source of growth, support, guidance, and inspiration tailored to the time in which you and others find yourselves. You squander a chance for your gathering to help, and not just amuse, you and others. Looking back, that's what I did when I barred my husband from my baby shower.

We were expecting our first child. My girlfriends offered to throw a shower for me. Like most people, we didn't spend any time thinking about why we were having a baby shower. It wasn't the first one we'd had in our circle of friends, and it wouldn't be the last. It was almost becoming a routine—that great enemy of meaningful gathering.

And so, with a date agreed on, my girlfriends went straight into logistics.

I was excited. The problem was, my husband was, too. When I told him about the shower, he asked if he could come.

I thought he was pulling my leg. Then I realized he was serious. He really wanted to attend my baby shower.

At first I thought it made no sense. But in time I wondered if he had a point.

I always value a circle of women in my life, but that wasn't my highest need in this case. If I had thought about my gathering need more deeply at that moment, it probably would have been something about preparing both my husband and me for our new roles and the new chapter of our marriage as we welcomed our first child. I was becoming a mother. Anand was becoming a father. But we were also, as our doctor pointed out, transforming from a couple to a family. If I had been more thoughtful about it, I would have sought out a gathering that helped us make that weighty transition. But the structure and ritual of most baby showers—women-only, playing games, opening presents, making something crafty for the baby—were based on a different purpose. Traditional baby showers, I realized, were rituals for expecting mothers and a collective way to help a couple defray the costs of tending to a new life. The assumed format of this ritual—women gathering around women—reflected an era when the only person who really needed to prepare for parenting and a new transformative identity was the mother. But what should a baby shower look like when the purpose it was designed around no longer reflects the assumptions or realities of the people it's technically for? (Should it even be called a "baby shower"?)

Baby showers aren't the only form of ritualized gathering that suffers from a purpose problem. Many of the ritualized gatherings in our more intimate spheres—weddings, bar mitzvahs, graduation ceremonies—have been repeated over time such that we become emotionally attached to the form long after it accurately reflects the values or belief systems of the people participating in it.

Today in India, for example, one such clash is arising over the structure and content of marriage rites within the gathering of the traditional Hindu wedding. In the traditional format, the rites end with a man and woman taking seven steps around a fire, at each step saying a vow to each other. These *pheras*, or rounds, are visually striking and, for many Hindu families, steeped in meaning and tradition. It's often the photograph plastered on living room walls that children grow up staring at and imagining for their own weddings one day. But some younger couples are beginning to feel that the actual spoken words of the vows depict an outdated view of marriage: The man directs his wife in the first vow to "offer him food"; the bride agrees to be "responsible for the home and all household responsibilities"; only the bride vows to "remain chaste," with no such requirement made of the man; four of the groom's seven vows relate to children, but all of the bride's vows relate to the groom; and so on. The underlying assumptions of the vows describe an ideal of marriage that many no longer want. But when they suggest changing the ritual, to better reflect their actual values, the parents are shocked, and often deeply hurt, seeing it as a rejection of their traditions. The form itself has come to carry power, because of the repetition through generations, even when it no longer serves the ostensible purpose of the wedding for *this* couple.

Ritualized gatherings are hardly confined to the intimate

realms of baby showers and weddings. They affect our institutions equally. Of course, ritualized gatherings are never ritualized at the beginning. The initial idea emerges to solve a specific challenge. We need to find a way for the public to understand the differences between the candidates' positions. We need to find a way to get our sales team excited about a new product. We need to find a way to raise money for a new community center in the neighborhood. A structure is designed to bring people together around that need. Then that gathering—say, a presidential debate or a sales conference or a gala fundraiser—gets repeated again and again, year after year, and often the elements of the gathering become ritualized. That is to say, people begin to attach meaning not just to the meeting's purpose but also to the meeting's *form*. A specific gavel is always used. A certain turtleneck is always worn. People come to expect these elements of form and even take comfort in them. Over time, the form itself plays a role in shaping people's sense of belonging to the group and their identity within that group: *This is who we are. This is the way we do things around here.*

This attachment can be powerful when the form matches the purpose and need of the group. But as with the case of the courtroom, when the need begins to shift and the format is solving for an outdated purpose, we can hold on to the forms of our gatherings to the detriment of our needs.

When Dean Baquet took over as the executive editor of *The New York Times* in May 2014, he inherited an almost seventy-year-old gathering that no longer fit the needs of the newsroom or of readers. The "Page One" meeting at the *Times* was one of the most consequential meetings on earth. First conceived in 1946, it had evolved into the gathering where editors decided which articles would make the next day's front page. These choices helped to set the news agenda for the world.

In the meeting's heyday, its purpose was clear, and its format and structure logically derived from that purpose. The meeting was actually in two parts: a 10 a.m. session and a 4 p.m. session, after which the leadership would reveal "the lineup" of articles for the next day. For years, it took place at the *Times* building in a third-floor conference room around a massive wooden King Arthur–style table, with twenty-five or thirty editors packed into the room. Editors pitched their lead articles, called "offers," making their cases for pieces they thought belonged on A1.

"The desks would come with their best stories and offer them to the Olympic gods, and then would be grilled, and battle it out to see what would make it," one editor recalled to me.

As the meeting was repeated decade after decade, it gained the quality of a ritual. It was a badge of honor to participate in it. It became a rite of passage for young editors. When new reporters joined the *Times*, they would often be invited to sit in the meeting as part of their orientation. "The 4 p.m. meeting became the stuff of lore," Kyle Massey, a *Times* editor, has written.

By the time Baquet arrived, however, it no longer necessarily made sense to organize the most important meeting at the *Times* around the print front page. The majority of readers accessed articles online rather than through the physical edition. The home page and the print front page were entirely different animals; the former might feature dozens of different stories throughout the day. And according to an internal 2014 report on innovation at the paper, the home page's "impact is waning" as "only a third of our readers ever visit it." More and more readers were accessing online articles through social networks, drastically reducing the curatorial power of the editors. Besides, by the time the front page of the physical newspaper reached subscribers' doorsteps, the article would have spent hours or even days online.

The *Times* needed to adapt to the new realities of the digital age, and changing its anachronistic meeting was a way to reflect a commitment to change—and to help spur it. "It was no longer good for our readers to focus so much on print. But it was also bad for the journalists," Sam Dolnick, an assistant editor on the newspaper's masthead, told me. "We changed the meeting as a deliberate way to change the culture and values of the newsroom. We wanted people to think less about print, so we needed the meeting to be less about print. We used the meeting as a way to shift the values and the mindset" of the newsroom.

Changing how the editors gathered—what they talked about, how much time was devoted to what, who got airtime—offered a way to nudge the culture of the newsroom toward new digital re-alities. Baquet wanted the morning meeting to become a place for discussion about how *Times* reporters and editors should be cov-ering the news that day, across all platforms. He hoped for practi-cal discussion as well as time for larger philosophical debates.

"To my mind, in the ideal world, the meeting should be where we surface the stories we really have to focus on for the day, and sometimes that's obvious, like when you have a terror attack downtown, and sometimes it's less obvious," Baquet told me. He also wanted to shift the newsroom's focus toward the content of the stories and away from their placement. "It should be plat-form-free. It's just, what are our best stories?" he said.

And so Baquet changed the structure of the meeting to match a new purpose. He changed the venue and physical environment of the meeting. The storied King Arthur–style table was removed, and plans were made to construct a new Page One meeting room with glass walls and red couches—a more relaxed environment to facilitate a broader discussion about the news. The day I attended a meeting, in the fall of 2017, it was still in transition. The new room was still under construction, and the meeting was held in a temporary conference room on the second floor with a large square table in the center and a dozen green swivel chairs around it. The top editors all sat in a row on one side, with editors from the various desks seated on the other three sides. The Washington bureau chief had dialed in on speakerphone. There was a second row of chairs lining the walls for other staff and their guests. A flat-screen TV was fixed to the wall opposite the leadership and set to the *Times* home page, which would refresh to show the changing interface every few minutes.

Baquet also shifted the timing of the meetings. In an ever more rapid news world, 10 a.m. had become too late for a morning meeting, so he moved the meeting time to 9:30 a.m. He split the afternoon meeting into two meetings: a 3:30 p.m. meeting with a much smaller group to decide what goes on the front page of the print paper and then a 4 p.m. meeting to look at the next day's coverage.

As he transformed the hallowed meeting, he communicated his reasons for doing so to the entire newsroom. He understood he was changing things that people had grown accustomed to. In an email to his staff on May 5, 2015, he wrote, "The idea is for us to mobilize faster in the morning so we can get an earlier start on setting news and enterprise priorities, and to move the discussion of print Page One out of the afternoon meeting in order to focus on coverage regardless of where it appears, as well as to plan our digital report for the following morning."

But changing the timing and setting would not have been enough to uproot the values inculcated by the old gathering format. The meeting would also have to be run differently. Whereas the meeting used to begin with pitches, on the morning I was there it began with an audience report on the number of views certain stories had attracted the night before and other audience statistics. To start with a focus on what readers rather than editors thought signaled a major change in *New York Times* culture. Editors of various desks were asked to share what they were working on. As they did, those on the masthead and a smattering of others would ask specific questions about a piece and what the focus would be.

These questions began to reveal a new *New York Times* in the making. A piece on a new tax proposal drew this question: "One of the things I think a lot of readers want to know is: What does this mean for the rich?" At one point, there was a debate about whether a certain article about a new health study merited a mobile news alert, which signals breaking news and goes out to all *Times* subscribers. Behind the specific query was one of those larger philosophical questions: What merits the "breaking news" label? At one point, the editor in charge of digital asked why a certain piece, if it was ready, couldn't be published now rather than waiting for 3 p.m., when it was scheduled. In asking that question, he was pushing his editors to think differently about when a piece goes live.

"We want to get people focusing on what the experience of *The New York Times* is right now, or in the next two hours, on their phone," Clifford Levy, the deputy managing editor who oversees all digital platforms, told me. "I think there's still a bit of people planning things out, which is great, but the here and now is just so super-important, and changing that metabolism in the newsroom has been our long-term project." While that metabolism doesn't change overnight, daily gatherings are a powerful tool for adjusting it.

The meeting is still very much a work in progress, however. After all, people still informally call it the Page One meeting.

Perhaps you, too, have new needs and realities that don't fit into the templates of gathering that you know. Perhaps you go with the flow of the old templates, hoping things will work themselves out. There is nothing terrible about going with that flow, about organizing a monthly staff meeting whose purpose is to go through the same motions as every monthly staff meeting before it. But when you do, you are borrowing from gatherings and formats that others came up with to help solve their problems. To come up with the formats they did, they must have reflected on their needs and purposes. If you don't do the same and think of yourself as a laboratory, the way the Red Hook Community Justice Center and *The New York Times* have done, your gathering has less chance of being the most it can be.

COMMIT TO A GATHERING ABOUT *SOMETHING*

The television show *Seinfeld* was, famously, a "show about nothing." When people come together without any thought to their purpose, they create gatherings about nothing. Yet many people sense this without being told, and they lay the foundation of a meaningful gathering by making the gathering about *something*. I want to challenge you to follow their example—but to go further and deeper.

Most purposes for gatherings feel worthy and respectable but are also basic and bland: "We're hosting a welcome dinner so that our new colleague feels comfortable in our tight-knit group," or "I'm throwing a birthday party to look back on the year." These are purposes, but they fail at the test for a meaningful reason for coming together: Does it stick its neck out a little bit? Does it take a stand? Is it willing to unsettle some of the guests (or maybe the host)? Does it refuse to be everything to everyone?

These may seem like unreasonable criteria for a meeting or poker night or conference. You may well ask, Why does my gathering have to "take a stand"? It's not the Battle of the Alamo. I have heard this question before. Virtually every time I push my clients to go deeper with their gathering's purpose, there is a moment when they seem to wonder if I am preparing them for World War III. Yet forcing yourself to think about your gathering as stand-taking helps you get clear on its unique purpose. Gatherings that please everyone occur, but they rarely thrill. Gatherings that are willing to be alienating—which is different from *being* alienating—have a better chance to dazzle.

How do you do this? How do you arrive at a *something* worth gathering about? What are the ingredients for a sharp, bold, meaningful gathering purpose?

Specificity is a crucial ingredient. The more focused and particular a gathering is, the more narrowly it frames itself and the more passion it arouses. I have discovered this anecdotally through my own work, but one of my clients has collected the data to back it up.

Meetup is an online platform for creating offline gatherings. People use Meetup to coordinate thousands of in-person meetings around the world for a range of purposes. Over the years, the company has helped millions of people gather. When its founders began to study what made for a successful group, a surprising observation came to light. It wasn't always the big-tent groups, being everything to everyone, that most attracted people. It was often the groups that were narrower and more specific. "The more specific the Meetup, the more likelihood for success," Scott Heiferman, its cofounder and CEO, told me.

To organize a group on the Meetup platform, one of the steps you have to take is to give your group a name and write a description about what the group is for. To increase the likelihood of success, Heiferman and his team started to encourage organizers to put more specificity in the title of the group, not just in the description. The tactic "makes it more visible and clear, and it's exciting to find something that is specific that fits you," he said. When an organizer in Istanbul or London or Toledo writes a group name, the more adjectives she uses to describe the group, the more likely the group will have what Meetup calls "tightness of fit."

For example, "LGBT couples hiking with dogs" would have a tighter fit (and presumably be more successful over time) than "LGBT couples hiking" or "couples hiking with dogs" or even "LGBT hikers with dogs." Because, as Heiferman explains, "the who is often tied to the what." Specificity sharpens the gathering because people can see themselves in it.

However, "if you get really specific, then there won't be enough people, so there's that balance between being not too tight of a fit and not too loose of a fit to draw out a sense of togetherness and identity and welcomeness and belonging."

Uniqueness is another ingredient. How is this meeting or dinner or conference unique among the other meetings, dinners, and conferences you will host this year? I once visited a teahouse in Kyoto, Japan, where I participated in a traditional Japanese tea ceremony to learn from their wisdom on gatherings. The tea master there told me of a phrase the sixteenth-century Japanese tea master Sen no Rikyū taught his students to keep in the front of their minds as they conduct the ceremony: *Ichi-go ichi-e.* The master told me it roughly translates to "one meeting, one moment in your life that will never happen again." She explained further: "We could meet again, but you have to praise this moment because in one year, we'll have a new experience, and we will be different people and will be bringing new experiences with us, because we are also changed." Each gathering is *ichi-go ichi-e.* And it can help to keep that in the forefront of our minds as we gather.

I sometimes think of this as the Passover Principle, because of a question that is ritually asked at the traditional Jewish seder on that holy day: "Why is this night different from all other nights?" Before you gather, ask yourself: Why is this gathering different from all my other gatherings? Why is it different from other people's gatherings of the same general type? What is this that other gatherings aren't?

A good gathering purpose should also be disputable. If you say the purpose of your wedding is to celebrate love, you may bring a smile to people's faces, but you aren't really committing to anything, because who would dispute that purpose? Yes, a wedding should celebrate love. But an indisputable purpose like that doesn't help you with the hard work of creating a meaningful gathering, because it won't help you make decisions. When the inevitable tensions arise—guest list, venue, one night versus two—your purpose won't be there to guide you. A disputable purpose, on the other hand, begins to be a decision filter. If you commit to a purpose of your wedding as a ceremonial repayment of your parents for all they have done for you as you set off to build your own family, that is disputable, and it will immediately help you make choices. That one remaining seat will go to your parents' long-lost friend, not your estranged college buddy. If, on the other hand, you commit to the equally valid purpose of a wedding as a melding of a new couple with the tribe of people with whom they feel the most open, that, too, is disputable, and it implies clear and different answers. The parents' friend may have to stand down for the college buddy.

If I had applied these criteria to my own baby shower, here's how it might have gone. If I had sought out a more specific purpose than celebrating the coming of a baby, I might have settled on the idea that my husband and I were setting out to do something for which there was little precedent: to parent equally. Because of the rarity of the practice until recently, there isn't much wisdom or folklore about how to make it work. Instead, there are articles warning of how hard it is to "have it all" and studies informing us about how treacherous equality can be for intimacy. A more specific purpose suited to our needs might have helped us navigate these relatively uncharted waters.

As for uniqueness, what might have made the shower different from many others' showers was the equal participation of the father and other male guests in the ceremony.

And it is disputable that a baby shower should include a man, and, what is more, be reorganized around his and potentially other men's presence. Disputable in a good way. We wished to be witnessed in our community as a couple parenting in full and actual equality, not as a mom raising a child with a dad who "helps." This is a disputable way of life, and a shower designed to help us get there would have had a disputable purpose. Similarly, in the Red Hook community court, it is disputable that people involved in the justice system all want the same thing. In a Hindu wedding ceremony, it is disputable that you can change the words of the vows and still have it be a "Hindu wedding ceremony." Again, disputable in a good way. There are certainly people who think that by changing the vows, you are cutting from tradition, not honoring it. Similarly, at *The New York Times*, there were certainly, at least for a time, journalists and editors who did not think that digital should be elevated above print. Each of these gatherings' purposes were disputable—and that's why, in part, they had energy behind them.

SOME PRACTICAL TIPS ON CRAFTING YOUR PURPOSE

When clients or friends are struggling to determine their gathering's purpose, I tell them to move from the *what* to the *why*. Here are some strategies that help them do so.

Zoom out: If she doesn't zoom out, a chemistry teacher might tell herself that her purpose is to teach chemistry. While teaching is a noble undertaking, this definition does not give her much guidance on how to actually design her classroom experience. If, instead, she decides that her purpose is to give the young a life-long relationship to the organic world, new possibilities emerge. The first step to a more scintillating classroom begins with that zooming out.

Drill, baby, drill: Take the reasons you think you are gathering—because it's our departmental Monday-morning meeting; because it's a family tradition to barbecue at the lake—and keep drilling below them. Ask why you're doing it. Every time you get to another, deeper reason, ask why again. Keep asking why until you hit a belief or value.

Let's look at how we might move from the what to the why of something as simple as a neighborhood potluck:

Why are you having a neighborhood potluck?

Because we like potlucks, and we have one every year.

Why do you have one every year?

Because we like to get our neighbors together at the beginning of the summer.

Why do you like to get your neighbors together at the beginning of the summer?

I guess, if you really think about it, it's a way of marking the time and reconnecting after the hectic school year.

Aha.

And why is that important?

Because when we have more time in the summer to be together, it's when we remember what community is, and it helps us forge the bonds that make this a great place to live. *Aha.* And safer. *Aha.* And a place that embodies the values we want our children to grow up with, like that strangers aren't scary. *Aha.* Now we're getting somewhere.

Sometimes asking why means helping people drill until they find an insight that will help them design the gathering itself. I was once advising a publicist who was hosting a book event. I asked what the purpose of the event was for her—what she wanted out of it. And she said something to the effect of "To make it the best book of the fall." If we had stopped there, it wouldn't have given her any guidance on how to design the book event. Nor, frankly, was it an inspiring reason to people outside that publisher. So we kept digging. Why do you think this book deserves to be the best book of the fall? Why does this book matter so much to you? She thought about it for a second and lit up, and said something like "Because it's a powerful rendering of how a story can completely change based on whose perspective it is." *Aha.* That was both meaningful and an insight she could begin to design an event around.

Ask not what your country can do for your gathering, but what your gathering can do for your country: I often press my clients and friends to think about what larger needs in the world their gathering might address. What problem might it help solve? Again, this may sound like too much to ask for a chamber of commerce or a church group. But if you think the problem of your country is that people from disparate tribes no longer know one another or communicate honestly with one another, that kind of insight and theory of the case can translate very plainly into a purpose of using your gathering to collide different tribes.

Reverse engineer an outcome: Think of what you want to be different because you gathered, and work backward from that outcome. That is the formula of Mamie Kanfer Stewart and Tai Tsao, who set out some years ago to improve the work meeting. Stewart grew up working in her family enterprise—which is behind the hand sanitizer Purell. The meetings she attended, Stewart told me, were "the absolute best part of the day." It was only when she set out into the world and discovered other companies' meetings that she realized how awful most of them are. That inspired her to study meeting behavior and how to fix it, and led her to start a business called Meeteor to help companies meet better.

Stewart and Tsao's big idea is that every meeting should be organized around a "desired outcome." When a meeting is not designed in that way, they found, it ends up being defined by process. For example, a meeting to discuss the quarter's results is a meeting organized around process.

What, they might ask, do you want to achieve from discussing the quarter's results? To make a decision on new projects so that work on them can move forward? To align as a team? To clarify plans and next steps? To brainstorm a list of ideas? To produce something? Figuring out your desired outcome brings focus to a meeting, and it does one more useful thing: It allows people to make better choices about whether they need to be there. It may even help a host decide whether a meeting is necessary for that outcome or whether an email will do.

This focus on the outcome may sound obvious in a business context but strange when getting together with friends and family. Yet working backward from an outcome can be helpful in personal settings, too. Even outside of work, you are proposing to consume people's most precious resource: time. Making the effort to consider how you want your guests, and yourself, to be altered by the experience is what you owe people as a good steward of that resource. You don't have to make a big announcement about this desired outcome. It's just something that might help you become clearer on why you are gathering. A Thanksgiving dinner animated by a purpose of getting difficult issues out in the open to break an impasse between family members is very different from a Thanksgiving dinner oriented toward levity after a grueling and stressful year. Knowing what you want to happen can help you make the choices to get there.

When there really is no purpose: If you go through these steps and find that you still cannot figure out any real purpose for your get-together, then you probably shouldn't be planning the kind of meaningful gathering that I am exploring here. Do a simple, casual hangout. Or give people their time back. And plan your next gathering when you have a specific, unique, disputable purpose that helps you make decisions about how the event should unfold.

THIS CHART MAY HELP

Here is a chart showing how you might move from gatherings about nothing to gatherings about *something*.

Gathering type	Your purpose is a category (i.e., you don't have a purpose)	Basic, boring purpose, but at least you're trying	Your purpose is specific, unique, and disputable (multiple alternatives)
Company offsite	To get out of the office together in a different context	To focus on the year ahead	· To build and to practice a culture of candor with one another · To revisit why we're doing what we're doing and reach agreement about it · To focus on the fractured relationship between sales and marketing, which is hurting everything else

continued . . .

Gathering type	Your purpose is a category (i.e., you don't have a purpose)	Basic, boring purpose, but at least you're trying	Your purpose is specific, unique, and disputable (multiple alternatives)
Back-to-school night	To help parents and kids prepare for the year	To help integrate new families into the school community	· To inspire parents to sustain on evenings and weekends the values the school teaches during the days · To help connect the parents to one another so as to make them a tribe
Church small group	To make the megachurch a smaller place	To help everyone feel like they belong	· To have a group that keeps us doing what we say we want to do · To have a trusted circle to share struggles without worrying about appearances
Birthday party	To celebrate my birthday	To mark the year	· To surround myself with the people who bring out the best in me · To set some goals for the year ahead with people who will help me stay accountable · To take a personal risk/do something that scares me · To reconnect with my siblings
Family reunion	To get the family together	To have a time together where no one is allowed to use phones	· To have a chance for the cousins to bond as adults, without spouses and children · To convene the next generation in the wake of Grandpa's death and create a more tolerant family reunion in line with the younger relatives' values

Gathering type	Your purpose is a category (i.e., you don't have a purpose)	Basic, boring purpose, but at least you're trying	Your purpose is specific, unique, and disputable (multiple alternatives)
Book festival	To celebrate reading	To build community through books	· To use books and a love of reading to build community across racial lines

THE MORASSES OF MULTITASKING AND MODESTY

In my experience, a lot of people don't gather with real purpose because they're not clear on what a purpose *is* or how you arrive at one. But many others, myself included, aspire to greater purpose in gathering yet often run up against two kinds of internal resistance. One comes from the desire to multitask; the other from modesty. Both reared their heads when a woman I know—we'll call her S.—decided to have a dinner party.

She came to me because she was confused about the dinner. It clearly wasn't an ordinary dinner; she seemed to have some unspoken need to make it special. But she wasn't sure why she was having it, which left her unsure of how to put it together.

When I asked why she was hosting, her initial response was "Because this couple had us over, and we need to pay them back."

This is, technically, a purpose, but it's not much of one. So I asked more questions. The more S. and I talked, the more unarticulated half-purposes slipped out: to continue a rotation of hosting among a well-established circle of friends; to bring more meaningful conversation into her life; to help her husband create new business opportunities.

These were all worthy reasons to gather, but they were in tension with one another. The goal of comfort didn't jibe with the goal of dining with people who might bring her husband business. The goal of entertaining her regular circle of friends ran up against the goal of great conversation, which can often be invigorated by new blood. S. was trying to jam several half-hearted mini-purposes into one dinner party. No gathering could possibly serve so many different purposes at once.

S. wasn't unaware of the desirability of gathering with purpose. She had come to me precisely because she knew that she wanted a more purposeful gathering. Despite knowing this, she ran into the instinct to multitask—to make a gathering do many things, not just something.

Through further questioning, I tried to get S. to commit to one of those many possible somethings: If she could accomplish anything with this dinner, how would she want her guests to walk away at the end? The more we spoke, the more her ideas flowed, and the more excited she became.

She realized before long that what mattered most to her was creating a gathering that interrupted the patterns of hosting that she had fallen into. When they were younger, she and her husband had met new people through his work. But as they aged, her husband started his own small company, their kids left for college, and they had begun to gather less often. They found themselves having similar conversations with the same people over and over. While she loved her friends, having dinners only with them didn't contribute to the sense of adventure and variety they valued in themselves. She decided what she wanted from the dinner—and from the dinners for which it might set a precedent—was novelty and freshness. She decided to put aside the demi-purposes of bringing her husband new business and reciprocating with her friends, and to zero in on connecting meaningfully with new people.

Making her gathering about one big something excited S., but it also scared her. She was scared because the dinner she was originally heading toward, however purposeless, was simple. It would likely have gone off without a hitch—uneventful, low-key, no pressure. To gather in the way I was guiding her toward was to commit to some big *something*.

"Who am I to gather in this way?" people often ask themselves. "Who am I to impose my ideas on other people? A big purpose may be fine for a state dinner or corporate retreat, but doesn't it sound too arrogant, ambitious, or serious for my family reunion/dinner party/morning meeting?"

This modesty is related to a desire not to seem like you care too much—a desire to project the appearance of being chill, cool, and relaxed about your gathering. Gathering well isn't a chill activity. If you want chill, visit the Arctic. But modesty can also derive from the idea that people don't want to be imposed on. This hesitancy, which permeates many gatherings, doesn't consider that you may be doing your guests a favor by having a focus.

So S. had grown clearer about her overriding purpose and hushed the voices telling her to do many things at once with her gathering. And now she overcame the pressures of modesty—the irksome questions that begin with the words *Who am I to* . . . With her new focus on novelty and freshness, she decided to invite three couples to dinner. One included a man whom her husband had recently met through a work project and had liked but hadn't incorporated into their socializing routines. One was a younger couple, former students of her husband's. And then the couple who had originally had them over for dinner.

My ears perked up at the mention of that third couple. I wondered whether this was one of those old, discarded half-purposes popping back out of the trash can. Why the last couple? I asked. Out of obligation?

S. replied that she actually did want them there, and that including one close friend at the dinner might seed a new notion among her existing group of friends that they don't always have to socialize in the same old ways. That was consistent with the new purpose she had settled on.

S. knew she wanted to have a single conversation among the group. And in keeping with the idea of new blood, she wanted a question that would reveal something about each person and connect the guests to one another. She and her husband, both immigrants, decided to ask the table about their conception of "home."

Her husband began: "When my mother recently passed away, I realized that visiting her was my last connection to my birth country. And that my orientation to home had changed. In this political climate, as the very notion of what it means to be American is being questioned, how do you think about what 'home' is for you?"

The group, a mix of immigrants and native-born Americans, explored the question together. The result was a beautiful, provocative conversation. The question fulfilled S.'s desired purpose, because it allowed both for hearing new people's stories and for talking about larger current events. The group laughed and questioned and even teared up, because the topic struck a chord that was both universal and deeply personal.

Days later, S. received a grateful email from one guest. It read: "I am still thinking about your amazing question. My husband and I continued to talk about it all the way home. And now we're even discussing it with our children! Thank you."

A gathering's purpose doesn't have to be formal, stiff, or self-important. It doesn't have to be philanthropic or achieve some social good. The Golden Retriever Festival in Scotland, which attracts hundreds of dogs and their owners, has an admirably clear, if cosmically inconsequential, purpose: to pay tribute to Lord Tweedmouth, the nineteenth-century nobleman responsible for developing that breed. The Coney Island Mermaid Parade, in all its naked glory, has a clear purpose: to celebrate the beginning of summer. Even sex parties have a purpose: to get laid in a judgment- and repercussion-free zone.

Having a purpose simply means knowing why you're gathering and doing your participants the honor of being convened for a reason. And once you have that purpose in mind, you will suddenly find it easier to make all the decisions that a gathering requires.

PURPOSE IS YOUR BOUNCER

The purpose of your gathering is more than an inspiring concept. It is a tool, a filter that helps you determine all the details, grand and trivial. To gather is to make choice after choice: place, time, food, forks, agenda, topics, speakers. Virtually every choice will be easier to make when you know why you're gathering, and especially when that *why* is particular, interesting, and even provocative.

Make purpose your bouncer. Let it decide what goes into your gathering and what stays out. When in doubt about any element, even the smallest detail, hark back to that purpose and decide in accordance with it. In the ensuing chapters, I will take you through some of the decisions you must make when you seek to gather better and more meaningfully, equipped with bold purpose. But I want to close this chapter with a story about a book festival I once advised—a story that suggests what happens when you come up with a purpose but are only semi-committed to it, and only semi-committed to using it to guide your decisions. When you don't use it as a bouncer.

This book festival takes place every year in a major U.S. city. It had once been a dream for its founders, and their purpose in those early days was nothing more and nothing less than to make it exist. They succeeded. It grew to attract thousands of visitors every year. Now they felt like they needed a new purpose. The festival's continuing existence felt assured. What was it for? What could it do? How could it make itself count?

The festival's leadership reached out to me for advice on these questions. What kind of purpose could be their next great animating force? Someone had the idea that the festival's purpose could be about stitching together the community. Books were, of course, the medium. But couldn't an ambitious festival set itself the challenge of making the city more connected? Couldn't it help turn strong readers into good citizens?

That seemed to me a promising direction—a specific, unique, disputable lodestar for a book festival that could guide its construction.

Now it was time to give this would-be purpose a trial run as a bouncer. If the purpose of this book festival was to weave the city more closely together, how would it change? What would we add to, and what would we subtract from, the gathering? We began to brainstorm.

I proposed an idea: Instead of starting each session with the books and authors themselves, why not kick things off with a two-minute exercise in which audience members can meaningfully, if briefly, connect with one another? The host could ask three city- or book-related questions, and then ask each member of the audience to turn to a stranger to discuss one of them. What brought you to this city—whether birth or circumstance? What is a book that really affected you as a child? What do you think would make us a better city? Starting a session with these questions would help the audience become aware of one another. It would also break the norm of not speaking to a stranger, and perhaps encourage this kind of behavior to continue as people left the session. And it would activate a group identity—the city's book lovers—that, in the absence of such questions, tends to stay dormant.

As soon as this idea was mentioned, someone in the group sounded a worry. "But I wouldn't want to take away time from the authors," the person said. There it was—the real, if unspoken, purpose rousing from its slumber and insisting on its continued primacy. Everyone liked the idea of "book festival as community glue" in theory. But at the first sign of needing to compromise on another thing in order to honor this new *something*, alarm bells rang. The group wasn't ready to make the purpose of the book festival the stitching of community if it meant changing the structure of the sessions, or taking time away from something else. Their purpose, whether or not they admitted it, was the promotion of books and reading and the honoring of authors. It bothered them to make an author wait two minutes for citizens to bond.

The book festival was doing what many of us do: shaping a gathering according to various unstated motivations, and making half-hearted gestures toward loftier goals. When you gather in the way that I propose in this book, first you set and genuinely commit to your purpose, and then the decisions will flow. Among the early choices will be whom you invite and where you convene them.

Two

Close Doors

. . .

PART ONE: WHO

The purpose-driven list

The guest list is the first test of a robust gathering purpose. It is the first chance to put your ideals into practice. As with the book festival organizers debating whether to change the way they opened author sessions, it is an opportunity to assess how committed you really are to those ideals, how willing to sacrifice invitations on the altar of your reason for gathering. I have worked with more than a few hosts who feel gung-ho about their gathering's daring new purpose only to have their courage melt under the pressure of deciding whom to include or exclude. The desire to keep doors open—to not offend, to maintain a future opportunity—is a threat to gathering with a purpose.

Inviting people is easy. Excluding people can be hard. "The more the merrier," we are told from childhood. "The more souls, the more joy," the Dutch say. "The more fools there are, the more we laugh," the French declare. At the risk of dissenting from millennia of advice along these lines, let me say this: You will have begun to gather with purpose when you learn to exclude with purpose. When you learn to close doors.

I take no pleasure in exclusion, and I often violate my own rule. But thoughtful, considered exclusion is vital to any gathering, because over-inclusion is a symptom of deeper problems—above all, a confusion about why you are gathering and a lack of commitment to your purpose and your guests.

Sometimes we over-include because we feel a need to repay an old debt of hosting, as S. did. Sometimes we over-include because we're sustaining a custom in which we don't really believe: "I couldn't not invite the marketing team. That would be a huge slap in the face. They always come." Sometimes we over-include because we don't want to deal with the consequences of excluding certain people, especially those gifted at making a stink. We cave in to the founder who no longer works at the company but wants to come to the leadership offsite, even though its purpose is to establish the new CEO's authority after the founder's exit. We yield to the aunt who happens to be visiting and presumes that her presence is additive when a couple's parents are meeting for the first time.

Faced with people who should not, in theory, be there but are hard to keep away, it can feel easier and more generous to go with the flow. But the thoughtful gatherer understands that inclusion can in fact be uncharitable, and exclusion generous.

The kindness of exclusion

I was once part of a workout group that wrestled with this very question. Is more merrier or scarier? At first, the group consisted of six friends who gathered twice a week in a park at dawn with a trainer. We toned our abs while trading stories and advice. The group was going strong—the highlight of many of our days. And then one of us planned to go on vacation. Because our practice was to prepay for a season, our friend would have lost her money. She had a "better" idea. She wrote an email to the group, introducing a friend of hers who would "substitute" for her while she was gone. A number of us were surprised and uncomfortable at the substitution, but we couldn't articulate why.

Several of us seemed to intuit that the proposed substitution violated the purpose of our gathering, but here was the problem: We had never actually discussed its purpose. One day, one of the members helped us figure out what was bothering us when she said, "This is not a class." What it wasn't helped us to see what it was. The undiscussed but shared understanding of our gathering was to spend time as friends while exercising. It was a hangout that used the convening mechanism of exercise, not an exercise class that happened to be attended by friends. We were a group of people with busy lives who wanted to find a regular, reliable way of reconnecting with specific other people we had chosen.

Once we talked about it and agreed that this was our workout group's purpose, it became easier to deal with the specific issue raised by our friend. We decided we wouldn't allow substitutions in the group, because a stranger might damage the intimacy and people's willingness to share. But it also would take time out of the workout to teach a new person, who might attend only once, the various exercises. After our unspoken purpose was voiced and reaffirmed, it became obvious that the *who* of the gathering was central to its purpose, and that, in this case, the more was scarier, not merrier. Adding one person, while seemingly generous, would have been uncharitable to the other five who had committed to the group based on assumptions of warmth, social ease, and space for honesty.

Even when you get clear on your gathering in this way, there is never an easy way to say "Please don't come." That's why so many of our gatherings end up being hijacked in the name of politeness. But here is what the skilled gatherer must know: in trying not to offend, you fail to protect the gathering itself and the people in it. I have learned that far too often in the name of inclusion and generosity—two values I care about deeply—we fail to draw boundaries about who belongs and why.

Of course, if inclusion is the purpose and identity of the gathering, a porous boundary is fine, even perhaps necessary. But gatherings with many other, wholly admirable purposes can suffer from over-inclusion.

Barack Obama's aunt once told him, "If everyone is family, no one is family." It is blood that makes a tribe, a border that makes a nation. The same is true of gatherings. So here is a corollary to his aunt's saying: If everyone is invited, no one is invited—in the sense of being truly held by the group. By closing the door, you create the room.

In my workout group, I was on the excluding end of an argument about inclusion. Some years earlier, however, in a different but similar situation, I was on the pro-inclusion side. It took me time to see the compassionate potential of the closed door.

The gathering was an annual weekend with friends that I'm going to call Back to the Bay. We were a tight group of friends who were part of a professional training program, and somehow the plan emerged for a trip to the beach, where we could relax amid the pressure-cooker environment of our program and be silly and light in ways we couldn't during the weekly grind. We played T-ball, barbecued, debated the proper sequence of alcohol consumption, and organized "dance-offs" late into the night. For two years in a row, it was the weekend everyone looked forward to, and its admittedly basic purpose was broadly assumed, if unstated: to spend time together, to have a release, to bond. We didn't give the purpose much thought, frankly, until it was tested.

When the third year rolled around, two members of our group had become romantically involved with people not in our program. They both wanted to bring their partners. After many emails and conversations about these potential additions, they were asked not to bring them. One dropped the issue and decided to go alone. It was still early in the relationship, and it didn't matter so much to her. The other student, however, was in a long-distance relationship, and, making matters more complicated, he was a soldier who would soon be deployed. Back to the Bay happened to land on one of his few remaining weekends with his girlfriend. Moreover, he wanted his girlfriend to witness him with his program friends, to see a dimension of him that she didn't know. He wanted her, in a sense, to know what had been meaningful enough to keep him apart from her. So he again asked the group about bringing her. First he was told that there wasn't enough space in the house we had rented. He offered that the two of them could rent another place nearby and spend the days with the group. That, too, ended up being denied, in an awkward and unforthcoming way. The soldier, our friend, decided not to come. It felt strange to a number of us, and it forced the group to grapple with the question of who belonged to it and what it was for.

This grappling surfaced truths about the group and its purpose that many of us who were part of it didn't realize. As revealed in my workout group, conflict often unearths purpose. What we all knew was that the group had developed its rhythms and rituals and had created a certain magic. What was not universally known was that an element of this magic was that it was a rare space for one member of the group, a gay man whose sexuality was known to his friends but hidden from the wider world, to be unselfconsciously himself. Some of us had no idea that this was a big part of what Back to the Bay offered—and not just to this classmate, but also to those who felt for him and who enjoyed spending time with the freest version of him. And what benefited him in the extreme benefited the rest of us, too, if more subtly. Here was a place where we all could show sides of ourselves without risk to our safety or career advancement—including somewhat endangered sides. No one had ever formally declared this the purpose of Back to the Bay, but for many it had come to be the unspoken and inalienable one. And so the friends who had this point of view and who dominated the group decided that outsiders would change the environment for everyone. War or no war, the soldier's girlfriend couldn't come.

Years later, our gay friend came out publicly and became a leader in his field. I like to think that this group of friends, nurturing this man and giving him a zone of safety and freedom, helped him along his way. Although I didn't like the exclusion at the time, I now see that it was right to exclude the two new partners. The more would have been the scarier. Keeping others out was what let our friend be out with us.

Looking back on the episode, it becomes clear to me that when you don't root your gathering up front in a clear, agreed-on purpose, you are often forced to do so belatedly by questions of membership that inevitably arise. This was also what happened with my workout group: We didn't think about what it was for until we found ourselves in an argument about who it was for.

To be clear, I don't recommend backing into purpose through the question of whom to invite. But the link between the two issues illustrates that the purpose of a gathering can remain somewhat vague and abstract until it is clarified by drawing the boundary between who is in and out. When you exclude, the rubber of purpose hits the road. When you're hosting a gathering with others, as opposed to hosting on your own, you should spend time not only reflecting on the purpose of the gathering but then also, ideally, aligning on it with the other hosts. Why are we doing this? Whom should we invite? Why?

To put it another way, thoughtful exclusion, in addition to being generous, can be defining. It can help with the important task of communicating to guests what a gathering *is*.

One of the most deft gatherers I know is a woman named Nora Abousteit. She once told me a story about her late father, an Egyptian immigrant to Germany named Osman Abousteit, that perfectly distills how who *isn't* invited can make the gathering.

Osman had arrived in the small town of Giessen, Germany, in 1957, to study for a Ph.D. in chemistry. He observed, to his chagrin, that there was no real place in Giessen for students to gather—no hangout where they could be themselves free from their professors and the boring grown-ups of the town. He decided to start Giessen's first students-only bar. He named it Scarabée in honor of the Egyptian dung beetle. Osman's instincts were right. His fellow students craved a hangout, and they flocked to Scarabée, which lived by its own carefree rules. For example, at a time when it was considered crass to drink beer out of a bottle rather than a glass, Scarabée served beer in bottles. And yet it wasn't this impertinence or the presence of those droves of students that gave Scarabée its legendary status. It was, rather, one very notable absence.

To get into the club, you had to show your student ID to a bouncer outside. A nonstudent would show up from time to time and would be denied entry. These exclusions helped underline the rule but also didn't make much of a splash. It was when the vice mayor of the town came by one day that the situation grew interesting. The bouncer denied him entry. The vice mayor protested. Osman came out to deal with the situation. He enforced the rule and kept the vice mayor out. And it was this more demanding and risky exclusion that cemented Scarabée's reputation. It was not a bar that happened to admit only students. It was a bar with a defining purpose for which it was willing to fight. Sixty years later, the bar is still hopping.

How to exclude well

So how, you might ask, do I exclude generously?

This issue comes up a lot when I'm organizing large, complicated meetings for clients. These are some of the questions I ask them:

Who not only fits but also helps fulfill the gathering's purpose?

Who threatens the purpose?

Who, despite being irrelevant to the purpose, do you feel obliged to invite?

When my clients answer the first two questions, they begin to grasp their gathering's true purpose. Obviously people who fit and fulfill your gathering's purpose need to be there. And, though this one is harder, people who manifestly threaten the purpose are easy to justify excluding. (That doesn't mean they always end up being excluded. Politeness and habit often defeat the facilitator. But the hosts still know deep down who shouldn't be there.)

It is the third question where purpose begins to be tested. Someone threatens a gathering's purpose? You can see why to keep him out. But what's wrong with someone who's irrelevant to the purpose? What's wrong with inviting Bob? Every gathering has its Bobs. Bob in marketing. Bob your friend's girlfriend's brother. Bob your visiting aunt. Bob is perfectly pleasant and doesn't actively sabotage your gathering. Most Bobs are grateful to be included. They sometimes bring extra effort or an extra bottle of wine. You've probably been a Bob. I certainly have.

The crux of excluding thoughtfully and intentionally is mustering the courage to keep away your Bobs. It is to shift your perception so that you understand that people who aren't fulfilling the purpose of your gathering *are* detracting from it, even if they do nothing to detract from it. This is because once they are actually in your presence, you (and other considerate guests) will want to welcome and include them, which takes time and attention away from what (and who) you're actually there for. Particularly in smaller gatherings, every single person affects the dynamics of a group. Excluding well and purposefully is reframing who and what you are being generous to—your guests and your purpose.

One common problem I run into is that in gatherings with multiple hosts, different people have different Bobs. If you find yourself in a situation where there is conflict over who the Bobs are, there is an additional question to ask yourself that I have found useful: Who is this gathering for *first*?

I once designed a multigenerational convening at a seaside resort for forty leaders involved in a political movement. I was working with the organizers, a team of four people from different organizations, to make the guest list. They had agreed on the initial list, but as often happens, new requests had come in, both from people who hadn't been invited and from guests who wanted to bring others. One influential donor had asked to bring a friend along to the meeting. One organizer thought that we should let her, worrying that she might not come otherwise. Another organizer argued that the friend was, effectively, a Bob. I prompted the organizers to ask themselves: Who was this gathering for *first*? The gathering was first for the forty leaders. If the organizers could get them to agree on a common vision, it would be a huge breakthrough for the movement. As the organizers teased out the purpose, they realized that part of the magic of the meeting would be to get these leaders to connect their various agendas to a larger cross-unifying theme. To do that, we would need to design a gathering where they meaningfully engaged with one another. In this case, we believed, bringing a close friend would keep that guest's attention at least somewhat focused on her friend, as well as provide a safety blanket to not engage as deeply as she might otherwise. She was told no. (She accepted the invitation anyway.)

Another time, I was facilitating a gathering for a company in Brazil to help its team think through the building of a new city. We had invited twelve experts from around the world to come in for a day and dream up radical new ways to design a modern, bold, sustainable city. At the last minute, the firm's executives asked if they could bring ten more people from their side to observe the meeting, effectively doubling the size of their group. Again, we had to ask, who was this gathering for *first*? The client. And what was the underlying purpose? To come up with bold ideas that the client would have the political capital and risk appetite to implement. In this case, we realized these extra people weren't actually Bobs. The gathering's purpose would actually be better served if more people observed the early stage of the process, getting excited by these pie-in-the-sky ideas. And they were people whose enthusiasm later in the process would be beneficial. We agreed to let them come and, because the observers were going to outnumber the participants, we tweaked the physical format of the meeting accordingly. We decided to highlight the role of the observers and turn their size into an advantage. We organized the room into two circles of chairs, one within the other. In the inner circle, we placed twelve chairs for the experts, whom I would facilitate through mini-talks and lively debate. On the outside, in a larger circle with chairs facing toward the center, we placed all the clients and their guests, who would sit on the periphery, without phones, observing and listening deeply. The added size and energy of the outside circle ended up creating an even more exciting environment for the people inside the circle. People were really listening to their ideas—a lot of people.

Good exclusion activates diversity

You might ask: In a world where exclusion becomes OK, aren't we moving backward? Isn't exclusion in gatherings something we've been fighting against for years? Isn't exclusion, however thoughtful or intentional, the enemy of diversity?

It is not.

I started my life as a facilitator by moderating racial dialogues. I am biracial. I believe in few things as passionately as I believe in the power of the unlike being brought together and made to figure out the world. I exist because of that.

But diversity is a potentiality that needs to be activated. It can be used or it can just be *there*. A citywide book festival whose audience is very diverse but whose organizers keep them in silence, looking up at the conversations onstage, isn't getting much out of that diversity. Giving readers time and a prompt to talk to one another would squeeze more juice and more insight from difference. On the other hand, at Back to the Bay, the diversity was well activated. A student who hid himself at school let himself become real in that space. And it was exclusion that allowed that diversity to be activated.

When I talk about generous exclusion, I am speaking of ways of bounding a gathering that allow the diversity in it to be heightened and sharpened, rather than diluted in a hodgepodge of people.

Consider the case of Judson Manor, a retirement community in Ohio that has limited its membership to two distinct, tightly bounded populations: college music students and retirees. This twist on a home for the elderly occupies a revamped 1920s hotel. In 2010, what was then your standard-issue retirement community decided to try an experiment after a board member heard of a housing shortage at the nearby Cleveland Institute of Music. It invited 2 and eventually 5 music students from the school to live with its 120 elderly residents rent-free, in exchange for giving recitals and art-therapy courses and spending time with residents. Organizers hoped the music students would serve as a tonic against isolation, dementia, and even high blood pressure. The idea was rooted in studies that show huge health benefits for the elderly when they interact with young people. The students would, in turn, receive what every artist dreams of—an eager, captive audience—and what everyone else dreams of: free housing. (These intergenerational housing experiments have also been tried in the Netherlands to much fanfare.)

The result is a great example of thoughtful exclusion and flourishing diversity, and of how they go hand in hand. No one could accuse Judson Manor of homogeneity: its very raison d'être is to collide the old and the young, two populations that are as divided from each other as any in many rich countries. But to fulfill that purpose well, it had to tightly define the who and the why. The head of Judson Manor, John Jones, was also keen to ensure that the age distinction didn't just coexist, but that it was activated.

"What is the match? And are they doing this for the right reason? Do they really have a genuine interest in integrating within our community? We just don't want this to just be a free apartment for the rest of their school time," Jones says in a documentary about the program. One imagines the experiment wouldn't have worked as well if it allowed in anyone of any age who wished to volunteer their time with old people. Or students of any background and any major. Or even music students who had their own apartments and planned to drop in when it suited them. In any of those cases, the experiment would have been diluted. More openness would have meant weaker activation of the age differential the home was seeking to bring together. There was a power in the specific age and moment of life these students were in that inspired the residents. When asked what was special about having these young people around, one elderly resident said, "That's where life is." And at the same time, the students benefit from having "a lot of extra grandparents," as one young resident put it. "It's crazy to think as I talk with the centenarians here, and sixty- and seventy-year-olds, that they've lived four of my lifetimes, some of them, and have all this experience that I can ask them about," another music student, Daniel Parvin, said. And it was the music that gave the relationship an initial focus.

Here is the lesson of Judson Manor as I see it: Specificity in gathering doesn't have to mean narrowing a group to the point of sameness. With certain types of gatherings, over-including can keep connections shallow because there are so many different lines through which people could possibly connect that it can become hard to meaningfully activate any of them. Excluding thoughtfully allows you to focus on a specific, underexplored relationship. An overly inclusive volunteer program at Judson Manor would have been similar to many volunteer programs at nursing homes. The tightly bound program transformed it from a service program into a *relationship* between young artists and aging ears.

I first came upon this idea of specificity in gathering across difference in college when I facilitated racial dialogue groups. The program I helped bring to my campus was called Sustained Dialogue. It was a small-group process developed by a veteran American diplomat that enabled people to have difficult conversations across lines of conflict. I was a student at the University of

Virginia, where the first question many people asked me, seeing a racially ambiguous face, was "What are you?" Other people had it far worse than I did, and when outright racial conflict flared up for the umpteenth time in UVA's fraught history, some classmates and I decided to explore whether the Sustained Dialogue process could encourage people to talk.

Over the next few years, we hosted more than two dozen year-long small-group dialogues. Each of them consisted of a group of twelve to fourteen students who committed to meeting every two weeks for three hours to delve into these topics and build relationships with students who were unlike them. I was a student moderator, and I led the weekly debrief sessions among the other moderators, which were designed to identify and cross-pollinate what we were learning.

As we began to experiment with the makeup of each group, we started getting reports from student moderators that the best, liveliest, most intense groups were those consisting of two groups locked in a particular historical conflict, as opposed to the more general "multicultural" groups. Year after year, it was the dialogues that focused on one specific relationship—the black-white dialogue, the Jewish-Arab dialogue, and, on another campus, the Republican-LGBT dialogue—that had the highest ongoing membership and the most heat (of the kind you want in a dialogue). These were also the groups in which the moderators felt that they were achieving profound breakthroughs rather than just having interesting conversations. But to keep the focus, we had to be willing to say no to students who weren't of those backgrounds and wanted to participate, and to thoughtfully defend our decision.

The matter of size

Sometimes after I have guided a client to do what we've talked about here, she is ready to exclude in a purposeful way. But the inevitable question arises: How do I tell people?

The most honest way is to point your would-be guest to your purpose. Your purpose isn't personal. Your gathering has a life of its own, and you might tell them that this is not the gathering best suited to them.

But it can also be helpful to blame size, and if you do, you aren't lying. For every gathering purpose, there is a corresponding ideal size. There is no magic formula for the chemistry of what happens in a room; it's not scientific. And yet the size of a gathering shapes what you will get out of people when you bring them together.

If you want a lively but inclusive conversation as a core part of your gathering, eight to twelve people is the number you should consider. Smaller than eight, the group can lack diversity in perspective; larger than twelve, it begins to be difficult to give everyone a chance to speak. Therefore, when you are figuring out whom to include and how to exclude, know that by jamming in those extra few people you are changing the nature of the interaction because of the size of the group. If, on the other hand, the purpose of your meeting is to make a decision, you may want to consider having fewer cooks in the kitchen. Additionally, decision-making bodies like the Supreme Court purposely have an odd number of deciders in the group to improve the probability of a decision.

In my experience, there are certain magic numbers in groups. Every facilitator has his or her own list, and these are obviously approximations, but here are mine: 6, 12 to 15, 30, and 150.

Groups of 6: Groups of this rough size are wonderfully conducive to intimacy, high levels of sharing, and discussion through storytelling. The Young Presidents' Organization, a network for CEO types, has developed a highly structured process that helps peers in groups of 6 thoughtfully coach one another through their problems. Groups of 6 are, on the other hand, not ideal for diversity of viewpoints, and they cannot bear much dead weight. To make the gathering great, there's more responsibility on each person. Churches often encourage their members to join "small groups" of 6 or so members, who meet weekly to have dinner and share prayer requests, pains, and joys. It helps make the church a smaller place.

Groups of 12 to 15: The next interesting number is around 12. Twelve is small enough to build trust and intimacy, and small enough for a single moderator, if there is one, formal or informal, to handle. (When multiple facilitators are required at a large meeting, it is customary to divide the number of participants by 12 to figure out how many facilitators are needed.) At the same time, 12 is large enough to offer a diversity of opinion and large enough that it allows for a certain quotient of mystery and intrigue, of constructive unfamiliarity. In Sustained Dialogue, our groups were always between 8 and 12 people. King Arthur's famous table had 12 seats. Jesus had 12 apostles. The U.S. presidential cabinet, which expands as new departments are born, now consists of 15 secretaries plus the vice president. In my work, I have found that 12, give or take, is the number beyond which many start-ups begin to have people problems as they grow. I sometimes refer to this as the "table moment," when an organization's members can no longer fit around one table. It is a milestone that causes more problems than you would imagine. I once worked with a technology company that hit this size and began observing conflict and mistrust in a culture that had previously been collegial. When the size of the group was still under a dozen, the entire company could grab a chair and sit in one conference room to discuss anything. Once the staff grew to 20, meetings started to exclude people. Exclusion was probably good for focus, but it changed the vibe of the company.

Groups of 30: Thirty starts to feel like a party, whether or not your gathering is one. If smaller gatherings scale greater heights of intimacy, the group of 30 or so has its own distinctive quality: that buzz, that crackle of energy, that sense of possibility that attaches to parties. Groups of this size are generally too big for a single conversation, although I've seen that done well with experienced facilitators and the proper arrangement of a room.

Groups of 150: The next interesting number lies somewhere between 100 and 200. When I speak to conference organizers who think about group dynamics, the ideal range I hear again and again is somewhere between 100 and 150 people. While they disagree on the precise number, they all agree that it's the tier at which, as one organizer told me, "intimacy and trust is still palpable at the level of the whole group, and before it becomes an audience." Spark Conference, an experimental gathering run by leaders in the media, began with 100 people, and found that 70 created a more intimate environment. Many so-called "unconferences," at which attendees improvise the agenda, are designed for 100 people. A Belgian hotelier I know recommended weddings of 150 because, she felt, that was the size at which everyone could see one another at the same time and thereby function as a kind of organism. This spectrum roughly matches what some anthropologists have come to regard as the natural size of a tribe. The group of 150 is one in which everybody can still meet everybody, if the intention is there and the effort is made. This number, 150, also matches the number of stable friendships that the anthropologist Robin Dunbar says humans can maintain, which has come to be called Dunbar's number. Above the "tribe" number, it's still possible to gather well, of course, but the unit of experience usually gets broken up into smaller subgroups.

Tides of humanity: Well beyond these gathering sizes is the sea of humanity. Think Bonnaroo, the World Cup, Tahrir Square, the Million Man March, the hajj in Mecca, the Olympics. These are gatherings where the goal is not so much intimacy or connection as tapping into the convulsive energy of a massive crowd.

PART TWO: WHERE

A venue is a nudge

You have your purpose in mind. You have your guest list in hand. Where will you gather?

The choice of place is often made according to every consideration but purpose. The cost determines the venue. Or convenience. Or traffic. Or the fact that someone happened to raise her hand and offer her deck.

When you choose a venue for logistical reasons, you are letting those logistics override your purpose, when in fact they should be working for it.

You might object: Isn't a room sometimes just a room? What's wrong with taking Morgan up on her offer of her deck?

Here is the problem: Venues come with scripts. We tend to

follow rigid if unwritten scripts that we associate with specific locations. We tend to behave formally in courtrooms, boardrooms, and palaces. We bring out different sides of ourselves at the beach, the park, the nightclub. As Patrick Frick, a fellow member of my tribe of professional facilitators, told me, "The environment should serve the purpose." When he is working with high-level teams and they give him a boardroom to facilitate the meeting in, he said, "ninety-five percent of my options are gone." Why? Because, Frick said, "people who walk into this room will immediately fall into the same pattern of behavior: The CEO sits at the top, and you're trained—you're absolutely trained and brainwashed—how to behave there. You take your place according to hierarchy, you know when you're allowed to speak, and so on."

Jerry Seinfeld once made a similar point to an interviewer about how rooms determine comedic success: "The room is doing eighty percent of the job. And every comedian has had this experience where he's been in a club, some rich guy sees him and says, Oh, I'm going to have this guy at my party. And you go to the party, and they put you on in a living room or in some weird party room. And you go in the toilet. And the reason is the context of the room does eighty percent of the work, in terms of giving you a position of advantage over the audience."

To paraphrase and distort Winston Churchill, first you determine your venue, and then your venue determines which *you* gets to show up. If figuring out the guest list is about deciding who best helps you fulfill the purpose of your gathering, figuring out the venue is about deciding how you want to nudge those chosen few to be the fullest versions of themselves and the best guests.

So how do you choose a good, purposeful location for your gathering?

Embodiment

You should, for starters, seek a setting that embodies the reason for your convening. When a place embodies an idea, it brings a person's body and whole being into the experience, not only their minds.

Larry O'Toole, the CEO of Gentle Giant Moving Company, based in Boston, makes use of embodiment when inducting new recruits. He leads groups of recent hires on a group run around Boston that ends with a race up the steps of Harvard Stadium. The choice of locale—compared with, say, an orientation conducted in an office—tells the new hires something about the place they have joined: To work here, you have to be physically fit, and just as important, when you are doing hard work, you should do it collegially, cooperatively, cheerfully, and with a sense of sport. Not surprisingly, year after year Gentle Giant gets rated as one of Boston's best places to work.

Embodying a purpose doesn't necessarily require going anywhere special. Sometimes just reconfiguring a room is enough. Wendy Woon runs the department of education at the Museum of Modern Art in New York. Her job is to help make a world-famous museum more accessible to the public. It is a challenging job in any museum, because the power in museums tends to lie with the curators. Sometimes it can seem that museums are being run *for* them and not merely *by* them. The goal of making a museum speak to ordinary people is often in tension with the curators' desire for exhibits that win them esteem among their fellow curators and the larger art world. The job of someone like Woon is to constantly provide a counterweight to that desire—to be the voice within the museum for questioning how art is presented and for ensuring that it's still accessible and connects to people's lives and experiences. Even if that means pushing back against the curators. Woon's role is to remind people that what curators may consider sacred isn't sacred—that a museum should adapt itself to speak to people.

As part of her job, Woon teaches a course for graduate students who aspire to become museum educators. It takes place in a classroom within the museum. On the first day of class, at 3 p.m. sharp, the classroom door opens. In the middle of the room is a huge mess of white chairs, all tangled together—a giant highway pileup of seating. The students pause, confused. They look around at one another and then at Woon. Their teacher watches quietly, giving away nothing.

Eventually the students begin talking to one another. Little by little, their confidence growing, their interactions becoming more amusing by the minute, they untangle the chairs and arrange them. As they do so, each student must decide what to do with his or her chair without instructions: Where should I put my chair? How close should the chair be to someone else's? Are we forming rows? A circle? If someone is not going along with the group shape, what should we do?

This is what I mean when I say that gathering well doesn't require money or fish knives. It doesn't require a fancy venue. The classroom that Woon uses is utterly ordinary—an unremarkable space in a building, and a city, full of remarkable spaces. By doing one simple thing—setting up the chairs in that crazy tangle—Woon makes the place an embodiment of her purpose. What was that purpose? To teach these future museum educators that nothing in a museum is sacred—not even a pile of chairs that at MoMA could have been confused for a work of art. And to teach them that art truly happens when people participate in it, and that a museum comes to life when people interact with it. "The reason I do this is to challenge traditional hierarchies of teaching and learning. The design of social space, physical space, and emotional space affects how people engage with ideas, content, and each other. And I wanted to show my students that you must actually *design* a 'space' for exchange and also then invite participation by design," she explains. Over the course of the ensuing weeks, she teaches these aspiring museum educators how to make such interactions happen—how to achieve the kind of participatory museum she believes in and fights to defend. But on that first day, at zero cost and to unforgettable effect, she embodies all that she wished to say.

I am no Wendy Woon, but in my own work I try to have my clients choose spaces and locations that resonate with their deeper goals. For a workshop on people trying to find their path forward in life, a twelfth-century monastery in southeastern France set on one of the routes to the Camino de Santiago, a literal path of pilgrimage. For an architecture firm discussing the future of cities, the Hollywood Hills, overlooking all of Los Angeles. For a comedian looking to take his craft to the next level, the famed writing room of the satirical newspaper *The Onion*. I have seen, over and over again, that when a location inspires a client and makes them feel closer to their purpose, it makes my job as a facilitator much easier, as they are already halfway there.

Consider your own gatherings. What if for your company's next sales training you assigned employees to each spend the day underground with a subway busker, to build their empathy and connect them with the most extreme version of what they do?

What if you held your next college reunion in a cemetery, reminding your classmates, directly if morbidly, that time is of the essence for fulfilling the ideals they professed in their youth?

Sadly, the failure to embody is more common. The unwillingness to do so can be almost comical. I once advised an organization that advocates for protecting oceans. It was hosting a team meeting near San Diego to give everyone a break from their stuffy East Coast offices. When I looked at the schedule, it was chockfull. I asked when they'd have time to go to the ocean. "Oh, we have too much to do to go see the ocean," the organizer told me. This was an organization that people were devoting their lives to because of their passionate love of the ocean. Spending time in and by the ocean could rejuvenate a strung-out team and remind them of their core purpose. This meeting didn't.

The Château Principle

The Château Principle, in its narrowest form, is this: Don't host your meeting in a château if you don't want to remind the French of their greatness and of the fact that they don't need you after all.

Every gathering with a vivid, particular purpose needs more of certain behaviors and less of others. If the purpose has something to do with bonding a group, you will want more listening behavior and less declaiming behavior. If the purpose is to get your company out of the rut of old ideas and thinking, the opposite may be true. What many hosts don't realize is that the choice of venue is one of your most powerful levers over your guests' behavior. A deft gatherer picks a place that elicits the behaviors she wants and plays down the behaviors she doesn't. The failure to follow this principle once cost a banker a lot of money, not including the château bill.

"I will argue until the day I die that the meeting place we chose killed the deal," Chris Varelas, an investor now settled in the Bay Area, told me. Back in 2001, Varelas was an investment banker—a managing director at Citigroup and the head of its technology banking group. He came onto a project representing Lucent, a New Jersey–based telecommunications company, in a massive proposed merger with Alcatel, the French giant. The deal was valued at more than $20 billion. It was a complicated merger, and after roughly a year of talks, the merger finally seemed to be lining up. One gathering remained: a face-to-face meeting for executives to do the final mutual due diligence.

Until that gathering, the two sides had done a good job of maintaining a useful fiction. This deal was "supposed to be a marriage of equals," Varelas said, but everyone quietly knew that Alcatel, being the more powerful of the two, "was going to be more equal." Yet until that point, according to Varelas, the perception that the two were equals had mostly held throughout the talks. It was a big part of why they had gone as well as they had— until a choice of venue upended the pattern.

The originally scheduled venue was a nondescript airport hotel in New Jersey, so that "no one would know what we're doing," Varelas said. Keeping details out of the media was an important priority, to avoid embarrassment on either side should the deal not happen and also to "avoid a leak, which can scuttle a deal if the market reaction is negative." At the last minute, however, a senior director of Alcatel fell ill and requested that the meeting be relocated to France. They chose as the forum for the talks the Château des Mesnuls, a castle about an hour's drive west of Paris, which was owned by an Alcatel subsidiary. "I'm pretty sure they used it regularly for offsites, which probably worked fine for internal rah-rah planning and strategy sessions but not for a merger negotiation," Varelas said.

It is a fifty-five-room château restored in the Louis XIII style, complete with Persian rugs, gold frescoes, chandeliers, and portraits of famous French soldiers—including, one presumes, those who have recently outwitted Anglo-Saxons who mistakenly thought themselves the equals of the French. Over the course of three eighteen-hour days, a few dozen participants—including the corporate executive teams, board directors, bankers, accountants, and lawyers from both sides—met in the château to nail down the final agreement. And then, in the final hours, after *The Wall Street Journal* had published news of the impending merger, including the agreed-upon price, Henry Schacht, the chairman of Lucent, walked out of the meeting, and the merger fell apart.

According to news reports at the time, the walk-out was tactical—the two sides were struggling to agree on board representation. But it was also emotional. "In Alcatel's failed effort to buy Lucent Technologies, the sticking point was pride," *The New York Times* reported. "Lucent officials are reported to have balked," the BBC said at the time, "because they did not believe that Alcatel was treating the deal as a merger of equals."

And why were they suddenly not treating the deal in the way they had dutifully treated it for a whole year? It is impossible to say. But Varelas maintains that it's because "the château brought the Frenchness out in the French.

"We're sitting in these ballrooms having these discussions," he said, "and you could just see the arrogance and hubris of

Alcatel employees. They became much more comfortable asserting their dominance than I know they would have if we had been
in Jersey." The French started saying things like "When we take
over" and, Varelas said, "It really pissed them off"—"them" being the Lucent executives. The Lucent side was aghast at Alcatel's
behavior, Varelas said. Lucent's chairman finally said, "We're out
of here." Deal off.

Seventeen years later, with many more mergers under his belt,
Varelas sticks to his theory. "I'm ninety-nine percent sure that the
meeting place reinforced or brought out the underlying assumption. It exposed the fiction that it was a 'merger of equals,' because it allowed the Alcatel people to be too comfortable in
asserting their dominance over Lucent," he said.

Even if you're not negotiating a multibillion-dollar deal, the
Château Principle may apply to your gathering. People are affected by their environment, and you should host your gathering
in a place and context that serves your purpose. In some cases,
hosting your gathering in a château may absolutely be conducive
to your purpose. But for the two companies, which needed the
French to remain modest for only one more day, it turned out to
be, at great cost, the wrong environment.

Five years later, the merger between Lucent and Alcatel finally
happened, albeit under the auspices of a new chairman and CEO
at Lucent. One presumes they stayed away from châteaus.

Displacement

So a well-chosen venue might signal to people what your gathering is ultimately about (embodiment). It might nudge people to

behave in the particular ways that make the most out of this coming-together (the Château Principle). And a venue can and should do one further thing: displace people.

Displacement is simply about breaking people out of their habits. It is about waking people up from the slumber of their own routines. As a facilitator, I seek to do that through the questions I ask and the exercises I run. But it is also possible to achieve a great deal of displacement through the choice of a space. As in the case of Wendy Woon, it takes imagination and effort more than anything else to achieve a little displacement. It is not more complicated than doing an activity in a place where people would think you shouldn't.

A dinner, for example, is generally thought best had on dry land. That, at least, is the conventional wisdom. However, one night in the Greek town of Kalamata, in the 1940s, the British travel writer Patrick Leigh Fermor and his friends had another idea. As the group was seated on the quay waiting for their meal to arrive in the searing heat, Fermor and his two companions silently picked up their iron table and carried it into the sea. They sat waist-deep in the water, patiently awaiting service. When the waiter emerged from the restaurant, Fermor wrote, he "gazed with surprise at the empty space on the quay; then, observing us with a quickly masked flicker of pleasure, he stepped unhesitatingly into the sea" with their dinners. The surrounding diners, amused at the spectacle, began to send the maritime diners wine in celebration of their insouciance. Perhaps not surprisingly, Fermor's *New York Times* obituary would note that his "tables" were "reputed to be among the liveliest in Europe."

A dinner party is not supposed to take place in an ocean. Which is why Fermor went there. And which is why you should think about where your next gathering ought *not* take place, and hold it there.

But, as in the case of Woon's classroom, displacement can also occur within a traditional location. Take, for example, the famed photographer Platon.

You'd probably recognize a Platon if you saw one. He shot cover photographs for *Time* magazine for many years and was a staff photographer for *The New Yorker* magazine. His signature style is a photograph taken so close to his subjects that you can see their pores. Platon has photographed every sitting U.S. president from Jimmy Carter through Barack Obama. He has done multiple portraits of Hillary Clinton and Donald Trump, well before they were presidential candidates. He has photographed world leaders from Angela Merkel to Tony Blair to Ban Ki-moon, the eighth secretary-general of the United Nations, and infamous despots from Russia's Vladimir Putin to Zimbabwe's Robert Mugabe, from Libya's Muammar Gaddafi to Iran's Mahmoud Ahmadinejad. Platon has photographed not only the powerful but also people who have challenged power, from the Burmese activist Aung San Suu Kyi (while still under house arrest), to Pussy Riot, to protesters in Tahrir Square, to Edward Snowden. And he's shot hundreds of celebrities, from George Clooney to Yoko Ono to Bono.

What's remarkable about Platon, though, beyond his litany of famous subjects, is what he is able to get these people to *do* in the room with him. It is in the interest of these leaders, many of whom have press secretaries and image consultants, to show a face that they want the public to see. It is in Platon's interest to get them to show something else, something real.

When Platon is able, he will have his famous subjects do the shoot in his studio in New York's SoHo neighborhood. However, for many subjects, he's not always able to choose the location. He's often given just ten minutes with a head of state to get the right shot, sometimes in a cramped hotel room, sometimes backstage at a university or concert or at the United Nations. In these cases, he can't control the space to the extent he'd like. But regardless of the context, he brings a decrepit, falling-apart, white-painted crate for his famous subjects to sit on. "I start by inviting them to 'step into my office,' which is funny, because usually I'm stepping into their office," he told me. This old white crate is a box that he's had every one of his subjects sit on. Apparently, sometimes a presidential advance team will see the box and freak out: "We can't ask him to sit on that box." Then Platon tells them who else has sat on that box, and they always acquiesce.

Platon is displacing his subjects from the context that they're in and is, through this physical object, connecting them to all the other photo shoots (and therefore people) who have come before them. He may have seven minutes with a president, but those seven minutes are going to be defined by his space and context, not theirs. After years of lugging it around, when the box finally fell apart, he had his assistants remake the new one to look as old and weathered as the original. It had become the gritty symbol that temporarily displaced a leader from his throne.

Perimeter, area, and density

The above pointers should help you choose your overall environment. Once you do, you will be faced with more practical questions about rooms and tables and chairs and the sizes of things. A few notes, therefore, on perimeter, area, and density.

PERIMETER

Metaphorical doors aren't the only doors that need closing in a purposeful gathering. The artful gatherer is also mindful of physical doors. Gatherings need perimeters. A space for a gathering works best when it is contained. Photographers and choreographers often close all the doors in a room to, as Platon explained to me, "make sure the energy isn't leaking out."

This rule is commonly violated in restaurants. Tables are often set up so that there is no "head" of the table, with chairs facing each other in two rows. I once went to a dinner at a restaurant with five friends. Our table was three square tables pushed together, with three chairs on each side. Throughout the evening, the conversation never really took off. It was difficult to have one conversation, as the person in the middle had to look left and right, as if watching a tennis match, and eventually the table broke off into two separate conversations. The two ends of the table remained "leaky." It didn't feel cozy or intimate. We should have simply asked the waiter to remove one of the square tables and moved two people to the ends. We would then have had a contained space (through the placement of our bodies) and it would have been easier for us to talk, to share—to come together.

A contained space for a gathering allows people to relax, and it helps create the alternative world that a gathering can, at its best, achieve. It can be as simple as putting down a blanket for a picnic rather than sitting on the endless expanse of grass; or temporarily covering the glass walls of a fishbowl conference room with flip-chart paper to create a modicum of privacy. Or if there's an extra chair at a meeting that is not going to be used, removing it and closing the gap between people. One underground party planner explained it to me like this: "If you are on a picnic blanket, you will hang out around your picnic blanket. It's not because there's a fence around it; it's because your picnic blanket is your mental construct. It's not about sitting on a blanket versus sitting on the grass; it's about claiming that mental space and making it yours and comfortable and safe."

A game designer named Eric Zimmerman once told me about an experiment he and his colleagues designed for an exhibition in Los Angeles. The board game they created was surrounded by four curved walls that approximated a circle, so that when you stepped inside to play, it felt as if you were in a cave. Passersby were intrigued and players ended up becoming so addicted to the game that well after day had given way to night, they kept playing. At last, after the organizers took down all the other sets, they had to remove the four walls, though they left the board game intact. As the walls came down, one by one the players lost interest in the game and dispersed, despite the game remaining playable.

"When the walls came down, even though we didn't take away any of the pieces of the board game, they didn't feel like continuing," Zimmerman told me. "The energy was dispersed." Once the game's perimeter was gone, its players lost their sense of being in an alternative universe.

MOVING ROOMS

You don't have to bring your meeting to the ocean (though I highly recommend it) to make it memorable. Studies show that simply switching rooms for different parts of an evening's experience will help people remember different moments better. To ensure people will remember the distinct parts of your party, Ed Cooke, an expert on the workings of memory, suggests having several interesting phases over the course of the evening, each of which occurs in a different space. "That way, in your recollection, the fuzz of conversation doesn't all kind of blur into itself, and become just a single 'it was fun,' but instead you can remember specific things that happened at each point. You go on a journey; there's a narrative," he said.

AREA

The size of a gathering's space should serve your purpose.

I once walked into a fortieth birthday party that had all the right ingredients: a beautiful venue, delicious food, an open bar, a lively band, and two hundred guests. But for some reason, I kept looking over my shoulder all night, waiting for the party to begin. It felt like the room was still empty even after all the guests had arrived. You had to physically walk over to another part of the room to meet new people because everyone was standing so far apart. I spent most of the night hanging out with a small group of friends I already knew and didn't take any social risks. Even when the band came on, people congregated but hung back and didn't dance. What went wrong?

The space was too big. The room was gymnasium-sized. There was never a moment when you accidentally bumped into someone, you turned around and met someone new.

Another time, I was running a two-day gathering to brainstorm future uses for the Presidio, a large park and former U.S. Army military fort in San Francisco. The evening of the workshop, the Golden Gate National Parks Conservancy opened the event to the public. People were invited to come and hear presentations from museum educators across the country about what makes an engaging space. We wanted to start with cocktails to warm up the gathering and tried to embody what we were talking about.

As the guests started to arrive, one of the architects at the meeting realized that the space where we were gathering was far too big to make it feel like a cocktail party. Thinking on her feet, she took all the flip-chart stands we had been working with throughout the day and placed them in a semicircle that cordoned off a small section of the room. As people filtered in, rather than taking over the entire space, they started to cluster together between the flip charts and the classroom-style chairs that had been set up for the talk. Within minutes, the place was hopping. The quick-thinking architect had a sense of the right size of the area the group needed to gather in and saved everyone from what might have been a disappointing and low-energy event.

Just as we go into autopilot on the location of our weekly staff meetings, we also tend to accept the default setup we're given. If there's a table in the middle of the room, we leave it there. If the chairs are set up on two of the four sides, we don't move them, even though it would create more intimacy if we did. So next time you're in a gathering venue, remember that something as simple as a few flip charts can allow you to transform the feel of a room.

DENSITY

What the architect understood that night was the appropriate human density for the event. And I have since learned that event planners and space designers actually have rules of thumb for event density. Billy Mac, an event planner, swears by the following parameters for the number of square feet required per guest for different vibes:

Examples: Square Feet Per Guest	Sophisticated	Lively	Hot
Dinner party	20 sq. ft.	15 sq. ft.	N/A
Cocktail party	12 sq. ft.	10 sq. ft.	8 sq. ft.
Into the night/dance party	8 sq. ft.	6 sq. ft.	5 sq. ft.

Source: Apartment Therapy blog, https://www.apartmenttherapy.com /party-architecture-density-how-to-plan-a-party-5359.

He suggests dividing the "square feet of your party space by the number to get your target number of guests." If your entertaining space is 400 square feet and you want a sophisticated dinner party, invite 20 people. If, instead, you want a "hot" dance party, invite 80 for that same space. Mac says one of the reasons party guests often end up gravitating to the kitchen is that people instinctively seek out smaller spaces as the group dwindles in order to sustain the level of the density.

Three

Don't Be a Chill Host

. . .

Now you know how to craft a bold and clear purpose for your gathering and how to close doors based on it. The next step is to think about your role as host. How will you run your gathering?

"CHILL" IS SELFISHNESS DISGUISED AS KINDNESS

When I raise the question of the host's role to clients or friends, whether in preparation for business meetings or family get-togethers, I am often greeted with hesitancy. This is because to talk about their role is to talk about their power as a host, and to talk about that power is to acknowledge that it exists. This is not what most people want to hear. Many people who go to the serious trouble of hosting aspire to host as minimally as possible.

But who wants to sail on a skipperless ship? Time and again, as in the case of S., who was debating whether to do more with her dinner party, I urge those I advise to own their power and lift a hand to the wheel. Time and again, they resist.

I once was in Washington, D.C., helping organize a meeting about poverty policy with a group of federal and state leaders. The hosts took my suggestion to hold an intimate, single-conversation dinner the night before the meeting, to give participants a chance to bond. The idea was for them to go deep, take risks, and even shift their mindsets to make their policy deliberations the following day more human.

After it was planned, one of the state leaders couldn't make the dinner but wanted to attend the meeting the next day. I strongly urged that the organizers say no. The dinner wasn't an aside; it was a core part of the design of the gathering. The full group would have bonded, creating the potential for an entirely different, more generative dynamic for the meeting. Then one person who didn't go through that process would show up a day late and affect the entire group by her unchanged mindset. The four organizers, averse to conflict and worried about upsetting an important leader, resisted my advice. They wanted to let the state leader decide. Finally, the senior woman in charge listened to me and told the state leader: You are welcome at both parts of the gathering or neither part. She attended neither. After the dinner, seeing the shift that had occurred in the group through the meaningful personal conversation that evening, the organizers understood why it would have then been disruptive to bring in an uninitiated member the next morning.

On another occasion, I was at a housewarming party on a rooftop in Brooklyn. After dinner, the gathering had hit a lull, with people milling around, debating whether to leave or stay. I sensed this, and suggested to the hosts a game of Werewolf, a dynamic, intense group game invented by a Russian psychology professor that could bond the seated guests, reverse the tide of ebbing energy, and spice up the night. One of the hosts seemed eager to play the game and give the group a focus. She looked around and saw some of her guests eager as well, and a small handful with skeptical looks on their faces. The skepticism of this minority intimidated her, and she abandoned the idea, not comfortable using her power as host to bring them along. It was less a risk to do nothing. The moment passed, people broke up into smaller groups, and we lost the critical mass. The next day, she texted me that she wished we had played.

A journalist I know went to the trouble of gathering a dozen peers for a ten-year reunion of their time as foreign correspondents. People came from out of town to attend the dinner at a Thai restaurant in New York City. The journalist is someone who had taken my advice in the past. And so, of his own accord, he decided that he wanted at some point in the evening to interrupt the sidebar conversations and invite everyone to reflect on what that time abroad had meant to them. He wanted to create a moment of focus that would activate the evening's intended purpose. But at the last minute, he backed down, fearing that the idea would be too domineering, or too earnest, or both.

A ubiquitous strain of twenty-first-century culture is infecting our gatherings: being chill. The desire to host while being noninvasive.

"Chill" is the idea that it's better to be relaxed and low-key, better not to care, better not to make a big deal. It is, in the words of Alana Massey's essay "Against Chill," a "laid-back attitude, an absence of neurosis." It "presides over the funeral of reasonable expectations." It "takes and never gives."

Let me declare my bias outright: Chill is a miserable attitude when it comes to hosting gatherings.

In this chapter, I want to convince you to assume your proper powers as a host. That doesn't mean that there's one way to host or one kind of power to exert over your gathering. But I do believe that hosting is inevitably an exercise of power. The hosts I guide often feel tempted to abdicate that power, and feel that by doing so they are letting their guests be free. But this abdication often fails their guests rather than serves them. The chill approach to hosting is all too often about hosts attempting to wriggle out of the burden of hosting. In gatherings, once your guests have chosen to come into your kingdom, they want to be governed—gently, respectfully, and well. When you fail to govern, you may be elevating how you want them to perceive you over how you want the gathering to go for them. Often, chill is you caring about *you* masquerading as you caring about *them*.

THE PROBLEM WITH CHILL

Behind the ethic of chill hosting lies a simple fallacy: Hosts assume that leaving guests alone means that the guests will be left alone, when in fact they will be left to one another. Many hosts I work with seem to imagine that by refusing to exert any power in their gathering, they create a power-free gathering. What they fail to realize is that this pulling-back, far from purging a gathering of power, creates a vacuum that others can fill. Those others are likely to exercise power in a manner inconsistent with your gathering's purpose, and exercise it over people who signed up to be at your—the host's—mercy, but definitely didn't sign up to be at the mercy of your drunk uncle.

Isn't a host who lets people make their own fun, talk to whomever they want to, the most generous kind of host? One of the most dramatic and convincing rebuttals to that possible objection took place in a classroom.

Ronald Heifetz is a popular professor at the Harvard Kennedy School and a well-known authority on leadership. On the first day of his class on Adaptive Leadership, he begins in the most peculiar way. Instead of walking into the room and taking attendance or launching into a lecture, he sits in a black swivel chair in the front of the classroom and stares at the ground with a blank, slightly bored look on his face. Dozens of students sit in front of him. He doesn't welcome any of them. He doesn't clear his throat. He doesn't have one of his assistants introduce him. He just sits there in silence, staring blankly, not moving an inch.

The students sit expectantly, waiting. The official start time of the class passes, and Heifetz continues to sit there, not saying a word. The silence grows heavier, more nerve-racking. By doing nothing, he is abdicating his command of the classroom, refusing to play the expected role of professor-host—presumably, in his case, given his area of scholarship, for some reason we students do not yet grasp.

You can feel the collective nervousness growing by the second. One person laughs. Somebody else coughs. There is a general, unspoken confusion among the students. They are disoriented. When the professor, the traditional classroom authority, doesn't play his role, he removes the guardrails of the classroom. The students are left to navigate the treacherous road themselves.

Someone finally speaks, saying (as best I remember it): "I think this is the class?"

With that, a popcornlike conversation, slow and measured at first, then gathering pace and fervor, breaks out among roughly one hundred strangers:

"Is he just going to sit there?"

"I don't have all day."

"No, I think this is the point."

"So what should we do?"

"Shhhh . . . Maybe he's getting ready to speak."

"Don't shush me. I have every right to talk."

Without the professor leading the way, the students must deal with one another. Any of the hundred of them is, technically, free to speak (or yell or dance or laugh or attempt to take charge). No one is stopping them. But there are unspoken norms discouraging them from doing so. And even when those norms are put to the test, as Heifetz is doing by hanging back, each student has no idea how the others will react. Will one of them be strong enough, charismatic enough, or logical enough to convince the others what to do with the time? Or will they endlessly argue?

The popcorn of conversation goes on for what seems like an eternity but is really about five minutes. Eventually, Heifetz looks up at the class and, to everyone's great relief, says, "Welcome to Adaptive Leadership."

What is Heifetz doing? Launching a course on leadership by showing students what happens when you abdicate leadership. You don't eradicate power. You just hand the opportunity to take charge to someone else—in this case, the students. You are not easing their way or setting them free. You are pumping them full of confusion and anxiety.

AUTHORITY IS AN ONGOING COMMITMENT

As hosts of gatherings, clients and friends of mine sometimes agree to take charge. Their instinct is usually to do so once, early on in the gathering, perhaps by giving an overview of the agenda, or by leading a discussion about group norms, or by going over a set of instructions for a group game. Then, as far as they are concerned, their work is done. Having done their "hosting," they can pretend to be guests.

But exercising your authority once and early on in a gathering is as effective as exercising your body once and early on in your life. It isn't enough just to set a purpose, direction, and ground rules. All these things require enforcement. And if you don't enforce them, others will step in and enforce their own purposes, directions, and ground rules.

I once attended a dinner thrown by one of the more purposeful hosts I know. She seated her dozen or so guests around the table and then suggested we get to know one another by guessing one another's occupations. She had seen it done at another gathering and thought it was fun. We were game. She explained how it worked: Everyone at the table gets a guess (unless you know the person), and then the person says what he or she does for a living. We plunged in, making rather hilarious speculations about the first person as he tried to maintain his poker face.

With the game off to a good start, as the guests seemed to find comfort and laughter in one another, the host got up to get dinner ready. She must have felt that her work was done: Her gathering was on autopilot now. Leaving put her only ten or so paces from the table; it wasn't as though she had deserted us. But even this distance—more psychic than physical, since she was now focused on something else and only faintly following the game—created a problem. One of the guests, perhaps sensing the vacuum or perhaps doing what he always does, began to suck up a disproportionate amount of attention. He gave himself several guesses for each person instead of the allotted one, and when that infraction went unticketed, he began to ask follow-up questions to the guests after they revealed their occupation.

The host's (totally understandable) abdication had made space for a pretender to the throne. Thanks to this pretender, we spent forty minutes on just the first two people. It was completely unsustainable as a pace, and not very interesting. The problem was that no one was invested in the game or its rules besides the host. No one had even heard of the game before. When the host set the game in motion and left, there was no one at the table to enforce the game's rules or the norms of brevity and equality that made it work. But there was *someone* willing to enforce *something*—in this case, a guest willing to enforce his own idea that the rest of the group would benefit from hanging back a little and letting him conduct. He was wrong.

The man's casual evening oppression is the perfect illustration of an old quote from the political philosopher Isaiah Berlin: "Freedom for the wolves has often meant death to the sheep."

What ensued that evening was what so often happens when hosts fail to exert their authority and to enforce it as an ongoing commitment: Many guests get irritated. Some spoke up and, without explicitly maligning the man or the exercise, suggested that we move on and just talk. That was a good suggestion, but other guests were equally right in pointing out that this approach wouldn't be fair, since some people had now been elaborately introduced to the group and others remained unknown. Even after retaking her seat, the host laid low. We spent the entire night on the exercise. People were grumbling throughout—grumbling being the preferred weapon of guests who feel poorly governed and unprotected by their host.

So remember, if you're going to compel people to gather in a particular way, enforce it and rescue your guests if it fails.

And the next time you host a gathering and feel tempted to abdicate even a little, examine the impulse. What is compelling you to hang back? If it's something logistical (like the need to heat up food or to step out and take a call), you might find that a willing guest is much happier to get assigned to play temporary "host" than to be oppressed by some friend of yours for the better part of a night. Often, though, something deeper is at work: a reluctance that you convince yourself is generous.

It's not just with strangers at a dinner party that hosts abdicate their power. I once advised a company that was suffering from painful quarterly meetings because of a misunderstanding of generosity. Three-hour meetings would turn into seven-hour marathons without anyone's explicit consent. Agendas would be built, only to be thrown out the window once the executives actually gathered. The meetings would be diverted to one or two topics that a few felt passionately enough about to advocate for in the moment, and the rest didn't feel passionately enough about to protest.

There was ostensibly an executive who was supposed to run

these meetings. But the problem was that the entire company was based on the core value of equality. This executive would begin most meetings by going over the agenda, but then, like our dinner host, hope the rest would take care of itself. While the meetings might start on topic, inevitably one of the executives would have a burning issue he or she would want to discuss, and in trying to be generous to that peer, the host wouldn't enforce the agenda. And no one else would either, in part because the others didn't think they could if they were "equals." Quarter after quarter, the participants left meetings frustrated, having made few substantive decisions or pushed any agenda forward. And though he was telling himself he was governing in a generous manner, the host was also protecting himself. His underlying belief was that in the current setup, even if the group was collectively worse off for it, it did him no favors to rein in his fiercer colleagues. With no source of enforcement, the meetings became dominated by informal sources of power: tenure at the company, professional success, force of personality.

Is your laissez-faire approach really doing your guests the favor you imagine it is? Does your agenda-free meeting help the young analyst? Or does her chance of adding something useful to a discussion among seasoned experts depend on her being able to prepare in advance? Does your talk-to-whomever-you-want approach help the quiet guest speak at all if not given a protected turn? Does open seating at a teachers conference help the three newcomers who end up sitting clumped together at the end of the table every time?

An essential step along the path of gathering better is making peace with the necessity and virtue of using your power. If you are going to gather, gather. If you are going to host, host. If you are going to create a kingdom for an hour or a day, rule it—and rule it with generosity.

THE WONDERS OF GENEROUS AUTHORITY

At this point you may be wondering: If I am to rule my gathering, what kind of ruler should I be?

The kinds of gatherings that meaningfully help others are governed by what I call generous authority. A gathering run on generous authority is run with a strong, confident hand, but it is run selflessly, for the sake of others. Generous authority is imposing in a way that serves your guests. It spares them from the chaos and anxiety that Heifetz knowingly thrust upon his students. It spares them from the domination of some guests by other guests that the dinner host unwittingly enabled. It wards off pretenders who threaten a purpose. Sometimes generous authority demands a willingness to be disliked in order to make your guests have the best experience of your gathering.

But what does generous authority look like in the practice of gathering?

Generous authority is Richard Saul Wurman, the founder of the TED conference, walking onstage in Monterey, California, holding a pair of scissors. He walked toward Nicholas Negroponte, the founder of the MIT Media Lab, a speaker, friend, and longtime attendee who, despite his familiarity with its norms, had violated its policy forbidding neckties by wearing one that day. Generous authority, in service of the larger gathering and its values, compelled Wurman to approach Negroponte before he could start his talk and theatrically cut off much of his tie. Which he did.

Generous authority is the comedian Amy Schumer facing down a heckler at a comedy show—hecklers being a perfect example of those pretender authorities waiting to rule if the host shows any weakness. Someone yelled a non sequitur from the audience, "Where'd you get your boots?" Schumer hit the heckler back hard: "On the corner of You Can't Afford Them and Stop Talking to Me." She was funny, but she was also implicitly using her power to prevent one heckler from ruining the show for others.

Generous authority is Daisy Medici's arduous effort to equalize who gets to speak when wealthy families get together to make decisions and plans. Medici is a financial adviser (with a very good name for a financial adviser) who facilitates when the patriarchs and matriarchs of moneyed families convene their extended tribes for what are often difficult conversations. Generous authority is Medici's awareness—and gentle counterbalancing—of the tendency of in-laws often to stay silent, deferring to the blood relatives, and of the elders to edge out their adult children, even though it is those children who will live with the consequences of, say, selling off a family business or giving money away.

Generous authority is not a pose. It's not the appearance of power. It is using power to achieve outcomes that are generous, that are for others. The authority is justified by the generosity. When I tell you to host with generous authority, I'm not telling you to domineer. I'm saying to find the courage to be authoritative in the service of three goals.

PROTECT YOUR GUESTS

The first and perhaps most important use of your authority is the protection of your guests. You may need to protect your guests from one another, or from boredom, or from the addictive technologies that lurk in our pockets, vibrating away. We usually feel bad saying no to someone. But it can become easier when we understand who and what we are protecting when we say no.

When it comes to using our power to protect guests, we could learn from the Alamo Drafthouse, a movie theater chain founded in Austin, Texas, with locations now in several cities. How many times have you been in a movie theater, trying to watch the show, and one or two rows behind you are people loudly stage-whispering to each other? Or the person next to you takes out their phone and the radiating white light competes with the big screen? How bad does it have to get for you to say something? Perhaps you say something and nothing happens. Perhaps you say something and a conflict breaks out, ruining the movie for even greater numbers of people.

What sets the Alamo apart, in addition to its large seats and its food and beverage service during the show, is that it practices generous authority. Most movie theaters, like so many hosts, focus primarily on their own host-guest relationship, overlooking the audience's internal relationships: that of guest to guest. The Alamo does not make this mistake. Someone there seems to have realized that other theaters outsource the role of enforcer to their patrons, which is a role a paying customer should not have to play. And so when you watch a film at the Alamo, you see an announcement that warns you not to text or talk during the show, which many theaters have. But here's the clincher: If you do, you will get one warning by the staff. If you do it a second time, you will "be ejected." And if you, as a customer, see another customer breaking one of the rules, you can simply put up your "order card" at your table and the theater will take care of it. (Customers also write down food orders on the same card to signal the waiter, so the anonymity of the snitch is safe.) The waiters deliver on the promise by serving as enforcers. I can attest that they do their job.

When one guest was kicked out for texting, she left an angry voicemail on the theater's machine: "I've texted in all the other theaters in Austin and no one ever gave a fuck." She continued, "You guys, obviously, were being assholes to ME." She went on and on, ending with "And I'm pretty sure you're being an asshole on purpose. So thanks for making me feel like a customer! Thanks for taking my money, asshole!"

The Alamo, confident in the generosity of its authority, reveled in the message. The company turned the voicemail into an advertisement. It ended with the words "Thanks for not coming back to the Alamo, TEXTER!" The ad went viral. The company's CEO, Tim League, explained the company's policy and strict enforcement of it: "When you are in a cinema, you are one of many, many people in the auditorium. When the lights go dark and the movie begins, every single movie fan in the room wants to be absorbed into and get lost in the flickering images on the screen. A light from a cellphone, a screaming baby or a disruptive teen cracking jokes all pull you out of the magic of the movies. Providing an awesome experience for true movie fans is the reason we

DON'T BE A CHILL HOST

opened the first Alamo Drafthouse back in the mid-'90s, and it is the exact same philosophy we adhere to today."

What sets the Alamo apart from other theaters is not the fact that it has a no-talking and no-texting policy. It is, rather, that it pledges in a detailed way to enforce those policies and that its employees faithfully do. And the Alamo is willing to face the wrath of its guests. Its employees use their authority to protect the other guests and the larger purpose of their gathering. The Alamo, contrary to the texter's voicemail rant, isn't "being an asshole on purpose." Rather, it is working to protect the purpose of the gathering: to enjoy the magic of the movies.

The theater has created a separate program, Alamo for All, where it lifts the noise and technology rules entirely and allows people to move around during the movie. The theater hosts these film experiences to serve a different purpose: to create a radically inclusive, accessible movie theater for children (including crying babies) and guests with special needs. Because the Alamo knows the needs of some patrons can be at odds with those of others, it has created two separate gatherings that serve two separate purposes: one to protect its guests from noise and distraction, the other to protect its guests from exclusion and inaccessibility.

To protect your guests in this way can be challenging, because the anger of the shushed is concentrated, while the gratitude of the protected is diffuse. Anyone who has ever moderated a panel—that most lamentable of gatherings—knows the feeling. But very talented moderators like David Gergen, the CNN political commentator and consigliere to many American presidents— get used to the idea of taking one for the team, even if the team doesn't even realize what is being done on their behalf. When

Gergen hosts a panel and Q&A time comes, he often instructs the audience: "If you would, identify yourself, be fairly succinct, and remember that a question ends with a question mark." When an audience member inevitably begins making a long statement, Gergen interrupts repeatedly if need be: "Can you put that into a question? . . . Can you put that into a question? . . . Is this leading to a question?" It may seem to some that he is being mean, but in fact he is protecting the rest of the audience who waited or paid to hear from the head of state or a famous author or a political activist, not a fellow audience member.

That is protecting your guests: anticipating and intercepting people's tendencies when they're not considering the betterment of the whole of the group or the experience. The questioner at a panel who makes a statement often doesn't realize that she is making a statement, as odd as that might seem. The relentless self-promoter at a cocktail party probably wouldn't sound the way he does if he could hear himself. People aren't setting out to be bad people at your gatherings; bad behavior happens. But it's your job as a host—kindly, graciously, but firmly—to ward it off.

A few years ago, Elizabeth Stewart realized that she would have no choice but to step up in this way. She was the founding director of Impact Hub Los Angeles, which is part business incubator and part community center. Even though the organization she ran was about the growing of businesses and the nurturing of entrepreneurs, Stewart knew "that we had to guard against the transactional relationships that permeated the start-up coworking spaces." She continued, "I knew we had to be different through ground rules and setting up norms that supported something different." So Stewart introduced a rule in all Hub LA membership orientations: Members could only talk about what they "sold" if someone asked for help or asked about what they did. She was protecting her guests from being seen only as potential customers or investors and protecting the gathering from becoming crass. "It had to be about people getting to know each other as people first and foremost and sharing their ideas second. That's where the rule came from. We tried to create a culture that was sensitive to inquiry and invitation," she said.

Protecting your guests doesn't have to consist of loud interruptions or fierce rules. It can be done through small, almost unnoticeable interventions that happen throughout a gathering: rescuing a guest from a long, one-sided conversation in the corner of your party; shutting down a domineering employee at work with a joke; asking someone to stop texting.

Protecting your guests is, in short, about elevating the right to a great collective experience above anyone's right to ruin that experience. It's about being willing to be a bad cop, even if it means sticking your neck out. And it's generous, because you're doing it for your guests so that, as at the Alamo Drafthouse, they don't have to.

EQUALIZE YOUR GUESTS

Another vital use of a host's authority is to temporarily equalize your guests. In almost any human gathering there will be some hierarchy, some difference in status, imagined or real, whether between a sales vice president and a new associate at an all-hands meeting or between a teacher and a parent at back-to-school night. Most gatherings benefit from guests leaving their titles and degrees at the door. However, the coat check for their pretenses is you. If you don't hang them up, no one else will.

Thomas Jefferson understood that. The United States was, in his mind, a bold bet against inherited hierarchy. Jefferson was wise enough to understand that this ideal of equality should not remain an abstract concept. It should also dictate how he and other American leaders lived their lives—and, yes, organized their gatherings. Jefferson believed a new republic needed new protocols.

One of these new protocols involved the seating of dinner guests. A dinner party was a formalized affair in European society, where people were seated according to rank—all the more so in official and diplomatic settings. Jefferson got rid of this tradition, declaring, "At public ceremonies, to which the government invites the presence of foreign ministers and their families, a convenient seat or station will be provided for them, with any other strangers invited and the families of the national ministers, each taking place as they arrive, and without any precedence." Seating people "pell-mell," as it was called, offended some people who had enjoyed the benefits of status, including a British minister to the United States named Anthony Merry. Merry, his "large and equally offended wife," and another diplomat all withdrew from official Washington society. According to *The Thomas Jefferson Encyclopedia*, "The ensuing social tempest came close to clouding the course of American foreign and domestic policy, but Jefferson stood firmly behind the principle at the root of pell-mell: 'When brought together in society, all are perfectly equal, whether foreign or domestic, titled or untitled, in or out of office.'" He wanted his gatherings to reflect this ethos. (Unfortunately, the ethos didn't extend to his slaves.)

More than two centuries later, another American president

sought in his own way to equalize people and he, too, ruffled feathers, and got a few laughs, when he did. President Barack Obama noticed that men were far more likely to both raise their hands and be called on in public question-and-answer settings. So he started an experiment. Whether addressing students at Benedict College, workers in Illinois, or even his own press corps, he would insist on taking questions in "boy, girl, boy, girl" fashion. If no woman stood up with a question when the women's turn came, Obama would wait until one did.

You don't have to be the leader of the free world to equalize your guests. You just have to be aware of the power dynamics at your gathering and be willing to do something about them—as were the founders of the Opportunity Collaboration conference.

The conference was started in Ixtapa, Mexico, in 2009 to bring together leaders "dedicated to building sustainable solutions to poverty." From the beginning, the hosts knew they were up against formidable power dynamics in the anti-poverty field: the organizations with the grant money held much more power than the grantees who implemented the programs on the ground. The organizers believed this dynamic thwarted the work of reducing poverty. As Topher Wilkins, the conference's CEO, explained to me, "When I attend a traditional conference, it's like fingernails on a chalkboard." He added, "I think they do more harm than good. It's promoting the same hierarchy that leads to how economic development gets done, and it's that structure that we actually need to break down if we're going to solve these problems in the first place."

Wilkins and his team set out to design a gathering that would counterbalance rather than reinforce the hierarchy between donors and grantees. They invited 350 people to spend a week together in Mexico, and they spared no opportunity to embed equality into the gathering. They used nametags with first names in giant letters and last names in small letters, and—heaven forbid—they did not include organizational affiliations. They began the conference with a three-hour town hall, giving attendees a chance to "witness who we are as a community," Wilkins said, and "very openly talk about the things that are preventing us from working together in the first place." People seized on the chance to speak truth to one another and to power. Grantees said things like "Every time I go to a potential funder, it's like going to the gynecologist. You have to show them everything!" Donors responded: "I hear that, and it's really horrible. For me, it's also difficult because I have to make decisions that change people's lives, and there's a lot of responsibility and stress around that." The organizers even had people role-play the grievances of the other side to foster empathy.

Opportunity Collaboration had a larger purpose in mind: to solve the problem of poverty by equipping those who fight it to do so more effectively. That greater effectiveness, the organizers felt, would come from greater openness, greater collaboration, and, above all, greater equality. So after picking the location and guests, these organizers knew that they needed to claim their own power as hosts capable of equalizing their guests. If they could make the different tribes of anti-poverty warriors stand on level ground and hear one another democratically, perhaps they could begin to change how the field works in general.

This democratization of gatherings isn't just for presidential occasions and poverty conferences. Many parties and other social events could benefit from some assertive equalizing. It was in part because the writer Truman Capote understood this that he was able to make his Black and White Ball such a great splash.

On November 28, 1966, the Monday after Thanksgiving, Capote invited 540 of his "closest friends" to the Plaza Hotel in New York for a masked ball. It was unlike any party the city's society had ever seen. Not because of its lavishness (the invitation was for 10 p.m., and spaghetti and hash would be served at midnight). Not even because of the location. But because of who attended, and what they were told to wear.

Capote invited princesses and politicians, Hollywood stars and writers. The party was held in honor of Katharine Graham, which was itself an unusual move as she was a recent widow. Although she would go on to run *The Washington Post* during two of its most consequential decades, she was relatively unknown at that moment. Capote, whose bestselling book *In Cold Blood* had recently been published, invited the maharani of Jaipur and the Italian princess Luciana Pignatelli, as well as the middle-class family from Garden City, Kansas, who had hosted him while he was doing research for the book. And in addition to mixing all these worlds, he asked everyone to wear masks. "There was something radically democratic in the notion of inviting these very famous people to a party and then telling them to hide their faces," said Deborah Davis, an author who has studied the ball.

For Capote, who loved a good party, the role of the masks was a deliberate act of subversion. As celebrities streamed in, the act of blocking their faces, even if just a little, created a parity that rarely existed in their social universe. (He even had thirty-nine-cent masks on hand for the guests who "forgot" theirs, to enforce the rule, Alamo Drafthouse–like.) The guest list was sent to *The New York Times* the next day, and the symbolism of all those people in the same room shook up people's notions of who and how people could mix.

CONNECT YOUR GUESTS

A third use of generous authority is in connecting your guests to one another. One measure of a successful gathering is that it starts off with a higher number of host-guest connections than guest-guest connections and ends with those tallies reversed, far in the guest-guest favor.

As with the protecting and equalizing, the connecting of guests is something that no one is against in theory. Who doesn't want their guests to come away from a gathering having gotten to know one another? But the question, once again, is whether you are willing to use your authority and stick your neck out in order to make those connections happen. Whether you are willing to risk looking like a fool, or going too far, or even annoying people, in order to foster the linkages you claim to believe in.

I was once facilitating a one-day conference on a working farm. The topic was the future of grass-fed beef, and the organizers had convened about 120 people who were involved in different aspects of the grass-fed beef ecosystem. At the time, grass-fed beef represented a tiny percentage of the beef sold in the United States, and the organizers had invited people who wanted to see that percentage grow. In the room were ranchers, farmers, investors, beef buyers from grocery chains and delis, chefs, and consumer advocates. But they didn't all know one another, and in some cases, they had very different reasons for being there.

The organizers had scheduled a day full of panels, speakers, and updates from the field. But we knew that a key element in making them think of themselves as a group would be to build their sense of community. By the end of the day, we wanted them to feel as though they could pick up the phone and call anyone else in the room. So I set myself the goal of figuring out how to provide each participant with an opportunity for meaningful small-group conversations with at least three-quarters of the other guests. Yet the only way I could think of to actually do this was to have them get up and move to a different table after every speaker. It was a hassle, and people often resist packing up their belongings and moving.

Nonetheless, we decided to do it. After every speaker and every coffee break, I reminded them that it's hard to build a movement if you don't know who's in it. So each person had to move to a different table. At their new ten-seat tables, they would have a chance to introduce themselves to new people and answer a question relevant to the day or the most recent speaker. In order to deliver on the larger purpose of connecting the group, I had to be willing to face a few grumbles about moving belongings and not being able to talk to friends. I had to operate as a representative of their future selves—happy they met new people, surprised by new connections with people unlike themselves—and actively go against what their present selves demanded.

By the end of the day, the mood at the gathering was anything but grumpy. In fact, it had turned festive. A number of participants approached me and said that they had never before felt so connected to so many new people so quickly. We had gone through a lot of technical information about the grass-fed beef industry, but we hadn't sacrificed connection on the altar of our agenda. We believed we could do both. And we did.

The moral of this story is that connection doesn't happen on its own. You have to design your gatherings for the kinds of connections you want to create. And, again, it doesn't have to be elaborate and complicated. I once heard of a couple who found a clever way to seed connection among their wedding guests. At the entrance to the reception, they left a hint to each guest to seek out another specific guest they were told shared one similar interest—for example, to find the avid skier who once quit a management consulting job to become a ski instructor. They knew that, absent such instructions, friends and family who knew one another would seek one another out and stick together.

Some intentional gatherers actually encourage these guest-guest connections to form in advance of the event itself. Chris Anderson, who now runs TED, recently started a new tradition. Some weeks before the big conference he throws in Vancouver, he hosts a dinner for speakers based in New York who are in the final days of writing and memorizing what are supposed to be "the talks of their life." Before the dinner, those speakers are all connected individually to him or one of his colleagues. After the dinner, they are connected to one another. They become a tribe who can navigate the sometimes intimidating halls of the massive conference. A grueling and intimidating process becomes less scary, and a gathering becomes more intimate. One group of speakers who were brought together in this way still gather from time to time in one another's homes well after the conference, because they found such kinship in one another.

HALF-GERMAN, HALF-EGYPTIAN AUTHORITY

I have encouraged you to own your power as a host, and to do so not to aggrandize yourself but to protect, equalize, and connect your guests. Now I want to talk about one of my favorite role models for generous authority: Nora Abousteit.

Abousteit is an entrepreneur living in New York City. Born in a small town in Germany to a German mother and an Egyptian father (the one who started the students-only bar), she has spent her career building communities of people who make things by hand. The founder of CraftJam, an organizer of social crafting events, Abousteit gathers in the course of doing this work, and she gathers in her personal life. A lot.

She is, you could say, an extreme gatherer. She hosts and attends more gatherings than most people I know, and she hosts more generously and seriously as well. Abousteit will think nothing of gathering forty people in her home for a banquet multiple times a year. She cohosts large dinners on the eves of conferences around the world. She hosts regular brunches for anyone who happens to be in town on a Saturday. Her home has an open-door policy, and she hosts friends of friends, even if she has never met them, to give them a temporary sense of belonging while they navigate a new city. In all she does, she incarnates generous authority—protecting, equalizing, connecting.

Abousteit uses her authority to protect her guests in ways small and large. At her formal seated dinners, she informs guests that they can't show up late. "People warm up together," she tells me. "They get to a certain point, and there's a certain kind of energy, and it's a collective experience." By letting people come whenever they want, Abousteit understands that she would be failing to protect those who showed up on time. In that same spirit, if two friends are in a corner catching up with each other and ignoring the rest of the group, Abousteit has no problem saying to them, "Catch up on your own time." She is protecting those who may not have the luxury of catch-up buddies at the dinner, and whose chance of having a good time depends on other people being open to conversation with a stranger.

She equalizes her guests by holding everyone to the same standards. At one banquet she hosted, she ended the evening by suggesting that the group of forty go around the table with each person sharing a single piece of culture, broadly defined, that truly moved them that year. She insisted that each person get only sixty seconds to do so. And then she equalized her guests by enforcing that sixty-second rule mercilessly. Whether it was her mother-in-law, her husband's colleague, or a high school friend, at sixty seconds, Abousteit said, "Time's up," and the group moved on.

Abousteit connects her guests to one another as if it's her job. At one party she hosted, as friends streamed up the stairs to the main room, she stood at the top with a big smile on her face, welcomed each guest, and told them that she loves nothing more in the world than the people she loves meeting one another, and that they have one job before dinner: make two new friends. And because she's so authentic and explicit about it, people make an effort to talk to new people, in part because she's given them the social cover to do so.

One way Abousteit helps her guests connect is by priming them to take care of one another. When she gathers a large group of people who are sitting at separate tables, she assigns roles to a guest at each table, which gives them something to do and an excuse to talk to the others around them. A "Water Minister" ensures that everyone has full glasses of water. A "Wine Minister" keeps the wine flowing. At another dinner, with people seated banquet-style next to others they didn't know, when the food arrived in big bowls, she explicitly invited her guests to "serve each other and not worry about getting served themselves." She explained: "In Egypt, we always serve one another first. When that happens, everyone gets food. You're not worried about yourself." Abousteit laughingly admits that she plays the Egyptian when greater warmth is required and it's helpful to be Egyptian, and she plays the German when greater order is required and it's helpful to be German. That night, the guests, a bit startled but also intrigued, began lifting bowls of quinoa salad to serve one another, everyone looking around to see if their dinner mates had gotten enough food. This small reorientation shifted the dynamic of the room. Instead of worrying about themselves, the guests relaxed and started to look out for everyone else. She had nudged people into relationships of care, even though many of them had just met.

Abousteit understands that generous authority is a commitment, and that she must sustain the protecting, equalizing, and connecting of her guests throughout the event. And it was this commitment, and the bewildered pushback it invited, that came to a head at the most important gathering of Abousteit's life: her wedding.

She had spent days with seating charts designing what she thought were perfect tables. They were low tables, in the Egyptian style, covered with multicolored silk cloths under a beautiful, enclosed tent. She sat groups of six people together at thirty tables.

She chose a smaller number than many do for wedding tables because she was more interested in group intimacy than group energy. She was marrying an American who works in China much of the time, and because she herself hailed from multiple places, the guests were from many different countries. At the tables, she tried to put together people who were different but somehow complementary. She considered the dynamics between individuals and the table's potential conversations as a whole. And to the dismay of some of her guests, she followed German tradition and separated couples by putting them at different tables.

At one point during the evening, Abousteit, looking stunning in her black-and-white wedding dress, walked around proudly, admiring her handiwork, visiting each table to greet her guests. Her deepest desire was coming true: the disparate parts of her life were melting into a tribe. Suddenly, she noticed something amiss: "I saw a couple where the woman was actually sitting on her husband's lap, telling him that she missed him. I was confused why this one table was different. I could tell right away, just from looking at the people, that the entire energy of the table was off." To the surprise and dismay of that guest, Abousteit walked over and marched her guest back to her original table.

Why had the aberration in her seating arrangements upset her so much? "They were breaking harmony," Abousteit explained. "They were only thinking about themselves and their own needs and not about the group. In a group, if everybody thinks about the other person's needs, everyone's needs are actually fulfilled in the end. But if you only think about yourself, you are breaking that contract." She continued: "I was really upset because it's not fair to the other people at the table." In that moment, Abousteit was thinking not about the guest who had departed from the seating order so much as the guests who were left behind. Obviously, none of her guests was going to get up and ask the guest to return—even if the absence did alter the dynamics at a rather small table.

The guest whom Abousteit shame-marched found her behavior authoritarian. But Abousteit saw it as being protective of the five people who were left at the table. In her mind, the dinner was a short part of a long evening, the only portion where couples were separated, and it was specifically designed to help her guests connect and interstitch the many disparate stories there.

When you are on the wrong end of one of Abousteit's gathering commands, it isn't fun. But I have never had any doubt about why she is ruling her gathering. It is always for the sake of her guests.

One of my favorite gathering documents is an email that Abousteit once wrote to a friend, offering tips for throwing a dinner on the sidelines of the South by Southwest Conference. It leaves no doubt about where her heart is:

1. YOU ARE THE BOSS. Hosting is not democratic, just like design isn't. Structure helps good parties, like restrictions help good design.
2. Introduce people to each other A LOT. But take your time with it.
3. Be generous. Very generous with food, wine, and with compliments/introductions. If you have a reception before people sit, make sure there are some snacks so blood sugar level is kept high and people are happy.
4. ALWAYS do placement. Always. Placement MUST be boy/girl/boy/girl, etc. And no, it does not matter if someone is

gay. Seat people next to people who do different things but that those things might be complementary. Or make sure they have something else in common; a passion or something rare is best. And tell people what they have in common.

5. Within each table, people should introduce themselves, but it must be short. Name, plus something they like or what they did on the weekend or maybe something that can relate to the gathering.

6. For dessert, people can switch, but best to have it organized: tell every other person at the table to move to another seat.

I love this list for how it distills the ethos of generous authority. In almost every instruction two things are embedded: compassion *and* order.

WHEN AUTHORITY TURNS UNGENEROUS

I'm sure you've been to many gatherings governed under the doctrine of chill. Conferences in which the "questioner" before you in line deprives you of the opportunity to ask something because his "question" turns out to be a soliloquy spanning two typed pages, and the moderator doesn't stop him. School-welcome picnics at which not so much as an opening announcement is made, leaving you wondering if you are actually at the school picnic or just a crowded portion of the park. Dinner parties at which you become an expert in start-ups—or at least the start-up of the really talkative guy next to you.

I'm also certain, though, that you've been to another, very different kind of gathering: one in which you felt not unattended or abandoned, but rather controlled, bossed around, taken for granted, even tricked—and very clearly for the sake of the host, not anyone else. Ungenerous anarchy—a.k.a. chill—is not the only enemy of generous authority. There's also the problem of ungenerous authority, to which we now turn.

If the sin of the chill host is leaving people alone for his or her own sake, the sin of the domineering host is controlling people for his or her own sake. It is running your gathering with an iron fist, and doing so in a way that is in service, above all, of yourself. Though there are no hard and fast rules, in my own experience, it is institutional gatherings that more often err on the side of ungenerous authority, the bureaucratic need for predictability translating into a rigidity that doesn't serve guests. It is personal gatherings that more often suffer from the problem of chill. That said, I have been to ungenerously anarchic institutional gatherings and ungenerously authoritarian personal ones. You never know.

The host most likely to succumb to ungenerous authority is the one who fears losing control. It is in the obsession with knowing how events will play out that we often make them go poorly for the guest, for the sake of calming ourselves. This was the case at one gathering I helped put together: the formal launch of the Obama administration's new Office of Social Innovation and Civic Participation, in the summer of 2009.

It was a new office, dedicated to a new idea: that sometimes the role of government is not to solve problems directly, but rather to play conductor to the orchestra of solution chasers around the country. The founding of the office sent a message that Obama, a former community organizer, didn't just believe in local solutions and active citizenship in theory. He was building an institution tasked with harnessing and promoting those ideas.

We wondered: What was the best way to launch such an office? This wasn't like launching a Treasury Department sub-agency. Our office represented new values and a new theory of where good ideas came from, and this deserved a different kind of launch. We made plans for an interactive conversation among President Obama and one hundred leaders in the social innovation sector. It was a rare gathering where the icons of the field would all be in one room—and a room in the White House, no less. Members of our team recommended doing a live, dynamic, fish-bowl conversation where each guest could step in and out of the dialogue circle at timed intervals while engaging with the president. But when we took our plans to the Office of Public Engagement, the gatekeeper for all public-facing gatherings, the staff there shot down every element of the gathering that was unscripted, that had any element of risk.

"We never know what he might say if it's unscripted," we were told of the president.

The event ended up being traditional—a highly scripted speech with guests seated in classroom-style rows in the East Room of the White House. What might have been an event that pushed forward a field and embodied its purpose—to look out to the community for solutions to the nation's problems—ended up being a staid, top-down ceremony. Because of the organizers' fear, it was an excessively controlled gathering. The organizers had claimed their authority, but their authority did not feel

generous. Rather than protecting their guests, they seemed motivated to protect their own jobs. Rather than connecting the invited leaders to one another, they had them listen to the president
and three other speakers. In the organizers' mind, the perceived
upside (galvanizing a group of leaders around the president's new
innovative initiative) was not worth the risk of the perceived
downside (the president making some offhand comment that
might cause other problems). This risk factor is among the biggest reasons many institutional gatherings leave the generosity
out of their authority.

If timidity can make gatherers ungenerous, so does navel-
gazing. I have a friend in the fashion industry who once invited me
to a fancy gathering to celebrate the 250th anniversary of a liquor
company. While the gathering overflowed with all the right ingredients for a swanky and memorable night—a welcome cocktail,
performance artists, a red carpet, a celebrity appearance, models as
waiters, and a tantalizing menu—it quickly became a self-serving
disaster—even though on the surface it appeared very generous.

There was one drink on offer: a strong cocktail made from the
brand's liquor. There were no alternatives except water. As we
were waiting for our drinks, we were strongly encouraged, repeatedly, to move into the main dining area as the program was going
to begin. At least we would be given some food to counterbalance
the liquor, we thought, only to discover that the food would be
served only after a presentation. We had been invited to a 7 p.m.
dinner, but the meal wasn't served until close to 10 p.m. There was
an MC managing the show, but there was only so much he could
do: It was clear he was following a script. As the guests sat quietly,
staring at the stage, without food or drink, the hosts showed video
after video explaining the work of the tasting committee, whatever

that was. We learned about the seven generations of family members that contributed to the legacy of this liquor.

As far as I could tell, few of us had arrived cynical of this event or of this brand. As the night wore on, I started noticing guests texting under the table, rolling their eyes, mock-eating their own arms. There began to erupt a small, if subtle, revolt. The experience of the audience was being totally ignored. By having us sit at specific tables, with no real way to move or get up or go anywhere, and with little opportunity to talk to one another, they were certainly using their authority. But what they gave us in return did not justify the freedom they were asking us to give up.

When the food finally came out, the hosts were so focused on the beauty of the delivery that they forgot the practical considerations of a roomful of hungry guests. For each table, a SWAT team of waiters marched out in a straight line, holding the plates, and then surrounded the table all together and served the course à la française (simultaneously to every guest). But the problem was that this process took a lot of time, and there were many, many tables to be served.

The printed menus on the table had filled me with excitement for the moment that was now, at last, coming. There would be, for saffron lovers, "Saffron Potato Crisp" and "Crab and Saffron Maki," "Scallop and Saffron Cream" and "Saffron Poultry." There would be "Cocoa Salmon" and "Chocolate and Mango Pie." When I finally got my plate, though, I was surprised to see how little there was on it. As we raised our forks to eat, the organizers now scolded us not to eat any of the "food" until the four members of the tasting committee came onstage to explain each dish that we were supposed to eat with the drink. First, they said it in French, and then it was translated into English. It was clear that it was important to the company that all four of these people were represented onstage.

I finally just started eating. I was done in five minutes, and looked around to see if I could get a second plate. No luck. What could have been a fun, interesting evening turned into a night to make fun of the hosts.

At this point, I and others grasped the deeper reasons for this dreary gathering: The event's purpose was to honor a small number of people. This was a celebration of the liquor company, by the liquor company, and for the liquor company. Everyone else was a prop. The evening was all form, no function. They hadn't woven us into their story, and we didn't feel a part of it.

The difference between Abousteit's imposition and the liquor company's imposition is this: Abousteit's authority was not about her. At her gatherings, the heavy hand demonstrably makes the gathering better for guests. She's not doing it to be the star. She's doing it so that each person gets an equal chance to be a star, to enjoy the evening, to come away slightly altered by the moment. With the liquor company organizers, the guests became the unwitting audience of a bad show. As one guest wrote to me later, "Why were we gathered? What purpose? What was the red thread that tied it all together?" He continued, "They forgot to do the basics: Frame the event. Here is why we are here."

The organizers neither connected the guests to one another, nor protected the guests from anyone, including themselves. In fact, they were the oppressors. And they forced the audience to protect themselves.

If you are going to hold your guests captive, you had better do it well. When a host fails to exercise power, the authority that pops up instead can be annoying, but it is hard to pin down. It comes from fellow guests whose names you may not even know. When a host exercises power badly, on the other hand, the anger has a clear focus. The wrath knows where to go.

HOW I RUINED THAT DINNER

So as a host, how do you get your power right? How do you not abandon your guests while ensuring that your power serves them? How do you strike that balance? Or to put the question in more personal terms: How could I have done it better that night I ruined dinner?

It was a dinner that my husband and I were hosting for ten guests. It was originally planned around a couple we wanted to have over, in part because they host us quite often. (I know: not a good purpose.) We then added six other friends to the evening. Some of the guests knew one another professionally, but not well; others had never met. It was an intergenerational group, ranging from people in their twenties to people in their seventies. My original intention was to be a cool, laissez-faire host. I would be unobtrusive. As each guest arrived, my husband or I let them in, poured them a drink, and led them to the living room, where there were nibbles arrayed on a small coffee table, surrounded by a circle of chairs and a sofa.

I thought that introducing people who already knew one another a bit might seem heavy-handed or overly orchestrated, and I was trying to create a relaxed tone for the evening. Each guest found a spot around the circle and then remained in it for much of the next hour, talking in small groups. The energy was low, and it felt a little forced. I was surprised because I thought the group would have enough in common to spark easy conversation.

I started to get nervous.

We invited people to move to the table for dinner, and at that point, one of the guests pulled me aside and said, "Can you please introduce us? There haven't been any introductions." In trying not to impose, I had left my guests underequipped.

I decided to reverse myself and take charge of the evening. I welcomed everyone and raised a glass. I thanked each of them for "sprinkling fairy dust on our family" in different ways over the previous year. Then I attempted to make an introduction of every guest. I hadn't planned what I was going to say, so I tried to wing it. I embarrassed the first guest in trying to honor her: I said something like "This date was chosen months out because of Elise's crazy calendar." She blushed, while everyone else looked a little wounded, thinking they were runners-up. Then I went around and tried saying something about each guest, but I messed up the details and was repeatedly corrected. "He grew up in Tennessee," I would venture. "Actually, Georgia," the guest said. I introduced some of the guests professionally, but other guests based on a personality trait. It got so bad that one guest said, "Hey, you said something about everyone's profession except for Zeb's." Then, as I became more flustered, I realized I wasn't sure of that person's current work, so I asked him to expound. I took forty-five minutes to do these introductions. My husband was cueing me to stop, but it was no use: I couldn't do half the group and leave the other half out. My husband finally had to tell people to please start eating while I finished the introductions.

In trying to course-correct, I swung from unstructured to

tyrannical—from an anarchy that didn't serve my guests to an authority that didn't serve them either. And I did both badly. I could have addressed the need for introductions in a number of creative ways: letting people ask each other questions, having partners introduce each other, asking each person to answer one fun question. But I did none of that. Instead, I took over without any forethought. And my mode of introduction neither connected the guests to one another nor provided paths to a group conversation.

The rest of the night was clunky at best. A few guests dominated the conversation. I would try to redirect it, but still raw from my introduction flop, I was gun-shy. I don't believe the guests left feeling particularly connected to one another. The conversation was disjointed. People fled right after dessert was served, saying they were tired. (Never a good sign when your guests say they are tired at 9 p.m.) I woke up the next morning feeling embarrassed and regretful.

I had tried out two kinds of authority that night, both of them wrong. I left people alone. And then I ruled them illegitimately. What could I have done better?

I could have started before the gathering even began. In my reminder email to the group the day before, I could have easily included a little fun background on each person, which they could read on their own time to get a sense of who would be there. As they walked in, I could have connected them, making a point of bringing each person around, even though it was a small group, and introducing them warmly to one another, saying a few nice things about each, as Abousteit's list advises.

Once at the table, if I was going to do introductions, I could have prepared better so that my comments would be warm and interesting and, more important, accurate and egalitarian. I could have found one beautiful detail about each person that no one knew. Or I could have asked a question at the beginning of the meal to connect the group, something like "What is on your mind for the year ahead for yourself? For the world?" And then, harnessing my inner Abousteit, I could have made sure that everyone answered it.

Briefly.

Four

Create a Temporary
Alternative World

. . .

S ometimes you need to spice things up.

So far, we have explored how to anchor your gathering in a meaningful purpose. How to close doors on the basis of that purpose. And how to be a host who takes care of your guests by taking the right kind of charge. These decisions will give your gathering a solid foundation.

Many of the people I work with don't realize they need to do this foundational work. I have to convince them to go back to basics. The question they often come to me with instead is the one we turn to now, and we can turn to it because we have gone through the foundation making: How do I mix things up at my next gathering?

If Internet-advice sites are a guide, the hunger for answers to this question is widespread. From SheKnows.com: "Ways to Spice Up Your Next Dinner Party." From the online-invitation company Evite: "5 Ways to Spice Up Your Office Party." From Wisdump: "Holding a Conference? Spice It Up with These Geeky Ideas." From the Catholic Youth Ministry Hub: "Twelve Ways to Spice Up Your Next Youth Group Breakfast."

Some of the tips you find on such sites work; some don't. But this genre of advice misses a larger point, which is that many of our bland gatherings cannot be saved by one-off interventions and tricks that are disconnected from the context of the gathering. A gathering's blandness is a symptom of a disease. We must treat the disease. And what is the disease? That the gathering makes no effort to do what the best gatherings do: transport us to a temporary alternative world.

So I will leave the micro-tips and micro-tricks of spicing things up to the Internet. In this chapter we will delve into a way of seasoning your gathering more deeply: designing it as a world that will exist only once.

THE RISE OF RULES

I began noticing the invitations a few years ago—invitations I personally received and ones people showed me. In some ways, they were conventional, asking people to a dinner, a conference, or a meeting. But they contained an unfamiliar, even jarring ingredient: rules for the gathering.

There was the group that called itself, with no apparent humility, the Influencer Salon. It gathers twelve strangers every month to cook and eat together. The invitation contained these rules: "Conversation: We ask that guests do not discuss their

careers or give their last names until after the presentation portion of the evening"; "Photography: Photos are only allowed during the presentation portion"; and "Attendance: People who
confirm and do not attend are unlikely to be invited again." (The
presentation, it turned out, was the serving of the dinner.)

There was a gathering called the House of Genius, which
started as an experiment in Boulder, Colorado, bringing together
a group of entrepreneurs and using their collective brainpower
to solve one of their problems. It came with its own set of
"House Rules," including "FIRST NAMES ONLY: Personal
information—last names, professions, etc.—are saved for last. In
the interest of maintaining pure collaboration, use first names
only until The Reveal"; and "COLLABORATE CONSTRUC-
TIVELY: Genius is about creative, actionable ideas for a greater
good. Criticism can be appropriate, but please keep it constructive. If you like something that has already been said, feel free to
'+1' the comment."

There was a so-called Jeffersonian Dinner, the invitation to
which warned that "you cannot talk to the person next to you,
you can only talk to the entire table."

There was a destination birthday party in New Orleans,
whose invitation came with its own rather charming set of rules:
"Limit your time in bed," "Don't stray from the herd, be a strong
follower," "Take tremendous photos but post nothing," "Commit to a conversation with a local," "Make up more rules as we
go," and "Don't miss the flight home."

There was a wedding invitation that said, "We invite you to be
Fully Present with us at our UNPLUGGED WEDDING. Kindly
turn off your phones and cameras."

There was even a Christmas party invitation that issued a rule about RSVPing: "We don't care if you come or go, but you must RSVP. If you don't RSVP, you won't be invited next year."

At times, these rules struck me as unreasonably demanding. Who are you to tell me who to talk to, which of my names I can reveal, what I can talk about, whether I seek alone time or not, whether I check my texts or not, whether I update my Instagram feed or not? These rules could seem like the stuffy old etiquette that ruled many older gatherings, but on steroids. What's nice about etiquette is no one clogs up your inbox about it. No one tells you what it is in advance. No one forces you to practice it. You just may not get invited back if you mess it up. Here was something different: people dictating the details of their guests' conduct up front and plainly, leaving nothing to the imagination or social cues.

It took me time to understand that what these gatherings signified was not a doubling down on etiquette but a rebellion against it. In the explicitness and oftentimes the whimsy of these rules was a hint of what they were really about: replacing the passive-aggressive, exclusionary, glacially conservative commandments of etiquette with something more experimental and democratic.

RANDOM KNOWLEDGE OF HOW OLD RICH PEOPLE WANT YOU TO BEHAVE

In sixth grade, I begged my parents to sign me up for Junior Cotillion. All my friends in northern Virginia were doing it, and I was not going to be left out, even if I didn't know what a "cotillion" was. My parents—since I was an only child and was raised in my early years outside the United States—were keen on sending me to things where I would have company, especially if they seemed very American. Thus they signed me up for what amounted to Southern charm school lite.

The National League of Junior Cotillions traces its origins back to the town of Lincolnton, North Carolina, and the year 1979, when a woman named Anne Colvin Winters began teaching etiquette. Winters was a former pageant winner and debutante in her hometown of Gastonia, North Carolina, who would go on to be a statewide organizer for Ronald Reagan's presidential campaigns, focusing on colleges and universities. The little classes she began in Lincolnton eventually grew into a national organization, with three hundred chapters in more than thirty states. Junior Cotillion offered students "a three year curriculum designed to give young people instruction and practice in the courtesies that make life more pleasant for them and those around them."

Among the skills that Junior Cotillion taught were proper telephone courtesy, acknowledgment of gifts, introductions, receiving lines, participating in group settings, polite conversation, paying and receiving compliments, sports etiquette, first impressions, dress code for all occasions, manners in the home and in public places, table manners, formal place settings, styles of dining (including American, Asian, and Continental), skills involved in being a guest, hostess, or host, and many other areas of social behavior.

Once a month, I put on stockings, a pleated navy polyester skirt, a white turtleneck that I tucked into that skirt, and my favorite floral vest, and I was driven to a local country club to learn how to make life more pleasant for those around me. The teacher, a South African woman, would roll out a table with a white tablecloth and show us proper table settings, down to the precise placement of a wineglass. She explained the correct way to send a thank-you note (promptly and by including a specific detail of appreciation), what to do when you drop a fork at a restaurant (never pick it up), and the steps of the foxtrot. I remember most classes ending with a formal dance lesson. (I was terrified of this part because it required pairing up with a boy to learn the steps, and I suffered from what my friends called "sweaty-hand syndrome.")

Cotillion was enjoyable, if not life changing. I enjoyed hanging out and giggling through much of it with my friends. I saw the inside of a country club for the first time. And I liked the graduation ceremony, because we got to have a dance party at the local Clyde's restaurant. But the lessons imparted to us didn't feel especially useful. I filed the teachings of Junior Cotillion into the deep recesses of my brain as Random Knowledge of How Old Rich People Want You to Behave.

There is no doubt that etiquette has a certain value. I'm the one who lobbied my parents to send me to Junior Cotillion, after all. Within a certain social milieu or professional class, it is helpful to have a common set of norms and behaviors. Sharing this common code allows people to coordinate more easily, to avoid embarrassing one another, and to minimize the social risk of situations.

These positive features of etiquette work particularly well in stable, closed, homogeneous groups. When like gathers with like, etiquette often does its work so well that no one notices its presence. In ancient Greece, when you were invited to a symposium, you knew there would be a chair for you, probably in a circle, perhaps in the host's bedroom, and that you had better prepare your liver and your larynx. If you were invited to a neighbor's home in Waterloo, Iowa, in the 1950s, you would know that after eating in the dining room, the group might wander over to the piano to sing songs together, many of which you, like everyone else, had learned in Sunday school. In Stockholm today, when you're invited to a crayfish party in August, you know that you might need to call back to mind the lyrics of the *snapvisor* and that you should be ready to down a shot of schnapps. And in Argentina, when families gather for a Sunday-afternoon barbe-cue, no one makes plans for the rest of the day. That would be silly. Because they know, after they eat platter after platter of meat, they will sit and talk, and then sit and talk some more—*sobremesa*, or "over the table," as it is called. Each of these situa-tions is lubricated by etiquette. A group of like-minded, similarly raised people gather enjoyably, over and over, by following an unspoken and long-standing code of being.

The problem is that more and more of us do not live in closed circles of like-minded, similarly raised people. Think of the last few gatherings you attended—a work meeting, a class, a trade show. Chances are, you sat next to and talked with people from places other than where you're from, people with different cul-tural norms, people of different races and religions and histories. And chances are, therefore, that you sat next to people who do practice etiquette—but etiquette different from yours, and per-haps even in conflict with it on certain points. When my Argentine friends used to show up to dinner parties in New York an hour late, they were confused as to why their friends were livid. They were experiencing a clash not of civilizations but of etiquettes.

When Jewish and Christian in-laws come together for the first time over Thanksgiving, and one side opens with the Lord's Prayer, as they always have, and the other family sits quietly feeling isolated, they, too, are experiencing a clash of etiquettes, not to mention belief systems. In the world we are becoming, there will be even more such clashes.

ETIQUETTE VS. POP-UP RULES

The rise of pop-up rules can be better understood against this backdrop. It is no accident that rules-based gatherings are emerging as modern life does away with monocultures and closed circles of the similar. Pop-up rules are perhaps the new etiquette, more suited to modern realities. If implicit etiquette, absorbed from birth, was useful for gatherings of closed tribes, whether Boston Brahmins or Tamil ones, explicit pop-up rules are better for gathering across difference. Rules-based gatherings, controlling as they might seem, are actually bringing new freedom and openness to our gatherings. To grasp why, we have to look into the differences between pop-up rules and etiquette.

The cotillion class I took is part of a long tradition of etiquette that goes back hundreds of years. In 1750, the fourth Earl of Chesterfield wrote a letter to his illegitimate son, Philip Stanhope, laying out advice that would come to be regarded as one of the founding texts of modern etiquette. "You have acquired knowledge," he wrote, "which is the Principium et Fons; but you have now a variety of lesser things to attend to, which collectively make one great and important object. You easily guess that I mean the Graces, the air, address, politeness." Among these "Graces" was the ability "to carve, eat, and drink genteelly, and with ease." One should avoid "awkward attitudes, and illiberal, ill-bred, and disgusting habits; such as scratching yourself, putting your fingers in your mouth, nose, and ears."

On the road from eighteenth-century etiquette to Junior Cotillion were many stops: the teachings of Emily Post, *Robert's Rules of Order* for business conduct, and various other sources of guidance on how not to mess up in polite society. Yet when I read the letters of the Earl of Chesterfield, what strikes me is how a few basic features of the etiquette approach to life were baked in from the start.

One of these is fixedness. Whether in the earl's instructions to his son or in the curriculum I absorbed at Junior Cotillion, there is a strong sense of permanence. These aren't the guidelines for this event or this month or this year; these are the enduring right ways to be. To practice these ways was to uphold a tradition. And because these codes wouldn't change, the assumption was that you needed to learn them early and on your own time, so that you would be ready to deploy them in society. "We truly believe manners will never go out of style and the skills we help children develop are the skills of a lifetime," the National League of Junior Cotillions declares.

The etiquette approach to life is also imperious. It is the opposite of humble. It shows minimal interest in how different cultures or regions do things. It upholds a gold standard of behavior as the only acceptable one for people who wish to be seen as refined. It is not interested in variety or diversity, or the idea of different strokes for different folks. At Junior Cotillion, we didn't learn the dances of Compton, Spanish Harlem, or Appalachia. We learned the foxtrot. We acquired its idea of the universal access code for appearing polite.

A third feature of the etiquette approach is exclusion. The value system behind etiquette is aristocratic. It is designed to help you stand out from the mob. The idea is to scale the social ladder, not collapse it. If everyone knew the foxtrot and proper wineglass placement, going to Junior Cotillion would no longer help students transcend the herd and be "among the most successful in their graduating classes," as its website promises.

If the standards of etiquette are fixed, imperious, and exclusionary, pop-up rules have the power to flip these traits on their head, creating the possibility of more experimental, humble, and democratic—and satisfying!—gatherings.

If etiquette is about sustaining unchanging norms, pop-up rules are about trying stuff out. The etiquette of not bringing up politics or religion at dinner applies, in the minds of those who believe in it, to all dinners, not just their own, and not just ones during an election year. But the rule of not saying your last name at a salon is a lark that expires as soon as the last guest has gone. In an etiquette-based gathering, the ways of behaving flow from your identity and define who you are. In a rules-based gathering, the behaviors are temporary. Whereas etiquette fostered a kind of repression, gathering with rules can allow for boldness and experimentation. Rules can create an imaginary, transient world that is actually more playful than your everyday gathering. That is because everyone realizes that the rules are temporary and is, therefore, willing to obey them.

If etiquette is about the One Right Way, pop-up rules make no such claims. They are free of the ethnocentric, classist pretensions of etiquette, because the rules they enforce are made-up. Their impermanence is a sign of their humility. No one is claiming that the withholding of last names is the mark of a cultured person. They are just saying that on this day, at this time, with these people, for this purpose, do not say your last name, and let us see what happens.

And if etiquette is about keeping people out of certain gatherings and social circles, pop-up rules can actually democratize who gets to gather. What could be less democratic than etiquette, which must be internalized for years before showing up at an event? A rule requires no advance preparation. Thus someone who has just arrived in a country and is unfamiliar with its culture, but is able to read an email, can fully, without embarrassment, partake in a rules-based gathering—but would struggle at a gathering full of etiquette landmines. It is not difficult as an outsider to comply with the rules of a Jeffersonian Dinner or a House of Genius event or one of the trendy new "silent dinners." But grasping whether a dinner party in Hamburg is the kind at which you should say "gesundheit" after a sneeze or rather shouldn't—that takes years of immersing in German social life, of learning codes and cues. If implicit etiquette serves closed circles that assume commonality, explicit rules serve open circles that assume difference. The explicitness levels the playing field for outsiders.

Etiquette allows people to gather because they are the same. Pop-up rules allow people to gather because they are different— yet open to having the same *experience*. In my observation, many of the people best able to gather across tribal lines these days are those willing to play with pop-up rules. When they do, they often end up creating that temporary alternative world I described earlier. By drafting a kind of one-time-only constitution for a gathering, a host can give rise to a fleeting kingdom that pulls people in, tries something new, and, yes, spices things up.

Let's now zoom in on one such gathering and see how it works—the Dîner en Blanc.

A KALEIDOSCOPE OF WHITE

Dîner en Blanc is a magical example of what a gathering can achieve when it is governed by explicit rules rather than hidden etiquette. It is a global dinner-party series that has hosted events all over the world, from Kingston to Singapore, Kigali to Bucharest. A dinner in a single city on a single night may have as many as fifteen thousand guests. An event occurs just once a year in any given city, but there have now been dinners in seventy cities on six continents. The dinners bring together people of all backgrounds, races, languages, and sexual orientations. People don't need to share a common language; they can come with whatever dietary restrictions they have.

What became a global phenomenon started as a personal invitation. In 1988, François Pasquier was returning to his native France with his family after two years living in French Polynesia. He invited a large group of friends to join him for dinner at his home to celebrate his homecoming. Then, realizing there wouldn't be enough space, he told them instead to meet at the Parc de Bagatelle, one of Paris's four botanical gardens. He asked each guest to bring a friend and to wear white to make it easier to find one another in the public gardens. The evening turned out to be memorable and electric and they decided to repeat it the following year, and again the following. Each year, there were many of the usual suspects, plus a growing number of newcomers. It expanded and expanded, all through word of mouth, each year more spectacular than the last. Once it outgrew the Parc de Bagatelle, they began hosting it in even more iconic venues in Paris— the Pont des Arts, the Palais-Royal, and the Trocadéro. The organizers tried to keep a certain continuity to the dinners by requiring that newcomers be invited by someone who had attended the previous year. Still, over time, the annual Parisian dinner has grown to more than fifteen thousand guests. And it began to spread around the world, from continent to continent.

And the not-so-secret secret of its spread is the invention of a rule-based format that allows the dinners to gather people who share very little in common.

On the appointed evening, thousands of locals dress elegantly in white from head to toe, with a dash of the spectacular—perhaps a boa, a fascinator, a top hat, a cane, angel wings, or white gloves. They arrive in pairs at one of a number of designated locations throughout the city. They are carrying picnic baskets full of champagne, elegant home-cooked food, glassware, white tablecloths, white flowers, and their own fold-up tables and chairs. They do not know ahead of time where this massive flash mob of a dinner party will take place. But they are sure it will be good.

The guests are escorted, typically in groups of fifty, from their meeting points to a surprise venue in the city, along with thousands of others. Once at the venue, they set about building a glimmering but temporary ant colony of white. They unfold their white tables, their white portable chairs, their white tablecloths. They array their tables in long rows, and the women sit on one side of each row all the way down, the men on the other. Each pair lays its own table with things brought from outside: glassware, porcelain, candles, fresh flowers, vases, napkin holders, and whatever else might add to the beauty of the evening. There is not a speck of paper or plastic to be seen.

There is no public announcement to begin, no MC guiding the night (in fact, it is explicitly forbidden). Rather, to signal the beginning of the evening, guests, reading one another's cues, grab their white dinner napkins and wave them in the air. It is time to eat. For ninety minutes, as the sun sets, this gigantic tribe feasts on three-course homemade meals. The food, like the tables and candles and everything else, is brought by the guests, and the hosts strongly encourage it to be homemade. (In recent years in certain cities, there has also been an option to purchase food from a vendor on-site.) The wine is white or rosé or champagne; there are few, if any, beer cans in sight. Dessert time comes—guests are encouraged to make something special: chocolate-covered strawberries, say, or individually wrapped macarons. During dinner, everyone remains seated; no one stands or wanders around. Marriage proposals have been known to happen at this hour.

People all over the world have described attending Dîner en Blanc as the best night of their year. One elderly guest in New York described it in this way: "Over the past three and a half years, I've been dealing with physical illness and challenges, and despite that, I've made sure that I attend the Dîner en Blanc every year, even if my doctors recommend that I didn't come, because I find it spiritually and emotionally and physically such a rejuvenating thing." He continued, "You really can't describe the emotions and the feelings that are involved unless you're here and feel them yourself."

As dusk yields to the summer night, you might notice every table lighting sparklers, signaling the evening's next transition. Guests stand up, find other friends, hug, toast, and begin to dance. The entertainment, always a surprise, begins. It might be an electronic violin, as at a dinner in New York; or choreographed dancers with paper parasols, as in Tokyo; or drums and guitar, as in Port-au-Prince, Haiti. The mood changes as the pulse of this coordinated tribe grows stronger. At midnight, a trumpet sounds. The guests wrap up their tables, pack their items, and collectively leave. Four hours after everyone sat down to eat, there's no trace of the evening.

A GAMBLE ON RULES

Why has Dîner en Blanc spread so well? Perhaps because of its intuition that etiquette would be inadequate to the task of gathering so many different kinds of people. Dîner en Blanc instead bet on rules—rules that would one day help a woman named Kumi Ishihara import the magic to Japan.

Thousands of miles from the Parc de Bagatelle, and many years after that original gathering, Ishihara one day saw a YouTube video of a flash mob dinner in New York. Born in the Japanese seaside town of Kamakura, Ishihara had moved with her family at age fourteen to Düsseldorf, Germany, where she attended a Japanese school and acquired a sense of herself as a nomad. After stints in Singapore and London, she returned to Japan in her late twenties and built a motley livelihood as a yoga instructor, creative consultant, and translator. When she saw this video of thousands of people in white, it grabbed her. "I was so amazed to watch this crowd of white gathering," she told me. She loved that it was a global phenomenon, connecting disparate people through the same experience. She knew she had to bring Dîner en Blanc to Japan.

She first needed to convince the French organizers to grant her a coveted Dîner en Blanc license. To maintain the dinner's integrity, the French organizers have developed a system of granting official licenses to organizers all over the world to host an official Dîner en Blanc. She convinced two Japanese friends who had more experience organizing large events to join her in applying and interviewing, and after two video conferences they won the license.

Ishihara now had to figure out how to bring this very public European dinner to a very private Japanese context. She and her fellow organizers needed Japanese authorities to give them space on public grounds for an admittedly strange-sounding event. They had to generate interest in the dinner among hundreds of people, most of whom had not heard about it before. Perhaps most difficult of all, they had to persuade these strangers to follow a set of intricate, unfamiliar protocols.

As an organizer, Ishihara was required to follow and enforce an extensive list of strict rules that she received from the organizers. She shared with me the following summary of them:

· If you receive an invitation, you need to bring one guest with you.
· The rows of tables have a male side and a female side.
· Wear white, including socks, shoes, headpieces.

· Dress formally and outrageously, but in good taste.
· Bring wine, champagne, or mineral water. No beer, spirits, or soft drinks.
· The square table must be between 28–32 inches by 28–32 inches and covered with a white tablecloth.
· No plastic, no paper. Only glassware and fine china.
· If you accept, attendance is mandatory. Rain or shine.
· Food must be "quality," ideally homemade; no fast food.
· There is no MC to the evening. Everything happens through group cues.
· No standing during the eating period. This is a formal dinner.
· Clean up behind you, with the trash bag you brought. Don't leave a trace.
· Organizers may host Dîner en Blanc only once a year.

Selling the dinner to Japanese people was going to be tough. Japan, Ishihara told me, doesn't have a culture of dining with strangers. While dressing in costume is common in Japan, white shoes are almost impossible to find. Tables with the exact right measurements would need to be ordered months in advance. People aren't used to registering for events through the Internet, or to schlepping and working so much to attend a party. It is difficult enough to get people to commit to come to your event, Ishihara said; people aren't used to paying for something they've never seen before. This was Ishihara's challenge: to get thousands of Japanese strangers to not only follow these rules but also be excited by them.

For months, she wrote daily Facebook posts on the Japanese

Dîner en Blanc page, to "get them in the mood," she said. She summarized for me in English the themes of her Facebook messages. "The story is not just about the day," Ishihara said. "It's over the course of the month at least, buying the candle stand that you like, the skirt that you like, so you're building momentum and excitement." She focused on different elements over the course of a few months. One day she wrote about the European-ness of the dinner: "It's like a banquet. It's very formal. You really have to dress up. At a banquet, you would never dream of having it on paper plates!" She explained to guests that the dinner was demanding on purpose: "This is a heavy-duty party. It's not just an easy picnic." Above all, she employed the Passover Principle that I wrote about in chapter 1, conveying that this was a special invitation for a special night, that it would happen no more than once a year, and that it was the inaugural Dîner en Blanc in Japan. "We are choosing this secret place, which no one else in Japan or anyone else has ever dined at," she said, recalling her post. "It will likely be the only time in your life you will dine there."

Some in Tokyo might have recoiled at certain rules, just as people around the world have. In Singapore, a debate arose about whether Singaporean food was "formal" enough, generating a firestorm of outrage about their "ancient colonial master mind-set." In Boston, a blogger wrote, "Um, so if I'm part of a same-sex couple, romantic or platonic, I can't sit with my guest? Because it will mess up the symmetry?" In Washington, D.C.: "No event has ever made me want to plan a paintball rampage like this one." In New Orleans: "This whole thing makes me feel like putting on an old Saints jersey and licking roast beef po-boy gravy off my forearm while doing the Cupid Shuffle." Organizers have been accused of being "snobbish," and their event "too expensive" (it varies by city but is roughly thirty-five to fifty dollars per person to register) and simply too much work for the guests. In Vancouver, two artists even staged an alternative "ad hoc, barely-even-organized, family-friendly" Ce Soir Noir to which 1,500 people turned out. And yet the dinner continues to spread from city to city, year after year, with longer and longer waiting lists. The waiting list in Tokyo was 11,000 people. The waiting list in Philadelphia has been as high as 26,000 people.

Having attended the one in New York as a fly on the wall, I can tell you the crowd was more diverse in every way than that at most New York parties I have attended—and more diverse than the clientele of most New York restaurants of comparable elegance. As a cohost of the New York event told *Time Out* magazine, "The beautiful thing about this event is that it's so diverse. The community here is from every background and every part of New York. It's truly a reflection of the city that we're in. It's brilliant to be a part of something that brings so many different people together, and to have everyone celebrate as one. You can put everything else aside, but at the end of the night, we're all wearing white."

Shane Harris, a political reporter who wrote about the Dîner en Blanc in Washington, D.C., made a similar observation. Harris touted the event as being "snobbery-free"—a rarity in a self-important city known for "its rigid social calendar and order." He wrote:

We may have been all dressed in white. But we were, as a lot, mostly African-American, followed by white, with a ribbon of Asian and Latino throughout. We were old. We were young. We were gay. We were straight.

I couldn't tell who was rich and poor. A woman in a stunning silk gown could have been an intern as easily as a partner in a law firm.

What these people were not was the type I'm used to suffering at so many social occasions. No one was looking over their neighbor's shoulder to see who they really should be talking to. No one asked what I did for a living. It was a delightfully douche-free affair.

In the elegant Washington soirées to which Harris seemed more accustomed, it's usually the clothes that come in all colors and the people who are overwhelmingly white. At Dîner en Blanc, it was the clothes that were white and the people who were of every color. I don't believe it's a coincidence. When the social code is spelled out, when it is turned into a one-night-only game, you don't have to know certain unsaid things, you don't have to have been raised in a certain way, you don't have to be steeped in a certain culture, you don't have to have parsed decades' worth of social cues. You just need to be told tonight's rules. This is the bargain that the rules-based gatherer offers: if you accept a greater rigidity in the setup of the event, the gatherer will offer you a different and much richer freedom—to gather with people of all kinds, in spite of your own gathering traditions.

On Ishihara's big night in Tokyo, 1,600 white-clad partiers showed up at the appointed hour, at the appointed place. Ishihara described what she felt during the waving of the handkerchiefs that opened the dinner: "We conquered this place." The people all around her were total strangers to most others in the gathering. But something about the scene and the strange, binding, liberating rules created a beauty and a sense of awe that brought people together, Ishihara said: "Your heart is already open, so you can be friends with anybody."

At the end of the party, a trumpet was blown to notify the guests that it was over. "Do you remember Cinderella?" Ishihara asked. "Cinderella would know at twelve midnight that she has to go. And here, too, people would automatically know that this midnight summer is over." She said that she felt herself asking, "Is it a dream or reality?" Such is the power of gathering openly and colorfully with rules. You create another world. And then it expires, and you begin all over again.

RULES VS. PHONES

Etiquette, as we've seen, is a problematic glue in modern society, because it makes it harder, rather than easier, to gather across differences. Nor is that its only drawback. Etiquette is also a hopelessly porous shield against the most powerful force of our age: addictive technology.

Anyone who gathers nowadays must, like it or not, cope with the reality that people are often elsewhere, thanks to their technological devices. Perpetual distraction is a curse of modern life and of modern convening in particular. People are often too busy to gather at all. Scheduling gatherings can be a nightmare. Coordinating people can be a pain. And when, against all odds, we do come together, our minds are in a thousand places.

How do you get people to be present at your gathering? How do you get them not only out from behind their screens but also not thinking about those screens? If people check their phones an average of 150 times a day, as some studies have shown, how do you ensure 50 of those check-ins aren't at your event? You may have everyone in one room, but how do you get people to be *here*?

For too long, in too many settings, our response to these questions has depended too heavily on manners, on unspoken norms—on etiquette. We have hoped that not checking your phone during dinner will become like not double-dipping a chip—something people know not to do without being told. (Clearly, neither norm has succeeded.) But etiquette is not succeeding against technology in an age of distraction. And if etiquette fails with large, plural groups because it is internalized and implicit, it fails against technology for an even simpler reason. An army of some of the smartest people alive are working feverishly to ensure that etiquette stands no chance against our addictive new technologies.

In 2011, Google acquired a small company called Apture, along with it its CEO, a man named Tristan Harris. He ended up working on the team that designed Gmail's inbox app and realized what he would later publicly say: "Never before in history have the decisions of a handful of designers (mostly men, white, living in SF, aged 25–35) working at 3 companies"—Google, Apple, and Facebook—"had so much impact on how millions of people around the world spend their attention . . . We should feel an enormous responsibility to get this right." Harris eventually published this sentiment in a 144-slide presentation titled "A Call to Minimize Distraction & Respect Users' Attention," directed to his Google colleagues. It is an impassioned plea to abandon the hobbyhorse of personal responsibility and manners—of etiquette—as the proper response to distraction. Making it an individual's responsibility not to be distracted, Harris told *The Atlantic*, is "not acknowledging that there's a thousand people on the other side of the screen whose job is to break down whatever responsibility I can maintain." Google appointed him to be its in-house "philosopher." His mission was to reflect on how technology was affecting human societies.

If etiquette doesn't stand a chance against the programmers of Silicon Valley, why would rules? Because rules are explicit and become an experimental game. There is a certain kind of fun in trying something for a bounded moment. The kind of restriction that might feel oppressive if permanent can seem compelling and intriguing when it applies sometimes, as part of a conscious effort to create that temporary alternative world.

"I AM HERE" DAYS

My husband and I once created an event of this kind, but inadvertently. We were just about to move to New York and eager to explore our new home. We wanted to get ourselves into a habit of exploring continuously; we didn't want to get stuck in the rut of the same few neighborhoods. Somewhere in our conversations, we agreed to set aside a full day every now and then for exploring a single unfamiliar neighborhood.

Soon enough, it was time for our first such day. We chose Harlem. We mentioned it to our friend Nora Abousteit, that paragon of generous authority. Without being invited, she announced, "I will come." What began as a newlyweds' romantic plan was now a social occasion—a gathering. Abousteit then said she was bringing a friend along (yes, she broke her own rule). Not knowing what we were doing, we agreed. And thus "I Am Here" days were born.

We had a friend who was a member of the Abyssinian Baptist Church, led by the Reverend Dr. Calvin O. Butts III. The church receives thousands of visitors every year, in part because of its famous gospel choir. However, because we were guests of a member, we were able to sit downstairs in the main pews, not upstairs with the outsiders. Before launching into his sermon, Reverend Butts surprised us by not only naming us but also reading our résumés aloud to the church. Everyone started clapping as we blushed. We were welcomed and greeted by dozens of members.

High on the feeling of that place, we went to have lunch at a nearby diner. At the diner, we talked about our different experiences of New York and about the manic pace of the city. Having now spent a few hours together, we started to share our fears and anxieties about living there, understanding the social codes, figuring out if we could afford to stay. Without much forethought, we then walked forty blocks south. What we were doing had begun to feel a bit like an investigation of our city, and someone suggested that we should see not only big institutions and restaurants but also private homes. That was where the action was. But how would we see a private home?

Suddenly, Abousteit remembered that she had a friend who lived nearby. On a whim, she texted him to ask him if we could stop by to say hello. To our surprise, he invited us for tea, and we got to see the inside of a beautiful home. We were so tickled by our luck that we decided to keep going, this time walking north to the Museum of the City of New York. There we learned all about the making of New York City—how its lands were leveled, how the farms were paved over, how skyscrapers could be built only in certain places. On our way out, we heard loud beats from a neighboring building and discovered a huge, underground dance party at four on a Sunday afternoon. We grabbed a beer and started dancing. An hour later, sweaty, we broke away and entered Central Park. We realized that we felt relaxed, peaceful, and full of energy, despite having walked so much. And we had barely checked our phones. At 7 p.m., we called it a day. We went home full of the people we had met, the blocks we had walked, the conversations we had had. Only three weeks after moving to a new city, we thought: Maybe we can find our people here. Maybe we can call this city home.

What began as a vague idea between the two of us turned into one of the most meaningful gathering rituals of our early days in New York. First there were the four of us, and then six on another day, and then eight or ten on another. In the beginning, there weren't any rules; we just stuck together the whole time. We began to gather on those Saturdays or Sundays in a way that felt different from how we usually spent time with people. We would choose a neighborhood and rotate "curation" of the day—basically, the role of deciding what to do. At first, it was relatively ad hoc, and the only real rule was that you had to come on time and stay the whole time. I didn't originally intend to have any rules. They evolved organically.

Almost by accident, my husband and I fell upon a gathering format that created some magic almost every time we used it. The "I Am Here" days came to fruition out of an intentional idea, but their structure developed naturally. Our constraints were natural ones: Choose an area that can be covered by foot; invite a group small enough to be able to sit together at a single table for meals; take into account the weather. We found that the days worked better when one person took on the role of curator and did some research ahead of time, to create a specific and enjoyable experience for everyone else—whether or not they knew anything about the neighborhood. We also found that the days worked best when everyone else agreed to submit to the curator's generous authority.

Our original motivation had to do with exploration and discovery more than presence. But as the days morphed from a two-person concept into a regular group expedition, and as more people became interested in attending them, including people we didn't know, I was forced to codify the practices that had emerged. People needed to know what they were signing up for. So I took what had basically been implicit, rendered it explicit, and sent these rules out to newcomers:

- If you're going to join an "I Am Here" day, be there from start to finish (all 10–12 hours).
- Turn off technology (unless it directly relates to the day).
- Agree to be present and engaged in the group and what's going on.
- One conversation at meals.
- Be game for anything.

Among these rules, it became clear that the two most important ones were spending a full day together and no technology. And they were powerful because they forced a degree of presence rare in New York and the tech-addled modern world. People had to come on time, stay the entire time—no coming and going.

When they knew that was the deal, they became more relaxed. They couldn't micro-coordinate. They were giving up the option of finding a better option. They were just here. And because we were all here, we enjoyed one another's company to the fullest. These rules allowed busy, stressed-out, perpetually distracted people to come together and simplify. "I Am Here" days worked because the rules created a feeling that it was "enough" simply to be there, because when you were "here," you were in another world.

We tend to associate rules with formality and stiffness, but in our "I Am Here" days we found that rules created intimacy. Each of us on his or her own was no match for the coding geniuses at Google and Facebook and Snapchat. But once presence was enshrined as a rule, a one-day-only attempt—temporary, humble, inclusive—overcame the power of the machines in our pockets and the churning of our brains.

We discovered from these experiments that spending twelve hours together as a group is fundamentally different from spending four hours together on three separate occasions. The longer you're together, the more reality sets in. You can only chitchat for so long. People (including you) get tired and cranky; walls start to come down. By the time late afternoon arrives, people begin sharing stories of their pasts, of their struggles with money, parents, religion—topics that don't always come up easily. And it was these conversations that truly mattered and made me feel less alone. I realized that there were others in the city who had left the homes they knew in pursuit of adventure but who, like me, treasured their families. That there were others who experienced setbacks in their work and wanted to talk about them but who, like me, didn't always want to be discussing work. That there were others who worried about money but who, like me, didn't want it to keep them from taking risks. And, most simply, that there were "busy New Yorkers" who were not only willing but also hungry to slow down and savor time with friends and even strangers.

The rules to be present worked because they weren't imperious. They were just the formula for these occasional days. And when we followed these rules, they changed our behavior, and they changed the way people saw and interacted with us. As we walked around neighborhoods, a present band of people, locals sitting on their stoops were curious about this strange nomadic tribe that seemed to operate on a different set of rules from everyone else's. We found ourselves sitting down with strangers and chatting with the owners of neighborhood bars. We once hung out with a local TV crew waiting for a story to air. We were invited to share cans of sardines in a garage in Red Hook. We spent time debating homosexuality with ultra-Orthodox Jews in a synagogue, and we got our fortunes read in one of the last working Daoist temples in Chinatown. On one magical night on Roosevelt Island—situated in the East River between Manhattan and Queens—we were invited upstairs to a bar owner's apartment to see the plant that a Chinese grandmother gave her New York–based grandson, the *Epiphyllum oxypetalum*, which blooms one night a year. (It was not the night we were there.) As we sat and sipped wine overlooking the Williamsburg Bridge, the bar owner pulled out his family album and shared photos of his grandmother. By lingering and listening, we witnessed a moment of beauty.

Why did we feel so freed by imposing these rules on ourselves? My friend Baratunde Thurston, a comedian and veteran of several "I Am Here" days, answers the question this way:

It's rare for groups of people to do things together for a sustained amount of time. We all carry with us the technical capacity to be anywhere, to check out of the present time or space. That means we always could be doing anything. So the active choice to do ONE thing and to do it with a fixed set of people is significant. I sometimes found myself feeling antsy with the rules. I wanted to text someone or look up information or just flip through Instagram because Instagram trained me to treat unfilled time as an opportunity to browse Instagram.

What "I Am Here" day offered was a different way to fill that time. Because of the rules, I could go deeper into the experience. I could observe something around me my phone would have caused me to miss. I could interact with a person next to me instead of thousands of miles away. And with the knowledge that I would spend an entire day with this one group, I could let go of the low-level anxiety caused by using every moment to anticipate the next. It didn't matter what else was going on. It didn't concern me where I had to be next. Because I decided to be HERE.

That's the point and the magic. In a world of infinite choices, choosing one thing is the revolutionary act. Imposing that restriction is actually liberating.

PUSH-UPS!

A diamond may be forever, but a gathering rule is just for right now. This is its power. It can make someone like Thurston feel liberated rather than oppressed because it is temporary, humble, and inclusive. It creates a world that begins when the gathering begins and ends when it ends. This fleeting quality of gathering rules allows you, the gatherer, to be creative with them. In setting your rules, you are not making a claim for how any other future gathering should be. A gathering run on rules is like Vegas—what happens there stays there. And so rules allow for an experimental spirit in gathering, whereas etiquette is that spirit's enemy.

At least that is what I told myself after making several senior Thai executives do push-ups in front of their colleagues. I was running a two-day retreat for a group of twenty consultants just outside Bangkok. In Thailand, and particularly at this firm, there was a very strong etiquette among the consultants that the client always comes first. Accordingly, it is understood that they pick up the phone at all hours of the night, leave family dinners to take calls, step out of weddings to reply to texts, and hop on planes if needed. This etiquette had helped to make the firm extremely successful in general. However, it was an etiquette that was threatening the success of this particular gathering: a retreat intended to build trust internally among the consultants. I had two eight-hour days planned, and everything designed down to the minute. Each two-hour section of the day was intense, with the consultants focusing on one another, having powerful and honest conversations, saying things they had been keeping from one another. Then the first break came. A number of consultants had scheduled calls with clients during the breaks. Not surprisingly, after fifteen minutes, they were finding it hard to get off the phone. We started the session again, but four of the consultants were missing. Their tardiness, even if in the name of being a good employee, was hurting the group and making the people who were in the room angry. And it was breaking trust, undoing all the work we had done in the previous two hours, because the latecomers' peers felt disrespected. The client-first etiquette was so strong, I began to realize, that I would need to counter it with an explicit, temporary rule.

As the stragglers came back in, one at a time, with sheepish looks on their faces, one of the consultants made a suggestion. It was said almost as a joke: "Push-ups!" Everyone laughed. I took the cue and decided that this would be our rule. The four tardy consultants, in suits and ties, heels and wingtips, looked at me like I was crazy. The consultants who had returned to the room on time started grinning and clapping. Before you knew it, all four consultants were down on the floor doing ten push-ups each.

It released the tension in the room, and it also introduced a new rule: If you're late, you can come in, but you first have to do ten push-ups. We had three more breaks that day, and by the third one, people were literally racing through the hallways to make it in time. After each break, people would shut the main room door on the dot with great ceremony. If anyone was even a few seconds late, everyone started cheering, and the condemned got down on the floor and gave them ten push-ups. The group collectively improvised a new rule to overrule, temporarily, their usual etiquette. By making it fun and harmless, if slightly embarrassing, they created a fleeting social contract that everyone bought into. The fact that the rule was physical and funny also added some much-needed lightness to the group.

In this case, their client-first etiquette may be good for the firm in general, but it was bad for that specific gathering. The push-up rule helped counterbalance that strong ethic for the alternative reality of our time together, an interlude that needed its own pop-up etiquette. Etiquette can, as I have said, serve a purpose: to maintain pleasantness and politeness and good behavior. But sometimes as a particular etiquette code grows entrenched in a culture, it crowds out the possibility of other ways of behaving that might be more appropriate for certain moments. The consultants' client focus was a good etiquette for most things, but it was an etiquette that left no space for the equally important ethic of caring for their colleagues. A gathering rule allowed us to create that space.

Harrison Owen, an organizational consultant, found this truth in his own way when he realized the limitations of conference etiquette. Politeness and feigning interest in others' work were such strong values that they crowded out the no-less-important value of learning. Owen wasn't a social engineer, and he wasn't about to rewire genteel networkers not to care about other people and their feelings—especially people they might need someday! He stood no chance of changing the etiquette. What he could do was temporarily overwhelm it. So he created a temporary methodology, called Open Space Technology, in which he embedded among other things one specific rule that helped counterbalance an implicit norm of politeness. It was called the Law of Two Feet, and it stipulated this: "If at any time during our time together you find yourself in any situation where you are neither learning nor contributing, use your two feet, go someplace else."

By creating the rule, Owen gave rise to an experiment: What happens at a conference when people are freed, even goaded, to leave a presentation that is not teaching them? Do the same feelings of offense take hold? Do presenters understand? Does it change the way people present? Owen later wrote that the purpose of his rule was "merely to eliminate all the guilt. After all, people are going to exercise the law of two feet, mentally if not physically, but now they do not have to feel badly about it." As in my workshop in Thailand, the rule counterbalanced an etiquette that is often helpful but, for this specific gathering, did not deserve to crowd out all other needs.

Sometimes a rule is useful when a gatherer wants people to connect in a way that normal social norms would discourage. For example, the Latitude Society, a controversial secret society in San Francisco that has since disbanded, used to design various rules at their gatherings to create a sense of belonging. One of my favorites, as shared with me by one of their talented "Praxis" facilitators, Anthony Rocco, was that you couldn't pour yourself a drink; someone had to pour it for you. This simple rule forced (in a playful way) people to interact. The rule took something most people wanted (a drink) and tied it to something that can be awkward initially: approaching someone you don't know. They knew that the old etiquette of pouring other people's drinks before your own had withered too much to expect strangers to follow it at their gatherings. So they made it a rule.

The proper use of rules can help you get so much more out of a gathering because it can help temporarily change behavior. Consider the case of Paul Laudicina, who realized that a bad habit had formed in the board of directors he was leading at A. T. Kearney, a global management consulting firm. Board members were constantly asking for more information and asking clarifying questions, and this was preventing the kinds of conversations that help a board reach critical decisions. At one point, when negotiations among board members were breaking down and tempers were flaring, Laudicina realized that people were asking questions in order to avoid making tough decisions. Curiosity was fine in general, but it wasn't useful given the purpose of this particular gathering. As the chair of the board, he introduced a new rule: Board members could only ask questions that were not asking for more information—that were building on what information there already was. For example, "What is blocking us from getting this done?" or "Who has a problem with this?" or "What would it take to come to agreement on this issue?" As opposed to "Can you give me last year's Q4 numbers?"

Laudicina ensured that all board members had the information they needed well ahead of the meetings and had ample time before the meetings to ask any questions that clarified the issues. By putting information-gathering questions off-limits, he forced his board members to have the kind of difficult but productive conversations that led them to state their positions more explicitly and reach decisions. As board chair, Laudicina had the legitimacy to introduce the rule. But the brilliance of the rule was that he changed the board's language. And by limiting and reorienting the language, he created a temporary alternative world in which they couldn't ask for more information. It forced them to create a world in which each was adding rather than staying still or even detracting.

Laudicina didn't need to create an entire world of rules to temporarily shift the world of the board meeting. He was able to identify the one behavior that he believed was stalling progress and create a temporary rule to overturn it.

Five

Never Start a Funeral with Logistics

• • •

U ntil now, we have explored how to give your gathering a purpose, and how to start making decisions based on it. We've discussed choosing guests and a location in keeping with that purpose. We've talked about finding your voice as a host to keep your gathering true to that purpose. We've experimented with formats and rules that may spice things up.

At some point, though, the big day itself will arrive, and our thoughts must turn from preparation to operation. What do you actually do with these people?

PRIMING

Before your event starts, it has begun

Your gathering begins at the moment your guests first learn of it. This may sound obvious, but it's not. If it were obvious, hosts wouldn't fail to host the pregame for their gathering as often as they do. In my experience, hosts often think of their event as beginning when you call the meeting to order or take your seats at the wedding or walk into your dinner party. In each of these cases, your guests have been thinking about and preparing for and anticipating your gathering well in advance of that moment. They have been experiencing your gathering from what I call the moment of discovery. The intentional gatherer begins to host not from the formal start of the event but from that moment of discovery.

This window of time between the discovery and the formal beginning is an opportunity to prime your guests. It is a chance to shape their journey into your gathering. If this chance is squandered, logistics can again overrun the human imperative of getting the most out of your guests and offering them the most your gathering can. Moreover, the less priming you do in this pregame window, the more work awaits you during the gathering itself.

Because so much gathering advice comes from experts in food and decor rather than from facilitators, that advice almost invariably focuses on preparing things instead of preparing people. This advice makes the pregame window about physical setup rather than human initiation, about the gathering space and not what it holds: people.

For example, Martha Stewart has published on her website a "Party-Planning Guide." It contains a helpful twenty-nine-item checklist for would-be hosts. Stewart covers what must be done weeks in advance ("Choose the type of party you want to throw") and what must be done in the hours before showtime ("Set up the bar, if it is not already done"). What struck me, though, is that only three of Stewart's steps involve communicating with guests, and each of these is logistical: mail or email invitations; let guests know what to make if it's a potluck; chase guests who haven't yet RSVP'd.

In this vision, people are to be corralled, not prepared. Compare this lack of human preparation to the kind of preparation that Stewart suggests for things: "1 Day Before: Wash and prepare salad greens and other vegetables, and blanch vegetables for crudités (keep these wrapped in paper towels). Refrigerate all separately, in airtight containers." This encapsulates the prevailing approach to gathering that I hope to change: fussing over the crudités and hoping for the best when it comes to the human beings. We deserve better.

One finds similar counsel from Rashelle Isip, a blogger, a consultant, and the author of *How to Plan a Great Event in 60 Days.* She breaks creating a gathering into the "10 Lists You Need to Make to Plan a Great Party or Event." There is the "Theme list," the "Budget list," the "Decoration list," the "Music playlist," and so on. The tips are helpful, but all ten focus on the logistics of things and people, not on the priming of the guests. It's not that these logistics don't matter. They absolutely do. But it is remarkable how little space there is in advice guides like this for getting people ready.

Contrast this approach with what occurs when hosts focus during the pregame window on preparing human beings and not crudités.

Four months after he got engaged, Felix Barrett, a prominent London-based theater director, received a key in the mail in an envelope marked "To be continued." He heard nothing else for months. "It was blissful torture," he later said, "the whole world suddenly took on a heightened hyper-real feeling, and everything was shrouded in mystery."

Barrett was no stranger to mysterious experiences, but he was used to being in the driver's seat when they happened. The artistic director of Punchdrunk, an immersive theater company in Britain, Barrett has shaken up his field with his staging of daring interactive plays. In his New York City version of Shakespeare's *Macbeth*, titled *Sleep No More*, your belongings are taken from you at the entrance, you are separated from your party, and you are given a white mask to wear for the duration of the show, a shot of liquor, and an invitation to explore five floors of an abandoned warehouse in Chelsea.

Now the tables were turned on Barrett. After that first envelope arrived, he waited. Eventually, another letter arrived: "Now we can begin." A suitcase was delivered to him at work. Inside, he later told *The New York Times*, he found a tide table, map coordinates, and a small shovel. He followed the coordinates and found himself on the banks of the River Thames. There, he dug up a box full of photographs of words on a computer screen. Those photographs told him that if he completed a series of challenges, he would be welcomed into a secret society.

For weeks, he would receive bizarre prompts from odd messengers: strangers, the words on a cat collar, letters in remote vacation spots. Each prompt included some kind of challenge that he would have to complete were he to enter this secret society. Barrett being Barrett, he obliged. He found himself doing half marathons and climbing between boats on ropes. Each individual challenge presumably took him one step closer to that secret society.

Then suddenly one day he was blindfolded, kidnapped, and taken to an old manor house where he was greeted by thirty men in hooded robes. They were his best friends. He was at the bachelor party of a lifetime—his own.

Barrett's friends understood two things well in organizing his bachelor party. First, that a gathering starts long before guests walk through the door. The clock of the gathering starts, so to speak, from the moment a guest becomes aware of its existence. For Barrett, the moment he received the key in the envelope, his journey into the gathering had begun. And from that moment onward, his friends knew that they were hosting Barrett all the way to the actual gathering. And that how they hosted him would shape how he showed up to the gathering.

The 90 percent rule

A colleague in the conflict-resolution field taught me a principle I have never forgotten: 90 percent of what makes a gathering successful is put in place beforehand.

Randa Slim is the director of the Initiative for Track II Dialogues at the Middle East Institute in Washington, D.C. Raised amid the traumas of the Lebanese civil war, she emigrated to the United States to pursue a Ph.D. in social psychology from the University of North Carolina at Charlotte. She has since become one of the leading practitioners of track-one-and-a-half and track-two diplomacy, in which current and former officials, alongside influential private citizens from multiple sides of a conflict, take part in dialogue in their personal capacities, to complement official diplomacy—often by having more honest exchanges than are possible in official negotiations. Over the past twenty years, Slim has run some of the most ambitious ongoing group dialogues in the Middle East.

One such project was a dialogue series in which she brought leaders from the United States and Europe together with leading

Arab Islamic and secular opposition leaders. The group met three times a year, for three days at a time, for three years, to build trust and find ground for new relationships between their respective countries. The group consisted of twenty influential citizens with the ear of their governments, but the freedom to speak as individuals.

Before the visas were obtained, before the agenda was built, before anyone got on a plane, Slim spent two years flying around the Middle East, using her own contacts, deep credibility, and fluent Arabic to identify the right guests and prepare them for the dialogue. In some cases, she would build trust with potential participants by sitting for hours while having tea with their family. In other cases, she had to convince party leaders to overturn established policies prohibiting meetings with former U.S. officials. She traveled vast distances into disputed territories to demonstrate goodwill, to prove that she was willing to take risks, much as she was asking her guests to do. For two years, Slim focused on securing political permission for the participants and preparing her guests for the dialogue. She knew how vital it was that her interlocutors trust her. You "need from the beginning to reinforce your interlocutors' belief that you will never bullshit them; you will never promise what you cannot deliver; that you will always be straightforward with them; that there are no hidden agendas," she told me. This is what she is getting at when she says that 90 percent of the gathering's success is set in motion before the actual convening. She calls it "the pre-dialogue dialogue phase."

Now, most of us aren't going to spend two years flying around the Middle East to pregame our gathering. I am telling you about Slim not to suggest that you copy her methods, but because there are lessons to be learned from the philosophy underpinning her approach.

One of those lessons has to do with the scale of the ask and the scale of the preparation. The bigger the ask—say, if you're having people travel long distances to attend your gathering—the more care, attention, and detail should be put into the pregame phase. You need to attend to your guests in this pregame window in proportion to the risk and effort you are demanding of them.

Another lesson is that the pregame should sow in guests any special behaviors you want to blossom right at the outset. If you are planning a corporate brainstorming session and you're going to be counting on your employees' creativity, think about how you might prime them to be bold and imaginative from the beginning. Perhaps by sending them an article on unleashing your wildest ideas a few days beforehand. If, for example, you are planning a session on mentorship in your firm, and you need people to show up with their guards down, send an email out ahead of time that includes real, heartfelt testimonials from three senior leaders sharing personal, specific examples of the transformative power that a mentor had on them. In Slim's case, she knew she was going to need her participants to behave with an almost irrational degree of trust. They would have to trust the process, trust her, trust the selection of interlocutors on the other side, trust that nothing terrible would happen to them when they returned home. Slim couldn't afford to cultivate that trusting behavior in them after they showed up. Because it would be important from the get-go, she nurtured it during the pregame.

One other lesson is that, whether in Middle East peace talks or at weekend dance parties, every gathering benefits or suffers from the expectations and spirit with which guests show up. It's hard to get a dance party started, for example, when people show up subdued and in the mood for quiet conversation. Similarly, if you're hosting a meeting at work and hoping to have an honest conversation in which employees share what they're actually experiencing, it can be harder to do if they show up cynical or defensive. Sure, you can try to change their mood when they arrive. But it takes more energy and sophistication on the part of the host and cuts into the time for the gathering. It is preferable to pregame.

Priming isn't hard to do

Lest you think you must become a peace negotiator to gather well, let me say that a thoughtful email can take care of the need to host your pregame. Priming can be as simple as a slightly interesting invitation, as straightforward as asking your guests to *do* something instead of *bring* something.

Consider the case of Michel Laprise, a writer and director at Cirque du Soleil and collaborator on Madonna's MDNA tour and Super Bowl halftime show. He decided one winter to host an end-of-the-year gathering at his home after a heavy season of touring. The problem was, he hadn't even had time to decorate his Christmas tree. He dashed off a quick email to his guests asking them to send him two photographs of happy moments they'd had in the past year.

When the guests walked in the door that evening, they found a Christmas tree decorated with twenty-four printed photographs, cut into small circles, of their own joyous moments: scuba diving, standing in front of a house bearing a "Sold" sign, wearing acrobat gear before a performance. They had a cocktail around the tree, marveling at one another's moments. "Suddenly they were not strangers or colleagues, but the personal part was there, and that started the dinner so well," Laprise recalled.

"I think people felt welcome the way they were, and that it was important for me and for the other people that we hear what's happiness for them," Laprise said. He didn't explicitly announce a theme for the dinner or the evening, but "just by doing the action of bringing something that represents happiness" that "just opened the whole evening on that," he said.

By dashing off that last-minute email and getting his guests to send photographs of themselves, Laprise had begun to host them during the pregame, not just from the formal beginning. By asking them to dig out photographs from the past year, he was getting them to reflect on it. He was priming them for a celebration of the year by having them rummage through it before they showed up. He was putting them into the state of mind with which he wanted them to pass through the door.

The tree decorations ended up sparking many conversations, and though Laprise hadn't intended it, the guests continued to talk about the year's highlights over dinner. "It was a Christmas of happiness," he said.

Laprise understood what many of us miss: Asking guests to contribute to a gathering ahead of time changes their perception of it. Many of us have no trouble asking guests to bring a bottle of wine or a side dish, but rarely do we consider what else we might demand of them in advance. Rarely do we follow Laprise's example of asking guests to perform a task that isn't really a task so much as an attempt to get them in the mood.

In my own work with organizations, I almost always send out a digital "workbook" to participants to fill out and return to me ahead of the gathering. I design each workbook afresh depending on the purpose of the gathering and what I hope to get guests to think about in advance. The workbooks consist of six to ten questions for participants to answer. For a gathering on the future of education at a university, I asked questions like "What is one moment or experience you had before the age of twenty that fundamentally impacted the way you look at the world?" and "What are the institutions in the United States and abroad that are taking a bold, effective approach to educating the next generation of global problem solvers? What can we learn from them?" For a gathering on rethinking a national poverty program, I asked questions like "What is your earliest memory of facing or coming into contact with poverty?" and "How are our core principles the same or different from when we started fifty years ago?" For a gathering of a technology company's executive team after a merger, I asked questions like "Why did you join this company?" and "What are the most pressing questions you think this team needs to address?"

I try to embed two elements in my workbook questions: something that helps them connect with and remember their own sense of purpose as it relates to the gathering, and something that gets them to share honestly about the nature of the challenge they're trying to address. The workbooks aren't so different from a college application in that sense: Sure, they give me a sense of the person and the dynamics of the group, but they also help the person think through the things they value before they arrive. I then design the day based on what I see in their answers. I also weave quotes from their workbooks into my opening remarks at the convening.

And the workbooks do one further thing: They inadvertently create a connection between each participant and me, well ahead of our time together, which makes my job much easier once I'm in the room. By crafting the workbooks and sending them out, I am sending the participants an invitation to engage. By filling them out and sending them back to me, they are accepting. The relationship, and the sharing of confidences, begins well before we enter the room.

A gathering is a social contract

Priming matters because a gathering is a social contract, and it is in the pregame window that this contract is drafted and implicitly agreed on.

Why is a gathering a social contract? Because it proceeds from an understanding between host and guest, sometimes stated and sometimes unstated, about what each is willing to offer to make it a success. Another way to say that is that all gatherings come with expectations. There are expectations of the host—that the agenda will be followed or that food will be served. There are expectations of the guests—that they will do their homework and come prepared with ideas; that they won't bring their three cousins along; that they will dance their heart out and get others to do so. These expectations are present whenever people gather, and the prevailing understanding of what they are constitutes a gathering's social contract.

As with purpose, it is often through conflict and disgruntlement that underlying assumptions about a gathering's social contract reveal themselves. Once, during a conference in Aspen, some friends of mine came back from a dinner irritated because of a violation of what they took to be its social contract. What had been billed as a large but social dinner at someone's home was, midway through the evening, transformed into a brainstorming session on the hosts' work project. The dinner guests, many of them not experts in the industry or particularly interested in "working" at the end of a long day, were suddenly expected to be advisers. My friends, who were among these nonexpert guests, suddenly realized that the dinner invitation was the lure; now they were on the hook to help the hosts make business decisions. Even though the hosts were paying for the dinner, the guests felt used. You never want your guests to think, "Hey! I never signed up for this."

A gathering's social contract is often invisible to us, even when we are carrying out its commands. For example, you may not think that last dinner party you went to had a social contract, but did you bring a bottle of wine or a six-pack of beer or a dessert? If so, why? Because of the implicit social contract that sounds too crass to say out loud: They were making you dinner, and you were helping defray the cost of hosting. Similarly, the social contract of a networking event may be something like this: I am paying forty-five dollars to attend this event; in return, you will ensure that there are better people here than I would meet on my own at the local bar. A social contract for a gathering answers this question: What am I willing to give—physically, psychologically, financially, emotionally, and otherwise—in return for what I expect to receive?

Among the burdens of hosting is drafting this social contract, starting with that moment of discovery. First things first, the host has the chance to frame the event. This is where your specific, unique purpose comes into play. For a funeral, are we coming together to "celebrate and remember," or are we gathering to "grieve and to mark"? Those different purposes imply different types of funerals and different moods and behaviors among guests. From the first lines of the invitation, there is an opportunity to get your guests ready for how you want them to show up.

The host can also set the context for the gathering. When I was invited to the sixteenth annual #Agrapalooza, continuing a summer tradition of made-up games and a drunken talent show at some friends' parents' house, building on the rituals and memories of all the gatherings before, I was being invited into a world, not just to an event. When I was invited to a Passover seder some years ago and the host indicated that it would be a unique one for her, as it was her first Passover without her mother, I was being primed, right from that moment of discovery, to understand the emotional swirl of the gathering. In fact, it is in setting the context that the Passover Principle—knowing why this night is different from all the other nights—first has its chance to be communicated to your guests.

And the host can, in drawing up this contract, begin to throw light on the fundamental bargain that is at the heart of many gatherings, whether or not we like to think of it in this way. I am in no way advocating for your gatherings to be made transactional. Rather, I am suggesting that it is impossible to gather without some kind of implicit deal. And when this deal isn't carefully crafted, and when people's expectations of one another are out of step with what people are willing to give, problems arise—as with that evening in Aspen. If you don't prepare people for the fact that you will be asking them for advice about your company, if you don't tell them that their phones will be taken away for the full day, if you don't warn them that they will be asked to share a personal story prompted by a question, you will often encounter resistance or worse. Trust me. And so part of the job of the pregame is to find ways, implicit and explicit, to communicate to your guests what they're signing up for by saying yes to the invitation.

Now, sometimes when I talk to clients or friends about this idea of a gathering's social contract, they fire back: What about mystery and surprise? You want me to spell everything out? But you needn't spell things out in order to prime your guests. Barrett's friends certainly didn't send him a contract to sign to inform him that he would be kidnapped. And yet at each step of the way he was given a taste of what was to come and given the chance to choose to keep going.

Naming as priming

So how do you make use of this pregame window to draft the social contract and set your guests' expectations? The chance arises with that moment of discovery I mentioned earlier: with the invitation.

When we invite people to our gatherings, too many of us spend too much time focusing on the wrong details of the invitation. Letterpressed versus engraved. Email versus Paperless Post. Black-and-white versus blue-and-white. This is what might be thought of as the Martha Stewart approach, elevating the readying of things over the readying of people.

The most important part of your invitation, though, is what it signals to your guests about your gathering and what it asks of them. And one way to send your guests a signal is to give your gathering a specific name.

To name a gathering affects the way people perceive it. The name signals what the purpose of the event is, and it also prepares people for their role and level of expected participation. If you're hosting a half-day gathering for your team to discuss a new strategy, do you call it a "meeting," a "workshop," a "brainstorming session," or an "idea lab"? Of these names, "brainstorming session" implies a heavier level of participation than perhaps "meeting" does. Part of what worked with our "I Am Here" days, I later realized, was that we gave it a name and that name primed people for what we most needed from them: presence.

Rachel Greenberger, an administrator at Babson College in Massachusetts, hosted a weekly meeting for students. She didn't want to call this time "office hours," because it sounded like an obligation as well as a one-way deal: The student comes to the professor for help and guidance. But Greenberger was running a food program and wanted to help students connect to one another, not just to her, and so she decided to call the weekly hour Community Table. Over time, the gathering has grown into the name; students now turn up with baked goods as well as notebooks. And in a way she couldn't have planned, the Community Table idea she began has now been transplanted to New York, where every month entrepreneurs, academics, activists, and students interested in food engage together around a table, giving and exchanging ideas and building a community.

In my own work, I don't call my sessions "workshops." I call them Visioning Labs. "Visioning" because I am helping people figure out their vision for their work, company, or life. And "Lab," short for laboratory, because it signifies experimentation and possibility, which is crucial to the process. Simply because of the name, I've noticed that people seem to show up differently. They're more open, since they're not sure what to expect from a Visioning Lab, and they are curious. These are some of the behaviors I need them to show up with in order to help them in a meaningful way.

Names help guests decide whether and how they fit into the world you're creating. Eve Biddle, cofounder of a creative community called the Wassaic Project in upstate New York, learned this lesson when she introduced an "Artist Mixer" to a residency program she was running. People weren't showing up, so she asked a few artists why. The evening, they told her, sounded "too nerdy." They were artists and free spirits. The word "mixer" perhaps sounded to some of them like something from the "sellout" lives they had avoided. She listened and renamed the evening "Happy Hour." Attendance shot up. A simple name switch altered people's sense of who the gatherer thought they were and what she expected of them.

Beyond the name, the invitation is full of opportunities for what I think of as priming language. This language doesn't have to be confined to text; it can consist of, or be buttressed by, images and video as well. Whatever the medium, the purpose of priming is to signal to people the tone and mood you're going for at your gathering. When the Walt Disney Company sent out invitations to its *Star Wars: The Force Awakens* premiere, the company reassured its guests that "parking for your Landspeeder, Sandcrawler or other transportation vehicle will be provided."

NEVER START A FUNERAL WITH LOGISTICS

Simple as that: This gathering will be playful, and it is for die-hards who live and breathe *Star Wars*.

And in keeping with an earlier chapter's commandment to be thoughtfully exclusive, being explicit with your guests ahead of time about what/who is in and what/who is out can help guests prepare for what is coming. Take, for example, a line from an invitation to an all-night dance party in Brooklyn, New York: "As we always say . . . bring your sexy single friends and leave those strollers at home. This ain't no Park Slope party"—a reference to one of the city's more family-centric neighborhoods. In this case, a bit of prosaic information is more than that: The relaying of details doubles as the priming of guests to know how to show up. Even the guest without children to bring receives a message from that line: This is going to be a rager.

After the kindling, a Kindle

The invitation is just the beginning. After the moment of discovery, it would be a mistake not to sustain the excitement. Once the invitation has done its work, there are many chances along the way to reach out to your guests and continue the priming. The thoughtful gatherer is conscious of these moments and uses them to set the tone of the gathering and groom the guests to uphold their end of the bargain.

I once saw this sustaining done inventively by a conference with a tough task: to lure high-level government officials to Detroit, and to make them prepare for it by doing a lot of reading. It was 2009. One weekday, my boss at the White House Office of Social Innovation and Civic Participation received a package in the mail. The conference organizers had sent her all the readings she needed to get through on a brand-new, fully loaded loaner Kindle. The Kindle was still a relatively new product, and I don't know that my boss had ever handled one. This boss, who received hundreds of pieces of mail and thousands of emails a week and frequently didn't leave the office until after 10 p.m., had, even before signing up for this conference, more backlogged reading to do than she cared to think about. But when that package arrived, with yet more reading to add to her backlog, she looked at the Kindle and smiled. Yes, the organizers were asking her to fulfill her part of the bargain to do the readings. But through the small design choice to send it on a loaner Kindle, they were able to capture an incredibly busy woman's attention and signal, "This one is going to be different."

This kind of priming is especially important when the host is demanding a lot or when the guest is of a particularly reluctant sort. Sarah Lyall, a *New York Times* reporter who once wrote about her experience of participatory theater shows in New York, describes herself this way:

> All of us have anti-bucket lists of things we do not want to do before we die, and mine includes any activity requiring potentially embarrassing public participation. Wearing a costume, declaiming before a crowd, playing spin the bottle, clapping along to a jaunty show tune, marching, chanting, speaking spontaneously into a microphone, ceding free will to a larger force, doing the hokeypokey and turning myself about—I have made it my business to avoid these things.

> The kinds of gatherings I specialize in creating could be terrifying to people who share this sensibility. That doesn't mean there

is no place for such gatherings, or that people with this inclination need to just take or leave it, or that they should not be invited. It means that some of your guests will share her aversion, and if you are going to ask anything of them, you have to be explicit about what you have in mind, and you are going to have to hold their hand from the moment you first let them know about your gathering/massive-opportunity-for-a-panic-attack.

USHERING

Between the priming and preparation and the actual opening of a gathering, there is another, often overlooked step: ushering. In many gatherings, your guests will benefit from being carried across a proverbial threshold, leaving the wide world and entering your small kingdom.

I am not suggesting that you carry your subordinates into your next Q4 meeting. (That would be uncomfortable and probably illegal.) Carrying guests across a threshold sounds intimate and serious, but what I am really telling you to do is manage your guests' transition into the gathering you have bothered to create. Hosts often don't realize that there tends to be unfilled, unseized time between guests' arrival and the formal bell-ringing, glass-clinking, or other form of opening. Make use of this no-man's-land.

Managing this entry is important because none of us shows up as a blank slate to anything. You have seven meetings in a row, and the fourth one goes badly, and you go into the fifth meeting distracted and spent. You walk into Thursday small group at your church after crawling through traffic to get your daughter to basketball practice on time. Right before entering a bat mitzvah, you receive a text from your boss that your article has been killed. If you don't create a passageway into your gathering for guests like these, they are going to be somewhere else in the most crucial moment of your gathering: the start.

Passageways and doorways

One way to help people leave their other worlds and enter yours is to walk them through a passageway, physical or metaphorical.

The world of immersive and participatory theater, knowing how many people dread public participation, has become very good at constructing such passageways. What can we learn from them about our own, much simpler dinners, meetings, and small groups?

Third Rail Projects is a New York–based theater company that specializes in this. I attended two of its shows to learn how it whisks guests into alternative universes so quickly. And at least in the two that I attended, *The Grand Paradise* and *Then She Fell*, the directors created literal passageways for their audience members to spend time in before the show actually "started." In *The Grand Paradise*, which is about a fading tropical resort in the late 1970s and the cultural values of that era, before we were let into the "resort," we were greeted by an overly cheerful activities director and given a lei and a tropical drink. We were then crammed into a small, closed room outfitted to look like the inside of an airplane. We were given instructions by an airline host and on the television screens above us about what we could and couldn't do and when we were released into "paradise." In

Then She Fell, an immersive theater experience inspired by the writings of Lewis Carroll and staged in an abandoned warehouse, the fifteen-member audience was first seated in a small reception area with a doctor character and given an "elixir" that looked like Jägermeister and a set of keys tied together by a black thread. We were greeted by the doctor, who explained that this room was a "liminal space" and that we were about to enter another world.

In both these shows, this spell of ushering is clearly distinguished from the actual show. The actual show, in our minds, hasn't yet begun. But the creators understand that they have an interest in shaping your total experience, and they understand that things have often begun before they have formally started. With that same understanding, one of the best-known performance artists alive, Marina Abramović, has created a replicable methodology that she uses to transition her audiences from the outside world into her shows.

Performance art is defined by the Museum of Modern Art as a live event in which "the artist's medium is the body, and the live actions he or she performs are the work of art." This art form, even more than others, is interested in the relationship between the audience and the artist. Abramović has become famous for performance pieces like her 1974 work *Rhythm 0*, in which she placed seventy-two objects on a table, including a gun with a single bullet, for the audience members to do to her whatever they wanted. More recently, in her piece *The Artist Is Present*, she sat in a chair for a total of 736-and-a-half hours as a stream of visitors took turns sitting in a chair across from her and looking into her eyes in silence. In each of her pieces, she is, like any good host, hyper-aware of the audience's ability to shape the gathering.

Over the years, Abramović has developed the so-called Abramović Method for Music, which includes a way of preparing her guests for these performances. When audience members arrive, they are asked to put all their belongings (including their cellphones) into a locker before entering the venue. Then they sit in a chair silently, wearing noise-canceling headphones for thirty minutes to block out all the distractions that keep us from being truly present. She thinks of this time as a palate cleanser. "The silence is something that prepares them for their experience," she told me.

In a show at the Park Avenue Armory, a massive performance space in New York City, sitting silently, the audience watched the pianist Igor Levit and his piano slide on a platform into the center of the stage. After thirty minutes, a gong sounded, signaling that the audience could remove their headphones. Only then did Levit play the opening note. One guest in attendance later described the thirty minutes of silence to me in various phases: At first, there was a lot of collective wriggling and shuffling as people quieted down and got used to sitting still. Then there was an overall calming and quiet. About halfway through the silence, though, you could begin to feel the anticipation and expectation build toward the performance. After all that time spent in anticipation, a critic later described the opening note of the aria as a moment of "hypnotic wonderment." This surely had something to do with the fact that he had been unplugged from the rest of the world for thirty minutes, primed to listen in a different way.

For Abramović's seventieth birthday party, she invited hundreds of friends and colleagues to the Guggenheim Museum for a celebration. When you walked in, you were immediately greeted by a row of women dressed in white lab coats bearing pocket mirrors and sheets of gold foil, standing at attention in silence. I was ushered over to the women, and one of them handed me a gold sheet and pointed to my lips. I looked around and realized that other guests had rectangular strips of gold covering their mouths. I picked up the strip, used the pocket mirror they held up, and placed the foil over my lips. Then the woman guided me to sit in a chair, in silence, and make use of the headphones. I didn't understand the meaning of all this, but at some level I didn't have to. Abramović had taken those moments before the action, in which people normally just mill around, and created an opening ritual for each guest. Gold-lipped and headphone-topped, I felt inducted into a secret society. Though I was intimidated to be there, I was wearing the signs of one who belonged.

When I asked Abramović about these passageways she creates, she said simply, "I want to take them from their comfort zone and into a new experience." And she realizes that people are more open to new experiences when the old is cleared away and some space is carved out for the new.

Now, I understand that you may hesitate to force your guests into a thirty-minute tunnel of silence or place gold foil on their lips. But there are many tiny ways you can create a threshold, a pause, before you and your guests cross the starting line together. And you don't need to be an award-winning theater producer to do it. The idea of helping people transition from one state to another is embedded in many rituals of traditional societies. It's the equivalent of a doctor taking off her jacket and putting on her white coat as she enters her office. It's the act of Muslims washing their hands and feet before prayer. It can be the removal of shoes before a Japanese tea ceremony. The only difference with modern gatherings is that the passageway is not prescribed. You need to create it. And one of the easiest, most natural places to create such a passageway is the doorway.

Arianna Huffington is a fascinating and controversial woman, thanks to her work in politics, media, and wellness. She is also a gracious and skilled gatherer. In 2013, she hosted a conference to explore the ideas of wellness that would eventually grow into her new company, Thrive. And she chose to host it in her living room in SoHo in Manhattan. It was essentially a business conference, and many of the participants were strangers to one another, and yet Huffington chose to greet them as if they were arriving at a wedding. She personally stood by the door for a good half hour or hour, first thing in the morning, and individually greeted each person who entered. She didn't have her chief of staff do it, and she didn't have her daughters do it. She did it herself. Because she did, she set a tone for the entire day. Yes, she was saying, we are at a conference, but we don't have to act like it. This is my home, and you are my guest.

When my sister-in-law was getting married, her then-fiancé's Scottish family had flown in for the festivities. The Friday night before the wedding, the entire Scottish clan was invited to my in-laws' home for a party. When the bus pulled up to the house and all the Scots stepped out in their finery, my husband and I spontaneously joined my father-in-law by the doorway and greeted each person as they walked in—dozens of them. This small welcome created a moment for virtually everyone on the groom's side to meet the bride's family, not at the end of the ceremony or during the reception but at the outset. This one act sped up the intimacy and the sense of permission to walk up to anyone over the course of the weekend, which many of us did. It was an initial act of tribe building, and it happened at the border of the gathering.

The psychological threshold

Sometimes there is no physical anteroom, as there was in those New York theater shows I mentioned. Sometimes it wouldn't be feasible to stand in the doorway and greet everyone. Sometimes the work of ushering must be done psychologically rather than physically. I once saw this done brilliantly by Baratunde Thurston, my comedian friend.

He had been asked to host a comedy event that was part fundraiser, part party. The venue was the Brooklyn Brewery. On the evening in question, it was cavernous, rowdy, loud, and full of people full of beer. I could tell that he had been put in a difficult spot. There actually wasn't a stage, or even an elevated platform. People had been eating and drinking for a while already; they were hanging with their friends and didn't look like they wanted to be interrupted. Even the music was no match for the volume of the talking. To make matters worse, most of the people there had no idea who Baratunde Thurston was, and despite the fact that he'd just been handed a microphone, these people were not about to stop their fun to listen to some guy's jokes.

Rather than screaming over people or just starting up his monologue, hoping that someone might take pity and listen, Thurston instinctively went into usher mode. He doesn't always do this, so the rowdiness of the crowd must have tipped him off to its need for some kind of transition. He took his microphone, his only identifiable form of power and authority, over to the liveliest person in one cluster of friends, and he asked that person to say their name into the microphone. After they introduced themselves, Thurston invited everyone else in the room to greet them and clap. Then he walked over to the next group and the next group in the same way, catching five or six of the loudest, rowdiest people in the room off guard by bantering with them, making some jokes, then, essentially, inviting them to support him in his mission to transform them from a crowd into an audience. Within ninety seconds, he had the entire room's attention. He walked back to the middle of the room and started his set.

No matter what environment you're given as a gatherer, you might ask yourself how you could create a transition of this kind—a passageway that tunes out the prior reality and captures people's attention and imagination. By doing so, you create a starting line and, even more important, you help your guests cross it as a collective.

If we think back to Felix Barrett's bachelor party, his friends did a great job of both priming and ushering. They primed him with the notes and tasks, so that he was constantly on guard for the next thing—and increasingly aware of the spirit of what loomed. Then, having primed him, they ushered him toward that opening by kidnapping him and bringing him to the venue. While I'm not (necessarily) suggesting that you kidnap your guests, I am suggesting that, like those bachelor party planners, you are prepared for all the moments leading up to the opening. One of the mistakes many of us make in thinking about this in-between time is believing that "it doesn't count." It does.

In everyday gatherings, it can be as simple as lighting a candle or making a welcome announcement or pouring every guest a special drink at the same time. But the final transition between the guests' arrival and the opening is a threshold moment. Anticipation builds between the initial clap of thunder and the first drops of rain; hope and anxiety mingle. And then when that opening moment finally comes, it is time to give your guests a message: A magical kingdom exists, and you are invited inside.

Missed opportunities

When gatherings fail to do this kind of ushering, they often waste their own potential. Consider the case of a feverish political rally that could have been so much more.

On April 6, 2016, Bernie Sanders, a senator from Vermont and a candidate for the Democratic presidential nomination, held a massive rally in Philadelphia. The line to get into the Philadelphia "Future to Believe In" Rally wrapped around the block. For security reasons, many people were in the stadium for close to three hours before the candidate ever appeared. When I hear that, I think: What an incredible gathering opportunity—three hours of ushering that could have been used not only to gear people up for the rally that day but also to build the Bernie Sanders movement. Only it wasn't.

Instead, thousands of people sat in the 10,200-seat arena and waited. There had been the prior world outside, and in a few hours, the official show would begin. There was little in between, even for a captive and die-hard audience that would have lapped up anything. Having worked with organizers, I can imagine exactly why these ones left this time unfilled: In their mind, the event hadn't started yet. This time probably wasn't on their "run of show." It was time outsourced to the security people, not the hosts.

So let us imagine what could have been done with that time. A few thousand fans of Bernie Sanders, a few hours, no candidate on-site. They could have had some volunteers work as facilitators to get people to sit in groups, or turn to a stranger, and talk about why they were there, what they believed the country most needed, and why they believed Sanders was the answer. They could have set up story circles where clusters of eight sat and shared their own experiences of being on the wrong end of America's economic divide. They could have used that time to create a movement. They had the complete attention of thousands of people, but because the time period was mentally scheduled under "waiting," they didn't make use of it. They didn't understand that they were already hosting.

LAUNCHING

So by now you have prepared your people in the run-up to your gathering and carried them across the threshold when they arrived. But what do you actually do at the opening of the gathering? How do you launch well?

Openings are a big missed opportunity in gatherings. They all too often underwhelm us, and they don't have to. After all, openings lay the track for a gathering. I once met the South African opera composer Neo Muyanga, who told me that he can listen to the first sixteen bars of any opera and know the system and framework of the rest of it—and, therefore, whether he's going to like it. "The opening bars inevitably set up a paradigm using elements such as volume, meter, and progression to invite a listener to eschew their mundane world for a time and to plunge down the rabbit hole into an alternate universe," he said. As he spoke, I realized that gatherings work in much the same way. The opening, whether intentionally designed or not, signals to guests what to expect from the experience.

In the first few moments of a gathering, we are all Neo Muyanga, reading cues and asking ourselves: What do I think of this gathering? Am I in good hands? Is the host nervous? Should I be? What's going to happen here? Is this worth my time? Do I belong? Do I want to belong? The opening is, therefore, an important opportunity to establish the legitimacy of your gathering.

Attention is at its highest at the outset. Because of what scientists call "cognitive processing constraints," we're not able to remember every minute of an experience. Our brain effectively chooses for us what we will remember later. Studies show that audiences disproportionately remember the first 5 percent, the last 5 percent, and a climactic moment of a talk. Gatherings, I believe, work in much the same way. And yet we often pay the least attention to how we open and close them, treating these elements as afterthoughts.

Don't kill the attention of mourners

The first change you should make if you want to launch well is to quit starting with logistics.

I once attended the funeral of a dear friend. The church was packed. Hundreds of family members, friends, and former colleagues gathered in a beautiful room to honor a man who had towered in his field and helped so many. As people entered the pews, they greeted one another. Many of them had been closely connected through this friend at some point but hadn't seen one another in years. Sadness hung in the air, and many of us were already crying. Then the minister got up and walked to the front of the room.

The moment was pregnant. All of us leaned in, eager for his words of comfort. He took a deep breath, looked out at all of us, and began. "Just so you all know, the family has invited us to join them afterward for a reception down the street at the rec center," he said (as best I remember). "But, unfortunately, I am told there is not enough parking at the venue. It's a short walk over, and I encourage you to keep your car here and walk over together afterward." In seconds, the potential energy of the moment had been squandered. We had all been hungry for consoling and coming together. The moment was ripe, and the minister had our attention. Yet perhaps because he didn't want to forget to make the announcement, he used his moment of launch to discuss parking. The minister had wasted what could've been an unforgettable opening to connect the tribe that had gathered around one man. Instead, he started with logistics.

The minister is hardly alone in this habit. Because we think the moments before we start somehow don't matter, any number of gatherings begin with throat clearing. Conferences that commence this way: "Before we start, there's a white Camaro with its lights on in the parking lot, license plate TXW 4628." Town halls that begin with announcements. Galas, full of people dressed in their finery, that launch with a long set of thank-yous to the event's sponsors. I'm speaking, in short, of every gathering whose opening moments are governed by the thought: "Let's first get some business out of the way." It may seem like I'm nitpicking, but what I'm proposing couldn't be more vital to the work of gathering better.

The politics of beginning

I imagine many people will, perhaps grudgingly, agree with me regarding events like funerals. In theory, no one believes in starting a funeral (or other intimate and personal gathering) with logistics. It's just a failure to live up to what we imagine would be best. But with other gatherings, ones where sponsors are involved and there are people to be thanked, I know many hosts will say: I have no choice. I cannot not start with logistics.

I disagree. What I tell the hosts I work with is this: However vital it may seem to start with this housekeeping, you are missing an opportunity to sear your gathering's purpose into the minds of your guests. And sometimes you are actually undermining that purpose by revealing to your guests that you do not, in fact, care about the things you claim to care about as much as you profess.

Every year, the Personal Democracy Forum hosts its annual conference in New York City. This gathering of hundreds of people brings together leading civic activists, technologists, community organizers, civil servants, and others interested in the state of democracy. In 2015, the theme of the conference was "Imagine All the People: The Future of Civic Tech." The organizers chose this theme because, they explained, "we want to take you into a future where everyone is participating, a future that we build together using technology appropriately, powering solutions to shared civic problems."

And so it was a bit jarring when, in the opening session that year, the Personal Democracy Forum began with one of the founders, Andrew Rasiej, turning the stage over to a representative of its "presenting sponsor," a Microsoft executive, to speak first.

What's the big deal? you say. Here's the big deal: In those first few moments, people are at their most ready to be inspired. They are asking: What is this really about? Who holds the keys? People have come, presumably, because they are attracted to the theme of the forum: the idea that democracy can be activated and more people can participate, not just the powerful and well-connected. And then, in those first few moments, the organizers end up replicating the very thing that gets in the way of democracy and the participation of people—money buying special access. By starting with remarks from a corporate sponsor—as opposed to, say, inviting various local community leaders onstage to speak in short bursts—they embodied the problem they were seeking to address.

Sponsors are there to amplify what you can do with an event. However, the moment the host of the event is not also the person funding the event, the event has two masters: the host and the sponsor. And their interests are not always aligned. This misalignment can arise throughout your gathering, but it is often most painfully clear in the opening and closing. So a host must be aware of the fact that handing over precious real estate to sponsors is never costless or neutral. As in the case of the Personal Democracy Forum, it may even raise doubts about the gathering's premise.

If you need some inspiration to push back against those sponsors, consider the case of George Lucas. When he was filming the original *Star Wars*, he wanted a bold launch for his movie. The Directors Guild of America protested. Most films at the time started by naming the writer and director in the opening title sequence—in this case, thanking the film's creators rather than its sponsors. It was how things were done. Despite the protests of the Directors Guild, Lucas decided to forgo opening credits entirely. The result was one of the most memorable beginnings in movie history. And he paid for it—the Directors Guild fined him $250,000 for his daring. His loyalty was to his audience's experience, and he was willing to sacrifice for it. You should be, too.

The cold open

The creators of television shows often find themselves in the same boat as Lucas was back then, and some have devised a solution that may be more straightforwardly applied to gatherings: the cold open.

The cold open is the practice of starting a TV show directly with a scene rather than with opening credits. In the 1950s, directors started experimenting with cold opens, seeking to sustain an audience's attention after the previous show ended and keep people from flipping to another channel. When *Saturday Night Live* starts with a skit of several minutes that sometimes seems like part of a news show or other program, and only later reveals itself when the performers scream "Live from New York, it's *Saturday Night*!" it is deploying the cold open at its best. The show understands that attention is everything in television, and once you have captured it, you can take care of business, thank people, attend to housekeeping.

Every gathering, to be sure, has logistical demands. People need to know where the bathroom is. People need to know where lunch can be found. There are often last-minute changes to announce. But people do not need to know this information at the very first moment of your gathering. It's not that you don't need time for logistics and the like. Just don't start with them. Open cold.

Honor and awe your guests

Once you bar the housekeeping from your opening, what should you actually start with? My answer is simple: Your opening needs to be a kind of pleasant shock therapy. It should grab people. And in grabbing them, it should both awe the guests and honor them. It must plant in them the paradoxical feeling of being totally welcomed and deeply grateful to be there.

This notion of honoring and awing is in some ways better practiced outside of gathering than within it. People who do things as far afield as writing novels and decorating hotel lobbies tend to be adept at this simultaneous work of making audiences feel flattered and unworthy. Any author will regale you in great detail with tales of how long she labors over her opening sentences. Ask hoteliers about the theory behind the practice of lobby design, and they will tell you what a difference certain tweaks make. Each of these is its own professional domain. What intrigues me is what their approaches have in common. When Melville opens *Moby-Dick* with "Call me Ishmael," and when the Four Seasons lobby greets you with flowers taller than you, both, I believe, are honor-awing.

In each of these openings, we are being made to feel slightly overwhelmed while at the same time made to feel welcome; our attention is gripped even as our nerves are soothed. When Melville addresses you, the reader, confidently and directly, there's a familiarity he's assuming, but there is also a confidence. He is not explaining an entire world to you. He is simply welcoming you into a world. Similarly, the flowers in the Four Seasons are stunning and maybe taller than you, and that awes you, intimidates you, makes you remember that you don't live like this back home. But of course the flowers are there for you, to honor you.

Few understand the art of honor and awe better than Dario Cecchini, an eighth-generation Tuscan butcher in the village of Panzano in Chianti, Italy. When you walk into the Macelleria Cecchini, a tiny butcher shop that attracts as pilgrims some of the leading chefs in the world, you instantly see Cecchini's mastery of openings. He hugs almost everyone who walks in, whether stranger or friend. He may hand a bewildered newcomer a cup of wine and a piece of bread spread with lard the moment they step into the shop. Most nights, after hours, right above the butcher shop, he seats thirty strangers at a long wooden table before a roaring grill. Before anyone gets a bite of his preparations, he raises two bloody Fiorentina steaks above his head, thundering, "To beef, or not to beef!"

His guests—some old friends, others who have wandered in off the street—are awed and captivated. Then, despite all the hovering staff, Cecchini serves the grilled meat onto the guests' plates himself, an attentive server who also happens to be an Italian celebrity. He is honoring his guests by engaging with them, even though he may not share a language with them. He moves around the table, visiting each guest, shaking hands, pausing and listening to stories, pinching cheeks, laughing heartily. Cecchini is fully alive in his butcher shop, and he makes you feel so, too. Cecchini is the man onstage, but he's also your host, your guide, your friend. As he models openness and passion, he wakes up those parts in you. Suddenly you find yourself turning to strangers, taking small risks, and asking unexpected questions, behaving differently than you would in a typical restaurant.

When you awe as a host, you are in a sense putting yourself—and your gathering—above your guest. When you honor, you are placing your guest above you. When you do both at once, as Cecchini does, you end up—with a hat tip to Groucho Marx—making your guests feel like valued members of a club to which they have no business belonging.

There are many ways to accomplish this honoring and awing. I once had a teacher named Sugata Roychowdhury, who, on the first day of accounting class, took attendance in a legendary way. Instead of lowering his head over a checklist and droning out names, he walked around the room, holding eye contact with the seventy or so new students in the lecture hall, and, one by one, pointed at each student and stated their (sometimes quite complicated) first and last names. They had never laid eyes on him before, nor he them. He took the entire class's attendance from memory. We were mesmerized. He must have studied our photos and practiced our names for hours ahead of time. This is an example of taking a totally banal element of gathering—roll call—and, with a few hours of effort, transforming it into a dramatic opening.

Professor Roychowdhury created an unforgettable moment that sent two important signals: that he cared deeply about his teaching and that he had a brilliance that might rub off on us if we made the effort to learn.

I don't want you to think that you have to be a famous Italian butcher or a brilliant accounting professor capable of memorizing seventy names and faces to honor and awe your guests. And so here is one more story of honoring and awing, applied in the most simple of contexts.

I had invited my stepsister and her husband for lunch. They

live in Washington, D.C., and my husband and I don't see them very often, but they happened to be visiting relatives in New Jersey one weekend.

Ten minutes before they were due to arrive, my husband walked into the living room confused as to why I hadn't set the table. In my mind, it was "just Lauren"—a casual meal with someone to whom I'm close enough not to need formality. Part of the intimacy of having her over, I thought, would be setting the table together when she arrived. But my husband thought we should make her feel special and insisted that we set the table beforehand. A minute after we finished, the doorbell rang. They were here. After hugs in the hallway, Lauren walked into the dining room and a look of surprise popped onto her face.

"Who's coming over?" she asked.

"You are!" Anand and I both said, laughing. She couldn't believe we had set the table for her, and she was clearly moved. I think she felt honored that we would make the extra effort for her, and she felt awed that we had set it so beautifully.

Fuse your guests

After the initial shock therapy of honoring and awing, you have your guests' attention. They want to be there. They feel lucky to be there. They might well be considering giving the gathering their all. Your next task is to fuse people, to turn a motley collection of attendees into a tribe. A talented gatherer doesn't hope for disparate people to become a group. She makes them a group.

The organization Tough Mudder creates weekend obstacle courses for the kind of people who like weekend obstacle courses. During these trials, participants can run through a field of live wires, swim in a dumpster chilled with 75,000 pounds of ice, and so on. While Tough Mudder is essentially a type of marathon, its opening rituals are very different from the rituals you might see at traditional marathons, which are individual in nature, with runners focused almost exclusively on their own performance.

At the starting line of a Tough Mudder race, every participant is asked to raise their right hand and repeat in unison the Tough Mudder Pledge:

As a Tough Mudder, I pledge that
- I understand that Tough Mudder is not a race but a challenge.
- I put teamwork and camaraderie before my course time.
- I do not whine—kids whine.
- I help my fellow Mudders complete the course.
- I overcome all fears.

Unlike a marathon, a collective physical challenge that is experienced individually above all, Tough Mudder is designed as a collective physical challenge that is experienced collectively. Its pledge primes the contenders to help one another physically and emotionally, even at a cost to their own personal success. Will Dean, the founder of Tough Mudder, told *Forbes*: "Tough Mudder was built on the principle that the true prize is to cross the finish line together. It is nearly impossible to complete many of our obstacles alone and this forces Mudders to ask each other for help. The interdependence that comes from this fosters an incredible sense of community and creates an investment in the success of others, not just yourself." Dean and his colleagues understood that to reorient their participants from competing to collaborating, they would need to do something at the opening of the race—this small but lasting act of fusing.

A pledge is one way to bind your guests, but there are others. Some of the most compelling approaches involve helping your guests see and be seen by one another. The simple act of your guests' acknowledging one another and confirming their own presence is a crucial step we often forget when we gather. In the Zulu tribe, this acknowledgment is baked into the very language of their call-and-response greeting:

Greeting: "Sawubona." (I see you.)
Response: "Ngikhona." (I am here.)

In the hustle-bustle of modern life in the West, we often skip this step. This is what happens in many churches when the pastor invites the congregation to shift its attention from the pulpit to one another and to wish a round of "Good morning" or "Happy Easter." This kind of invitation is missing from too many gatherings and can be especially powerful at the outset.

Jill Soloway, the writer and director, will rarely begin a day of shooting without the people who work for them (Soloway uses the gender-neutral pronoun "they") having connected in this way. Soloway, the Emmy-winning showrunner behind the series *Transparent* and *I Love Dick*, calls the ritual "Box." After breakfast, once all the actors and extras have arrived and the set and equipment have been arranged, Soloway or another director of a particular episode will decide it is time for Box. A production assistant will place a wooden box in a central area with plenty of space around it. As soon as the crew sees the box, people start gathering around in a wide circle while clapping and chanting "Box, Box, Box, Box!" The chanting persists until everyone has joined the circle and speeds up until someone hops up on the box to speak. Once someone is standing on the box, that person has the floor.

People share whatever is on their mind—worries about an old friend, a death in the family, how they're feeling about their own acting. "People get up on the box and they talk about their problems, they talk about their breakthroughs, and you cry and you release," Jay Duplass, who plays Josh in *Transparent*, told *The Hollywood Reporter*. "Things get purged prior to the workday that set the tone for the tenderness and brilliance that gets delivered," Trace Lysette, another cast member, was quoted as saying. "That's how Jill likes to work."

Soloway's commitment to fusing the tribe is so deep that they include the extras in the Box ritual.

Griffin Dunne, an actor in *I Love Dick*, remembers one extra who was supposed to be in a restaurant scene, sitting two tables over from the main action. The extra ascended the box one day. "This woman got up there to say that she's the manager of a bank down the street and that she'd never had this experience before of feeling involved, like a family," he recalled.

"Guest stars, and I'm not exaggerating, cry when they leave our set," Amy Landecker, an actor on *Transparent*, told Bustle.com. "They're so upset that they don't get to stay and that the rest of the business does not function that way."

Box usually takes twenty to twenty-five minutes, but it can go as long as forty minutes before they start the actual rehearsal. Soloway gives the ritual the time it needs. Christina Hjelm, who works as an assistant to Soloway, described to me how they close Box once the time is right and transition into rehearsal:

> Once there seems to be a lull in folks wanting to get up on the box, the AD will make a show of circling the crowd, giving any last takers the opportunity to hop up and speak. If no one hops up on the box by the time the assistant director has circled the whole crowd, the AD will then hop on the box and give their closing remarks. The closing remarks typically consist of any special shooting instructions for the day and safety warnings the crew needs to keep in mind while on set. They then end it by shouting the safe word of the day and having the crowd shout it back to them. Popular safe words on our sets have been "Bucky" and "Chicken."

Box is an opening ritual that connects a large team to one another, clears people's minds, and creates a passageway of sorts into rehearsal. "It turns into this collective moment for everyone to connect before we start working," Landecker has said. Box also creates a sense of authenticity—part of the secret sauce of making the show, and one of the values that its storylines explore—among the team. "We get to play, like children," Soloway told another interviewer. "Nobody has to worry about getting anything wrong." In around twenty minutes, the director transforms a bunch of actors and extras into a tribe, by making them *see* one another.

Baratunde Thurston once applied this idea of guests seeing and being seen to a get-together of friends. He was throwing a holiday party in his home and realized that all his guests didn't know one another. He was the hub connecting us spokes, and so he took it upon himself to make sure everyone who came got to know everyone else. And he did so by creating a unique opening moment for everyone.

As each guest arrived, Thurston would start clapping and yelling, *"Atención, atención!"* All the other guests would turn and look as he playfully yelled, "Announcing . . . Katie Stewart!" He then went on to tell the room a few details about Katie that others might be interested in: "I first met Katie at a surfing class, where it turns out she was the best surfer in the class. Katie moved to New York three years ago from a job in Kenya. She is a neighbor—go, Brooklyn!—and has two pugs. My favorite thing about Katie is that, despite having a crazy job, whenever I call her, she picks up." The other guests would burst into applause after each introduction. It was a bit of a shtick, but the introductions were funny, insightful, and unexpected, and Thurston owned it, so everyone went along.

In thirty seconds, he built each guest up while giving everyone in the room three or four pieces of interesting grist to connect to. He didn't reduce anyone to their profession. He'd leave some mystery (*I wonder what that crazy job is*). He did it for each guest, and each guest looked at once embarrassed, thrown off guard, and pleased.

His jovial, attention-getting introductions gave everyone in the room permission to look at one another, know something about one another, have a way into the horizontal ties that the evening had lacked at the outset. As a host, he was honoring each guest by spending time on them. Like Cecchini, he put himself "below" them by lifting them up. And yet by taking the time to pause the entire room and get everyone's attention, he was also putting himself above his guests. He used his generous authority to pause the gathering. Like Abousteit, Thurston rescued the guests from having to introduce themselves to others, and in the process he also created an ambient awareness for each guest of every other.

The importance of a group "seeing" one another may sound trivial, but it can be deadly serious. Until recently, when medical teams gathered to operate on a patient, studies showed that they often didn't know one another's names before starting. A 2001 Johns Hopkins study found that when members introduced themselves and shared concerns ahead of time, the likelihood of complications and deaths fell by 35 percent. Surgeons, like many of us, assumed that they shouldn't waste time going through the silly formalities of seeing and being seen for something as important as saving lives. Yet it was these silly formalities that directly affected the outcomes of surgeries. Even with such complex and intricate work, it was when the nurses and doctors and anesthesiologists practiced good gathering principles that they felt more comfortable speaking up during surgery and offering solutions.

If your gathering has an audience, there are other ways of making people aware of one another. Conferences tend to be terrible at this. They tend to be full of vertical connections between the stage and the guests but are short on horizontal linkages binding guests to one another.

Spark Camp, a weekend-long conference started by five friends in the media industry, was created in part to test if a more horizontally oriented conference was possible. It was founded on the belief that "conferences can be re-imagined as efficient, creative gatherings that further innovation and spark practical solutions to the challenges the industry faces." Like Thurston, the organizers of Spark Camp have learned how to use their authority to turn guests into a community from the beginning. On the opening evening, rather than asking seventy people to introduce themselves, the organizers take over. And, unlike me at that dinner party I ruined, they do it with preparation and care.

Right before the opening dinner, the organizers gather everyone and deliver "highly personal, whimsical" introductions of each person, ending with their name, according to a report by the conference. Andrew Pergam, one of the founders, explained the thinking to me:

> It's pretty simple: We'd been to enough other events where people write their own fancy introductions, listing every accolade in the third person, that we thought we should do it for them—but do it in a way that helped people stand out. We really believe that we invite the whole person to attend Spark Camp, and rather than an intro that focuses solely on their professional achievements, we wanted the intro to help round the individual out, personally.

As attendees, whom the organizers call Campers, recognize themselves, they are asked to stand. "You'll often see a lot of eyes darting around the room, and some careful deep thinking before someone stands up," Pergam said. The organizers "spend an inordinate amount of time doing research on an individual" and "find obscure details about someone's past and marry that with all of their other achievements." It not only spares the Campers the pressure of introducing themselves to dozens of other people, it also gives them easy ways to go up to one another later. Pergam said:

For one, it levels the playing field, with even the most accom-
plished among us relegated to our interpretation of their
background—and the whims of our Internet researching abil-
ities. We're implicitly saying, "We've invited you here to be
your whole self, not just your bona fides at work"; explicitly,
we're saying, "We take your accomplishments seriously—all
of them." And we'll often find people saying to each other,
"Oh, you're the fiddler!" or "Wait—you're the one who met
your husband at a beekeeping convention!"

You can even bond an audience while giving a lecture. For
example, observe a talented presenter like Esther Perel, a relationship and sex therapist and seasoned speaker who regularly
addresses crowds of more than one thousand people. In addition
to her intriguing content, Perel is so sought after because of how
she connects audience members to one another, signaling in subtle ways that they are not alone. If someone asks Perel a question
about cheating or divorce or boredom, before answering it, she'll
look out at the audience and ask, "How many of you can relate to
this question?" Or, "Who also wonders about this?" In that simple act, she transforms a one-to-many speech into a collective experience.

Moderators at conferences could learn from Perel. They tend
to overfocus on their panelists and the questions they are going to
ask. The talented moderator understands that even a panel is not
a stand-alone conversation. It exists within the context of a gathering. And so the solution might simply be to turn to the audience
in the beginning of the session and ask: How many of you consider yourself an expert on artificial intelligence? How many of
you are working in the field? How many of you are thinking

about this for the first time? How many of you just realized you're in the wrong session?

Whenever I do a Visioning Lab, whether it's at a government agency, a university, or a financial institution, within the first five minutes of my opening I always say something like this: "I want you to imagine you're building a spiderweb together. That each of you has strings coming out of your wrists that connect with the other thirty-two people here. We can only go as deep as the weakest thread will allow. Now, none of you are the weakest link." Everyone usually laughs nervously at that part. "No one's going to be voted off the island. But the weakest thread between two of you is what's going to determine how deep we can go together." I make this explicit, and I remind them of it during their breaks and at other moments of transition. Build a web, build a web, build a web. Because it's not about their connection to me. It's this psychological inter-stitching of the group that allows you and them to take risks, build together, and have the boldest version of whatever gathering they're having.

Above and beyond

For some gatherings, like your regular Monday-morning work meeting, honoring and awing may feel like trying too hard—though I would urge you to think about Jill Soloway's example. My own belief is that any kind of gathering can practice any of these elements at least a little.

But if you want to do more than a little, if you really want to go to the next level with your opening, here is some extra credit: Try to embody, with that opening, the very reason that you felt moved to bring a group of human beings together. Try to make your gathering's purpose felt in those first moments.

Daniel Barrett is an elementary-school teacher at Brooklyn Heights Montessori School. He told me that he and his fellow teachers purposefully launch the first day of school with students knitting. "We call it 'hand work,' and it's a way for the students to be quiet together and have something to focus on," Barrett said. "It's also meant to help with their handwriting because they're working on their fine motor skills." On the first day of school, the school brings in the first-graders for just a half day and begins to initiate them into the core principles of a Montessori-run school, one of which is community. So how does Barrett embody the idea of a community on the first day?

He takes a ball of string and throws it to a student, saying something nice to her. And then the child continues the practice, holding her part of the string and throwing the ball to another student and saying another nice thing, and so on, until the group has built a spiderweb of string. "If I tug my end of the web, everyone else feels it move, and that's what a community is," Barrett tells them. "All of your choices, all of your actions, large or small, will affect everybody else."

Barrett has found a creative, age-appropriate way to remind his students—his guests—why they're doing what they're doing. A thoughtful opening moment like that can change the course of a gathering—even one whose duration is measured in years.

Six

Keep Your Best Self
Out of My Gathering

. . .

We have spoken so far of gathering with purpose, and of making practical choices that flow from that purpose. You have absorbed my pleas to own your power as a host, but to rule generously. You have encountered examples of people spicing up their gatherings with rules and fleeting formats. You've been instructed what not to do in your opening, and what to do once you stop doing those things—and how to ready guests before it even starts.

Now your event is under way. The tracks are laid. Things are rolling. Your thoughts may turn to where many of my friends' and clients' thoughts do: the question of how to get those you gather to be more authentic. How do you keep people real? I have some suggestions. Fifteen, in fact.

15 WAYS TO MAKE A CONFERENCE—OR
ANY KIND OF GATHERING—SUCK LESS

Nowhere is puffed-up phoniness more palpable than at conferences. Nowhere else is the chance to have conversations across borders, identities, and professions so often wasted. Nowhere else are so many people with the influence to change things so frequently brought together, only for the resulting conversations to remain on the surface. They lurk there because everyone is presenting the best self they think others expect to meet.

If you had to pick the setting where this "conference self" is at its worst, you might well choose the meetings of the World Economic Forum, an organization that convenes the world's rich and powerful several times a year, most famously in Davos, Switzerland. Which is why, a few years ago, a colleague and I set out to see if we could hack the WEF. Could we create an anti-WEF on the sidelines of a WEF event? Could we induce people trained to present themselves as perfectly baked loaves to bring dough worth sharing instead? Might we have better conversations about what the world actually needs when people drawn from a dazzling array of backgrounds share their full selves, not just their puffery?

The event we decided to infect with our gathering ideas was an annual WEF conclave in the United Arab Emirates, a couple of months before the major event in Davos. The purpose of this earlier conference is, in part, to surface ideas and agendas for Davos. The WEF organizes dozens of "global agenda councils" on issues ranging from artificial intelligence to the future of the oceans. Each council is instructed to "provide innovative thinking on critical global issues and incubate projects, events, and campaigns for the public good." Nine hundred council members meet in the UAE for three days of meetings to discuss the work they have been doing throughout the year on their topics and to suggest new directions.

The people chosen to join these councils are invited because of their accomplishments and their strengths, not because of their vulnerability. For this reason, the meetings, and even the dinners and coffee breaks, can become like show-off sessions, with round after round of one-upmanship. Even when they were not competitive, the conversations I was part of often remained superficially intellectual, with little realness or emotional risk. It was like many conferences I have attended: you go, try to impress people with how smart you are, perhaps come away with a few new work opportunities. But it was difficult to have any authentic engagement. Everyone tended to behave like his or her own brand ambassador and press secretary. Given that this wasn't an insurance industry conference but an event about addressing the biggest problems of humanity, this superficiality seemed to interfere with our chances of doing so.

I had been invited that year to join the WEF Global Agenda Council on New Models of Leadership. According to a past report by that council, its focus was to understand and create an in-depth dialogue about the "profound shift in the context in which leadership takes place and in what it takes to flourish as a leader." Specifically, the council felt that changes in the world were "opening up a new leadership space." It said that space was defined by, among other things, "the emotional capacity of the leader (values, courage, self-awareness, authenticity)" as well as "the extent and depth of their social relationships and networks." Perhaps because of this focus, many of us on the council were struck by how the WEF's culture made it hard for leaders to develop along these dimensions. A colleague of mine on the council, a German marketing executive named Tim Leberecht, and I wondered if an experiment could change that.

Our experiment, perhaps not surprisingly, involved gathering differently. We suggested throwing a small dinner the night before the conference began, with members from various other WEF councils. Our goal was both simple and very complicated: to get people to turn off their networking engines and elevator pitches and get them to connect—humanly, authentically.

But how do you create an intimate dinner at a networking event? How do you get people to be vulnerable when they show up invulnerable? How do you create a work dinner that feels more like a rehearsal dinner? How do you take people who have come to hawk one idea or organization and restore them, for a night, into the complex, multifaceted human beings they actually are? How do you allow for weakness and doubt in people who normally exude certainty and confidence?

At first, we focused on the normal preparations: We booked a private room in a restaurant. We invited fifteen guests from various councils, many of whom we did not know but who intrigued us. To help focus the evening, we chose a theme: "a good life." We had used that theme previously on another project we had worked on and knew it was a rich topic—and one we were well prepared to moderate as a result. It was also purposefully *a* good life (as in, what do we think makes for a good life?), not *the* good life.

The night before the dinner, I had trouble sleeping. Why did we invite all these people? What if it doesn't go well? What if no one speaks? What if the theme doesn't work? I was worried about the actual conversation, the one part I assumed I could not shape ahead of time. I felt there was too much riding on our ability to facilitate a complicated conversation among fifteen strangers. And while we had spent so much time mastering every other detail down to choosing the opening welcome drink, we hadn't given much thought to the actual structure of the conversation. We were winging it. I wanted to make something intimate. But I had not actually designed for intimacy.

That day I had lunch with my mother and husband, who were with me on the trip. As we ate in a badly lit mall in Abu Dhabi, I shared my anxieties. Why would people share authentically? How was I going to decide who goes when? I put my facilitator hat on and started to think about potential structures. The most basic, and easily forgotten, gathering principle returned to me: We needed to design for what we wanted.

What if, instead of just introducing the theme of "a good life," we asked each guest, at some point in the night, to give a toast to "a good life," whatever that phrase means to them? OK, that was good. But what if people just waxed on and on about some grandiose idea of theirs?

Another idea: What if we asked them to start their toasts with a personal story or experience from their own life? We were making progress. But this was a lot to ask of people.

What if no one wanted to toast? What if everyone waited in long silences between toasts?

Then came the clincher: What if we made the last person sing their toast? I laughed when my husband proposed this, but he was serious. It would set a brisk pace for the evening and add some nice risk.

That evening, the guests arrived, not knowing what to expect, but people seemed intrigued and excited to be there. They were senior advisers to presidents, CEO types, journalists, entrepreneurs, and activists. We were split relatively equally by gender. The ages ranged from our early twenties to our eighties. People hailed from half a dozen different countries. We stood at the entrance of the room and handed each guest a welcome cocktail, warmly introducing them to one another. They saw their names written on cards and realized that there would be a seating order.

When we sat down, I raised my glass and thanked everyone for coming. I introduced myself and Leberecht. We described the theme and our reasons for wanting to hold this dinner. We explained the rules, including the singing rule and the Chatham House Rule (borrowed from the Royal Institute of International Affairs) that we had adopted, which allows people to talk about their experience of a private meeting and share the stories that emerge, but forbids specific attributions to any of the participants. We also instructed people to begin each toast by telling a story, and to signal when they were done by raising a glass to the value or lesson behind that story. And, at last, we began.

The first three toasts went quickly: The first toaster drew from the well of her own story to talk about a good life as a life with choices. ("To choice!") The second toaster spoke of her work in disaster-relief efforts and, as she did, became emotional. Her toast showed the group that it was acceptable to be human when you care deeply about something. In the third toast, a man talked about three elements he thought made a good life: to work for oneself, to work for others, and to have fun. He ended his toast by saying, "Two out of three ain't bad." Someone then burst into song, singing: "Two out of three ain't bad!" Everyone started laughing. ("To two out of three!") The group was starting to relax.

At that point there was a lull, and we took a break to eat and chat with the people around us. I began to think about what I was going to say. I had a distinct advantage going into the dinner, as I had known the theme in advance. I had a toast idea in mind. In that moment, though, I realized that I wasn't really taking a risk with that toast. An image came to mind of a good life, and it was a moment from when I was eleven. Then I thought: I can't share that with *this* group. My heart started pounding, a sign that I tend to interpret as saying, Do it. I took a breath, hands shaking, and clinked my glass. People seemed surprised that I was going to go so early in the evening.

I began with the idea that a good life is about seeing and being seen, and launched into a very personal story about a time when I had felt seen. This is roughly what I can remember of what I shared:

> When I was eleven years old, I got my period. I was sleeping over at a friend's house in Maryland and wasn't sure how to react. I didn't tell my friend, but went home the next day and told my mother. I was at an age where a lot of my beliefs and judgments about things came from other people's reactions, and I watched hers closely. When she heard, she hooted and hollered and lifted me up and swung me around, laughing with joy. She then danced all over the house celebrating. I learned that day, from her reaction, that being a woman was something to be celebrated. But she didn't stop there. Two weeks later, my mother threw me a period party.

People at the table began to laugh and clap in delight. Even the men, to my great relief. I continued. I shared the story of my period party as I could remember it:

She invited her female friends rather than mine, all older women who had passed through this important transition of womanhood themselves. I received presents from each woman. One guest gave me my first pair of pink lace underwear, because one of her favorite things about being a woman was "opening the underwear drawer and seeing a splash of color." They sang me songs, including my mother's favorite two songs: "On Children," by Sweet Honey in the Rock, and Crosby, Stills, Nash & Young's "Teach Your Children." That day, I knew I mattered. I was seeing, and I was being seen. I was being witnessed. And to me, that was a good life. And a small surprise for you all: My mother is here with us, sitting right over there.

My mother happened to be on another council at the forum. Because we have different last names, no one knew we were related. Everyone was stunned to realize that a woman who was sitting at the table, someone they might have known only as a World Bank expert on poverty, was also a mother who had designed a period party for her daughter. I was still shaking from telling such a vulnerable story, but I thought, What the hell, hoping it would crack others open.

The wine flowed and the toasts continued. One woman shared her mother's words on her deathbed: "I spent 90 percent of my time worrying about things that didn't matter. Don't do that." Once the topic of death was introduced, I noticed it showing up in several other toasts. After all, thinking about what makes a good life implies thinking about life ending, about it being of limited quantity. Another person now said in her toast that she was going to tell us something "weird" she does every morning, something she's never told others about. Every morning, she does a "death meditation," in which she imagines she has died, sees all the people she loves and all she's left behind in this world, and just hovers over the scene, watching. She then wiggles her fingers and toes and comes back, deeply grateful to be alive, perhaps a little more aware of what she values. It turned out that, for her, part of having and savoring a good life was keeping aware of death. She then raised her glass and toasted something like "To death!," signaling she was done. "To death!" we replied, glasses in the air.

As the night went on, tears welled more and more in the eyes of people speaking and the eyes of people listening. Not because they were sad, but because they were moved. Over the course of the evening, people stood up, one after another, and over and over again we heard some version of "I have no idea what I'm going to say" or "I hadn't planned on saying this" or "I've never said this out loud before." People dropped their scripts.

One man pointed out that certain superheroes wear their underwear outside their costumes. We laughed. It was a perfect metaphor for what we attempted that night—and what I am challenging you to cultivate in your gatherings. And, yes, at last, the final person sang. He closed his toast with a Leonard Cohen song. A line about cracks allowing for light shimmered over a room that had, for one moment, practiced letting go of that most consuming of worries.

It was a moving, beautiful night. All these people whose titles usually enter the room before they do left their egos at the door. They showed us fresh, raw, honest sides of themselves. The dinner pointed to what was possible at gatherings like this.

REALNESS CAN BE DESIGNED

After that moving evening in Abu Dhabi, we decided to take our format on the road. We called it 15 Toasts, after the number of people around that inaugural table, and we scouted for other stuffy gatherings that could use an injection of human feeling. One or both of us, and even some former attendees who felt comfortable facilitating, went on to host 15 Toasts dinners on the sidelines of events in South Carolina, Denmark, South Africa, Canada, and elsewhere. Everywhere it went, the format worked wonders. So I began to test it out on another type of gathering: ones where people *did* know one another, through work or family or otherwise. To my surprise, it still worked. And after hosting many of these dinners, and seeing groups of various kinds being authentic with one another in remarkable ways, I began to detect certain patterns in what helped the real and the revelatory to surface. In addition to setting the right environment (we always try to do it in private spaces, with low lighting, flickering candles, comforting food, and flowing wine), I have found there are certain approaches the thoughtful gatherer can take to encourage people to jettison the phony and the polished for the true.

SPROUT SPEECHES, NOT STUMP SPEECHES

One of these approaches is to seek out and design for what I call the "sprout speech," as distinguished from its tedious better-known cousin the stump speech. The stump speech is the pre-planned, baked spiel that people have given a thousand times. We all have stump speeches, and at many of the more formal and important gatherings we attend, it is our stump speeches that come out to play.

If the term "stump speech" evokes the strongest, most durable part of the tree, the part that is firmly in the ground, the sprout is, by contrast, the newest and weakest part of the tree. It is the part still forming. What I learned from 15 Toasts is that while we tend to give stump speeches at so many gatherings of consequence, it is people's sprouts that are most interesting—and perhaps most prone to making a group feel closely connected enough to attempt big things together.

So much in our culture still tells us to present our stump speeches when we are anywhere in the vicinity of opportunity, especially at something like a conference. But I keep stumbling on interesting experiments doing just the opposite, inviting people with impressive stump speeches to leave them at home and bring their sprout speeches instead.

One of these more forward-thinking gatherings is called House of Genius. (You may recall encountering it briefly in the chapter on pop-up rules—and, yes, some of the more interesting gatherings of our time may need better names.) House of Genius was founded by two entrepreneurs, Toma Bedolla and Tim Williams. The pair had gotten tired of networking events where everybody shared puffed-up sermons about what was working with their companies or jobs and few people shared what wasn't. They decided to experiment with a new format of business get-together—a format that would eventually be replicated around the world.

The format was this: A group of strangers would gather in a

room. Two or three of them would be entrepreneurs or other professionals with a problem. To get into the room, they had to apply for the chance to present their problem to the others. The others were people from varied fields who had applied to volunteer their time to solve someone's problem. A moderator would guide and tightly orchestrate the proceedings.

In both House of Genius gatherings I attended, I was struck by the moderators' ability to get people to share their challenges openly with strangers and to let the rest of us look under the hood. By inviting people to share their problems, House of Genius elevates authenticity over selling. They, too, have organized a gathering around our incomplete selves (and companies).

Both events I saw took place in conference rooms in coworking spaces in New York City. There was some time to mingle near the office kitchen before the event formally began. As people walked in, we were encouraged to meet one another but told that we couldn't discuss anything related to work. On one occasion, I started talking to a youngish man with blond hair wearing cargo shorts, and we both immediately realized we had to stretch a bit not to ask each other about work. We tried to chitchat. He asked whether I had taken any vacations recently. I think I asked him whether he had any pets. We both started laughing when we realized how bad we were at talking to each other about topics other than work. A number of questions kept accidentally bumping into the topic: "Have you been to one of these before?" "Yes," I said, "because I . . ." I stopped myself because I realized I couldn't tell him that I was studying gatherings, since it broke the no-work-talk rule. "When did you move to New York?" I asked. "Five years ago." "What brought you here?" "Uh, I can't tell you the real reason." More laughter. But we improved as the night progressed.

Later, I met the moderator for the evening. "Have you moderated before?" I asked.

"Yes, a few times."

"How did you get involved?"

"Um, we'll leave that for later."

"For the end?"

"For the Big Reveal."

"Oh."

Eventually a young woman, apparently the organizer, invited us to enter the room and take our seats. "First names only," we were reminded. As we wandered in, we were asked to take a name tag, grab a seat, and not talk about work. "You can talk about Disney World, but not work," she said. We started talking about Disney World. After the final stragglers came in, we were officially constituted as a "House."

The organizer welcomed us, gave us some background on the House of Genius, and reminded us of the purpose of the gathering and the rules, which were also posted on the wall. "Even in giving feedback, you can offer suggestions, but please don't talk about what you do," she told us.

That evening there would be two presenters, and each would get a roughly forty-five-minute session with the House. For the first five minutes, each one would make a presentation to the room about a challenge. We would then have two or three minutes to ask clarifying questions about the challenge, and the entrepreneur would answer them. Then everyone would have one minute to give their "first thoughts." (You can ask questions during this period, but the entrepreneur can't answer them.) And the rest of the time is a dialogue between the House and the entrepreneur. The moderator makes sure that everyone has a chance to talk and guides us on what makes good feedback: examples of past successes and failures, contacts because "we want to extend tonight into the future," and books and articles. At the end of the evening, we would have the Reveal, in which we would each share who we are and what we actually do for a living.

The first challenge-bearer was a woman running a social enterprise that was trying to build more inclusive workplaces. She wanted our help figuring out how to create true partnerships with employers and influence them to "think outside the box" when hiring. The second was a young man starting a travel app that would let people create and share their own guides with a larger community. He wanted our ideas on how to cultivate "loyal and rabidly engaged early users in this city with little budget and some connections."

In each of the conversations, I observed as the dozen or so of us began to figure out how we could help. In both cases, we needed to know more about each idea. But as we asked more questions, it made each entrepreneur more vulnerable. They had to give us more information: "So how many companies have you spoken with?" Not as many as they should have, maybe. Or our suggestions created more work for them: "Have you thought about partnering with job-training programs?" Or we pointed out their blind spots: "I'm not sure if your basic assumptions about why companies aren't hiring these populations are right." Yet if they could remain open to it, they would receive valuable help from smart people.

It was an interesting dynamic, and the more we got into the weeds of each company, the more I felt a desire to help these entrepreneurs. Had they come up to me at a networking event and pitched their idea with the usual puffiness, I may have been interested, but I doubt it would have tugged at my heartstrings. But seeing them there in the hot seat, knowing they had volunteered for this, to expose themselves and their ideas to strangers, made me feel compassion for them and made me want to use my brain and resources to push them forward. And in the rare moments when one of the problem-bearers would get testy or defensive, or withhold information, it was obvious to everyone, and it caused the helpers to pull back. It was like watching a group dance in vulnerability. The more the entrepreneurs shared, the more I could relate and the more I wanted to help. The stronger they seemed, the less they needed me and the less I could connect with their travails.

In some ways, this should be obvious. Being vulnerable with people makes them feel for you. Scholars like Brené Brown have been telling us this for years. But if it's obvious as a description of human behavior, it doesn't seem obvious to most of our gatherers. A gatherer is bringing people together. Sometimes, as at the House of Genius, the explicit goal is for people to help one another. But every time people gather, they are being brought into the opportunity to help one another, to do what they couldn't do or think up or heal alone. And yet so often when we gather, we are gathered in ways that hide our need for help and portray us in the strongest and least heart-stirring light. It is in gathering that we meet those who could help us, and it is in gathering that we pretend not to need them, because we have it all figured out.

A graduate school program I attended epitomized this paradox. At the Harvard Kennedy School, legions of brilliant, passionate students arrived with real questions and real fears and real wonderings about how to solve the problems of the world. All too often, however, they ended up intimidating rather than helping one another. In the classrooms where we were supposed to learn what we didn't already know, the culture taught us to avoid sounding stupid in front of one another. It didn't make sense to try ideas out loud, because these were your potential future bosses and partners and employees, and it was important to show your strength. In the early days of the semester, when people asked, "How are you?" we answered with smiling, and often false, positivity, falling into the terrible habits of politicians on the campaign trail: Never voice the truth; always be sparklingly upbeat. When we spoke of our pasts, we often spun like flacks on Capitol Hill: The up-and-down facts of our lives were smoothed into ascending narratives, our accomplishments were humble-bragged, and our personal brands were promoted.

Lisa Lazarus, a student one year ahead of me, had the gall to suggest that this was a lonely, miserable way to learn. She revolted by creating a small group called CAN, or Change Agents Now. The idea was simple: groups of six interested Kennedy School students would agree to meet every other week, for 3 hours at a time, and do the opposite of what they were doing for the other 333 hours of that fortnight. Against all odds, they—we—would be honest.

We would skip over all the parts that were working and dive straight into sharing what was not. We would tell authentic, painful stories—about parents who had abandoned us, about bullies who had taunted us, about poverty that had shamed us. We showed frailty, vulnerability, and fear; in fact, in an inversion of Kennedy School norms, weakness became more valued than strength.

We followed a loose curriculum that focused on sharing "crucible moments," a concept borrowed from Bill George, a professor of leadership at Harvard Business School and the author of

True North. Crucible moments, according to George, are challenging moments in our lives that shape us in some deep way and shift our lens on the world. They are stories that define us in our own minds—and that, nevertheless, seldom come up in the ordinary course of conversation.

My CAN group met every other Wednesday, and for our early meetings, we shared our life stories, focusing primarily on these crucible moments. We knew what we were signing up for, and we were curious about one another. I didn't know the students in my CAN group well, and the stories they shared—about their own childhoods, difficult decisions they'd made, relationships with their parents, hometowns, religious beliefs—made me see them in an entirely new light. It also made me feel safe showing my own different sides, sharing my own demons.

This series of gatherings, simple in their design, purposeful in their conception, transformed my experience of graduate school. The school became a different kind of place for me. Armor fell off; ears widened and mouths shrank; we learned to love one another for our flaws. The navy officer whose father was once homeless. The entrepreneur who grew up poor. The executive director who, in light of an absent father, became a second parent to her siblings. I began to see their behavior through a different lens. And rather than feel jealous or intimidated by their accomplishments, I began to feel empathy for them, because I understood their stories, just as they understood mine. Experiencing a different way of being in my CAN group led me to take similar risks with some of my peers outside of the group.

Lazarus had an insight about her peers: that we all wear masks, and that while masks have uses, taking them off can allow for deeper connection, shared growth, and more fruitful collaboration.

More than a decade after she started it, Lazarus's CAN group still meets.

NO IDEAS, PLEASE. WE'RE GATHERING

Another tactic that helps to undam realness in gatherings is a push for people's experiences over their ideas.

That evening in Abu Dhabi we had asked guests to give their toasts in the form of a story, but we had done so mainly as a form of quality control. We figured that anyone can tell a story from their life, and that such stories might be better than riffs on a theme people hadn't thought about. As it turned out, though, the emphasis on stories did something else as well, something we hadn't necessarily planned: It helped us feel connected. And it worked because we were explicit about it. We got stories because we asked for stories—we made a clear distinction in the prompt between people's concrete experiences and their abstract ideas.

Many gatherings would be improved if people were simply asked for their stories. And there are few institutions that have done more to demonstrate the power of this principle than The Moth, a series of gatherings that promote the idea and practice of storytelling as social glue.

The Moth was founded in the late 1990s by a Southerner named George Dawes Green who had grown tired of poetry slams. A novelist himself, he attended poetry slams to try to meet other writers and artists. But rather than feeling transported by the poetry, he would leave feeling irritated. "I felt something was wrong with them," he told me. Every poem, he said, "was told in this singsong voice. As soon as the poet stood up there, he'd begin to speak in this poetic language, and this wall would come down." That barrier, in his view, came from a prevailing idea of the poet as an ethereal and distant figure: "You were part of this deep tradition, and you gather your ideas from some connection that you had with God or with the powers of the universe. You were a shaman, and you were pulling this information down, and through you would come this exalted language—an almost non-human language." This may sound great to you. But to Green, at least, it was off-putting.

Despite his contempt for the slam scene, Green noticed when the poets *did* wow him. It was often during the preamble, an unscripted backstory poets would tell about the roots of their shamanic creation. "My grandpa would go fishing upstate," Green imagines one of the poets saying all these years later. "I remember having to get up so early." What struck him about the language in the preambles was that it consisted of "perfectly natural phrases," Green said, "and the audience would immediately perk up and be with the poet, because there was no longer a sense of artifice, a wall. And I was always fascinated by that." He started experimenting with a gathering format designed exactly around that moment, and The Moth was born. Two decades later, The Moth has ongoing programs in twenty-five cities and has presented eighteen thousand stories, often to standing-room-only crowds.

I told him about my experiences running 15 Toasts and asked him why, and when, he thought story works in a gathering.

"A moment a story works is usually a moment of vulnerability," he said. "You can't tell a story that's any good about how successful you are. Trump tries to do that." But when you touch this vulnerability, he said, "people feel this utter comfort. I went through that. I know exactly what that person is saying." Green has spent years studying the art and craft of storytelling. He explained some of the elements of a good story told simply:

> Story is about a decision that you made. It's not about what happens to you. And if you hit that and you get your vulnerability and you understand the stakes, and a few other things, people will intuitively find great stories to tell, and as soon as they do, we know them. We know them as human beings. This is no longer my boss's colleague. This is a real person who had heartbreak. Oh, I know *that*.

THE DARK THEME

If guests often bring their stump rather than sprout speeches to events, if they often talk of their theories rather than their experiences, then organizers can succumb to their own kind of phoniness. They insist on keeping gatherings positive, especially when choosing themes. The meaningful gatherer doesn't fear negativity, though, and in fact creates space for the dark and the dangerous.

If you recall that first 15 Toasts dinner, the theme we had chosen was highly positive: "a good life." Looking back, I don't think it was a great theme, and our guests evidently agreed. After all, it wasn't just one person who shifted the terms and tone of the conversation by bringing up death. We hadn't explicitly asked about death, nor did either of us introduce it ourselves. But as we spoke of the joy of life, there seemed to be a need to bring in the flip side of life. As we did, the conversation took on a new depth. People began to lean in more, no doubt thinking of their own mortality or that of those they loved. It made the evening richer and rawer.

As Leberecht and I began to spread 15 Toasts to other venues, we varied the themes: 15 Toasts to the stranger, to faith, to happiness, to collateral damage, to escapes, to borders, to Them, to fear, to risk, to rebellion, to romance, to dignity, to the self, to education, to the story that changed my life, to the end of work, to beauty, to conflict, to tinkering, to the truth, to America, to local, to the fellow traveler, to origins, to the right problem, to the disrupted, to the fourth industrial revolution, to courage, to borders, to risk, and, yes, to vulnerability. What we came to find over time was that the best themes were not the sweet ones, like happiness or romance, but rather the ones that had darker sides to them: fear, Them, borders, strangers. The ones that allowed for many interpretations. The ones that let people show sides of themselves that were weak, that were confused and unprocessed, that were morally complicated.

Sadly, themes like these are exiled from so many of our gatherings. Far too many of them, especially more professionally oriented ones, are run on a cult of positivity. Everything has to be about what's going well, about collaboration, about hope and the future. There is no space for what our guests were telling us they wanted at the dinners: a chance to pause and consider what is not uplifting but thought- and heart-provoking.

When I push this idea of darkening the theme on clients and friends, they often resist more fiercely than they do with most of my advice. So I am resorting to extreme measures to convince them, and you, of why it isn't just acceptable but also essential to create a space in your gatherings for the darkness to come in: I am outsourcing the job to a dominatrix.

I originally learned of Stefanie Zoe Warncke from a German DJ. He suggested that I meet a dominatrix he knew, as she was an expert in creating environments and scenes. I imagined some covert meeting at night in a parking lot. Much to my relief (or maybe dismay?), we ended up meeting for tea at a French patisserie in New York City.

Warncke, who goes by Zoe, trained as a lawyer and for years worked as a partner at a firm in Düsseldorf by day and as a dominatrix at one of the larger dungeons in Europe by night. She eventually left Germany and the law and moved to New York, where she still practices as a dominatrix. She sees her job as helping clients explore their darker fantasies in a safe space.

"I want to help people explore parts of themselves in a safe way," she told me. She said her interest in the work probably traced back to her own family environment growing up, a place where she "wasn't allowed to explore parts" of herself.

Why, I asked, was it important for people to probe their darkness? "I think it makes the world a better place," she said with a laugh. That sounded too simplistic. Why did letting people be dark make the world a better place?

She thought for a moment. "Because I think if they know who they really are, they don't have to compensate with anger or self-hatred or all those things," she said.

Warncke was touching on a concept that psychologists call the "integration of the shadow." I contacted Dr. David M. Ortmann, a psychotherapist and the coauthor of *Sexual Outsiders: Understanding BDSM Sexualities and Communities*. I described Warncke's work to him and asked him about it. He explained in an email that "integration of the shadow" is "a Jungian term that identifies that we all have shadow material (aggression, violence, nonconsensual fantasies, etc.). Disowning these parts of ourselves is not an effective way to deal with them, as what is disowned or ignored tends to grow (and often grow unconsciously). BDSM offers a way for shadow material to be integrated consciously." Of Warncke in particular, he offered: "I would say your dominatrix friend knows her work very well and would go further to say that she's doing something therapeutic."

At this point, you may be wondering what a dominatrix has to do with your next staff meeting or family reunion. I'm not suggesting you hire Warncke, but rather you *heed* Warncke. What she does in concentration you can do with an appropriate level of dilution in your gathering. The lesson she offers is that darkness is better inside the tent than outside of it. We all have it. It's going to be at your gathering. And if you bar it from the formal proceedings, it doesn't disappear. It shows up in ways that do your gatherings no favors.

THE STRANGER SPIRIT

One of the more improbable secrets of unleashing honesty and vulnerability in a gathering is raising the stranger quotient. Though it seems counterintuitive, it is often easier to get people to share when many in the room are unknown to them—or when they are helped to see those they do know with fresh eyes.

After one 15 Toasts dinner in New York, a guest was upset that a close friend of hers, whom she had brought to the gathering, had spoken openly of his depression. She pulled me aside afterward, feeling confused and betrayed that he would share with several strangers something he had never told her. Yet the man was making the same choice that many of us do in similar situations. It is often easier to confess parts of our lives with strangers, who have no stake in our lives, than with intimates who do.

The power of the stranger lies in what they bring out in us. With strangers, there is a temporary reordering of a balancing act that each of us is constantly attempting: between our past selves and our future selves, between who we have been and who we are becoming. Your friends and family know who you have been, and they often make it harder to try out who you might become. *But you're not the singing type! Why would you want to be a doctor when you hated biology in school? I guess I just don't see you doing stand-up.* Strangers, unconnected to our pasts and, in most cases, to our futures, are easier to experiment around. They create a temporary freedom to pilot-test what we might become, however untethered that identity is to what we have been. They allow us to try out new sides. In front of a stranger, we are free to choose what we want to show, hide, or even invent.

Some extreme gatherers so believe in this stranger spirit that they organize gatherings entirely for and of strangers—like the seventy-sixth birthday celebration of the Oxford professor Theodore Zeldin. Zeldin—a renowned historian of France and a famed philosopher, with a wild white mane—decided that year that he would hold a birthday party for people he didn't know. He issued a public invitation through the BBC for everyone who was interested to join him in Regent's Park in London at a particular date and time, and to celebrate his birthday by talking to someone they didn't know.

Hundreds of people showed up. Each of them was tasked with having a one-on-one conversation with a stranger. In lieu of food, at each setting was a Zeldin invention called the "Conversation Menu" that led the pairs through six "courses" of talk. Under the heading of "Starters" were questions like "How have your priorities changed over the years?" and "How have your background and experience limited or favoured you?" Under "Soups" was an invitation to ask, "Which parts of your life have been a waste of time?" Under "Fish": "What have you rebelled against in the past and what are you rebelling against now?" Under "Salads": "What are the limits of your compassion?"

FRESH EYES

The reality is, you don't have to invite the entire United Kingdom to your birthday party to raise the stranger quotient among your guests. If you host consciously, you can bring the stranger spirit to a gathering of people familiar with one another. When I have tried to do this with family dinners and team get-togethers, I have found that choosing the right question and structure can help people long acquainted see one another with fresh eyes.

A few years ago, my husband and I were going to India to visit our grandparents and extended family. We decided to gather both sides of our family for a dinner. There would be seventeen of us in total. Being well acquainted with large family dinners, I knew that if we didn't do anything to design the evening, cousins would gravitate to their own cousins, grandparents would talk among themselves, and most of the conversation would be small talk. We would eat, drink, get sleepy, and call it a night. Not necessarily a bad evening, but we wanted to make it special.

We decided to borrow from the 15 Toasts model, but with

some changes. Because there were multiple members of our families who had no problem singing in public, we scrapped the singing rule and instead had each toaster choose the next toaster. Borrowing from my CAN group's use of "crucible moments," we asked the group to share a story, a moment, or an experience from their life that "changed the way you view the world." Then we added the clincher: It had to be a story that no one else at the gathering knew. This was, in a sense, a rather wild requirement for a gathering of family members in a tight-knit society in which relatives are a bigger part of life than friends. But we thought it might give the dinner a shot at getting people who thought they knew everything about one another to see one another with fresh eyes.

A cousin began by saying something like "The birth of my children." But now the group, having already absorbed the rules and their purpose, immediately protested: *We already know that!* That false start and correction laid the groundwork for the others. People began to share stories that even their nearest and dearest had never heard before. Even if one or two people present did know a particular story, it was told that night in a way that revealed impacts or implications that no one had known. One aunt, a geneticist, spoke of being told as a teenager that she couldn't be a doctor because she was a woman. It shocked her into studying harder. Another aunt, a civil servant, talked about passing the Indian Administrative Service test, completing officer training, only to be put in a district magistrate's office for months on end, never being let into the field. She finally went out on her own in a truck one day because she couldn't understand why they weren't letting her do her rounds, and a local government official told her that she would always be treated differently, no matter how smart she was, because she was a woman.

As the toasts went on, I began to realize that something remarkable was happening. Our original goal had been to get our relatives to continue the weaving of families that had begun with our wedding. But now something even more interesting was going on: Fathers and mothers and sons and nieces were learning about their own family members in ways they'd never expected. When a family elder, now in his nineties, shared his story, he recalled a time fifty years prior when he was working at a large company and realized that the advertisement reels he was sending out to movie theaters were often not making it there or, if they were, not being played. He told us how he solved the problem. Suddenly, in this aging man who often stays quiet, in part because he is hard of hearing, the table saw a young, sprightly, inventive businessman. My grandmother, shy to speak in English, asked me to share her story, which I had learned only a few days earlier. It was the story of how she became one of the first women in her caste in the conservative city of Varanasi to attend Banaras Hindu University. She was the eldest of seven children, and her father adored her. He told her to go register for university and begin attending classes. Then he left town for a relative's wedding on her first day of school. When his neighbors complained that he was letting his daughter attend university and violating gender norms, he wasn't there to hear the complaints. When he returned, she was well into her classes, and he asked the same neighbors if they really wanted him to pull her out of school. Even if it was wrong for her to have started, should education ever be interrupted? The moment changed her perception of her father and educated her in how change happens (slowly and with people in privilege as protectors).

What was striking about the evening was everyone's willingness to embrace it. And to try something new. We began to see parts of one another with fresh eyes. A grandmother as a dare-devil college student. A grandfather as an innovative young executive. Aunts, who in Indian family gatherings are often relegated to the role of silent nurturers, as pioneers in their fields. It reminded me of how much there was left to know about people I thought I knew well. We weren't "strangers" by any stretch, but we found a way to design for the stranger spirit.

THE INVITATION MATTERS

If you want to try this type of gathering, centered on people's real selves rather than their best selves, you need to warn them. One of the insights we learned from 15 Toasts is that, in keeping with my approach to openings, you should tell people as explicitly as possible and at the beginning what you want in the room and what you want to be left at the door.

When I host 15 Toasts on the sidelines of a conference or another high-powered gathering, I tend to say in my welcome words that there is a typical dynamic to such events that we are hoping to avoid—the dynamic of showiness and puffery. Given our desire to counteract that, I invite people to leave outside the door those parts of their lives and work that are going great. We're interested in the half-baked parts. We're interested in the parts they're still figuring out. We're not interested in their preplanned speeches but rather in the words and thoughts still forming.

In the very different situation of the 15 Toasts format applied to family gatherings, a different kind of invitation was required. Normally at such dinners, no one reveals anything fresh or surprising. If we wanted to change up the kind of family dinner we were having, it required guiding people. So I told them to leave their familiar stories about themselves at the door and bring into the room those parts of themselves that might surprise even their kids.

When I work with business teams and do a 15 Toasts before a big meeting, there is another set of problematic dynamics to fend off. Teams often interact in well-worn ways, with the same people playing the same roles. So in my welcome I name that and tell the group that the whole point of this dinner is to try out another way of being together, to create space for everyone to show different sides of themselves and play different roles. By naming the way I anticipate they will be, and asking them to set that aside and try something else, I often get through to them. Often, but not always.

This cueing of people in the welcome doesn't have to be elaborate. Just a strong and suggestive hint. At the first 15 Toasts dinner, I said something about how we hoped the evening would feel more like a wedding than a conference. Someone joked, "Who's getting married?" Another guest said, "We'll vote at the end of the night!" People laughed, and I knew the night was taking off.

At each 15 Toasts since, I almost always say something like "Tell us something that would surprise us," or "Leave your successes at the door," or "There's no need to slip in an accomplishment."

I have also found that this leaving of things at the door is easier when people are seen for their virtues. People are still people, and, particularly in professional contexts, no one wants to look weak. But I have discovered that if I, the host, acknowledge and broadcast their strength, as individuals and collectively well in advance, it relieves some of the pressure people feel to flex during the event itself. I say something up front like "You're all here because you're remarkable." I acknowledge their remarkableness and then I add, "That said, we don't want to hear about your résumé or how great you are. We already know that."

HOST, REVEAL THYSELF

It isn't enough to signal what you want and don't want from your guests when it comes to sharing more honestly and authentically. Early in the gathering, you, the host, need to go there yourself. You need to show them how.

If you are hoping to help your guests be more real, you need to be real yourself. When I host these dinners, I make sure that every toaster has my full attention throughout the dinner. I listen deeply and show the kind of self that I am asking them to show me.

This is what I was doing when I spoke about my period party. In contexts in which I am at a disadvantage, I typically try to tell stories against type. I could emphasize other details about me so as to be taken seriously: studying at an engineering school or not knowing how to cook. Why on earth would I tell a story not only from when I was eleven years old but also about getting my period? Because few stories could have more clearly communicated to my guests that I was willing to be genuine and to connect with them—and that they might do the same.

The period story sort of just came to me, but a Dutch colleague of mine, Bernardus Holtrop, actually follows a principle about sharing in this way. I saw it in action when he and I (and many others) co-facilitated a meeting of a few hundred business leaders who had come together to create trusted circles of support with one another. Holtrop shared one of his pro-tips with us: To get the group to be vulnerable, he said, we facilitators needed to share an even more personal story than we expected our clients to. We would set the depth of the group by whatever level we were willing to go to; however much we shared, they would share a little less. We had to become, in effect, participants.

RISK MANAGEMENT

When you're asking people to go deeper, to share what they don't usually share, you must manage the risk-taking you are encouraging. Sometimes that means prodding people to take more risk; other times, it means soothing people afraid of taking risk.

The singing rule we established with 15 Toasts was a way of nudging people toward risk-taking. By creating a risk in not coming forward with a toast, we evened out the risk calculus. People had to decide which was worse: giving a toast early or singing. The singing rule also creates some playful drama toward the end of the night, when all of a sudden three or four people, realizing the risk of having to sing, start clinking their glasses desperately after each toast, making sure they are not last.

It is also important as a host to be attentive to the needs of different personalities. No one, however extroverted, wants to feel like they have no choice but to share a deeply personal story. One of the reasons choosing a general theme works so well is because there is a lot of freedom within that theme to choose the level of depth one wants to take. While we do ask that everyone present participate, we let people decide what and how much they want to share. And this level of choice is the difference be-tween people being game for the evening and people resenting it.

Leng Lim, a fellow facilitator and an Episcopalian minister, uses the analogy of a swimming pool to talk about people's dif-ferent comfort levels. He hosts a range of gatherings, some at business schools, some at his farm, and he told me that he invites intimacy in all of them. But he is explicit about letting every par-ticipant choose their desired level of depth.

"I draw a swimming pool," he said. "There is a deep end and a shallow end. You can choose whatever end you want to enter. If you want to tell us your deepest secrets, you can. Or you can be superficial, and getting wet means being real, so bring something that is real for you." It is important, Lim said, to offer an "invita-tion to intimacy, but depth is a complete choice." Allowing each person to choose what and how much they want to expose was vital to making 15 Toasts intimate without being pushy.

Seven

Cause Good Controversy

. . .

E nough about warmth. Let's talk about heat.

I am often called in by gatherers who are looking for greater authenticity, but who are more interested in spice and heat than warmth and fuzziness. The skilled gatherer knows not only how to make people share and connect, but also how to make things fruitfully controversial.

While the last chapter was about bringing people closer together through what they share in common, this chapter is about making good use of what divides us in our gatherings. It is about how to turn up the heat. My belief is that controversy—of the right kind, and in the hands of a good host—can add both energy and life to your gatherings as well as be clarifying. It can help you use gatherings to answer big questions: what you want to do, what you stand for, who you are. Good controversy can make a gathering matter.

DO NOT *NOT* TALK ABOUT SEX, POLITICS, AND RELIGION

You may have grown up, as I did, hearing the adage to avoid talk of sex, politics, and religion at your gatherings. This commandment to avoid the dangerously interesting is widespread. Personally, I believe that few things are as responsible for the mediocrity and dullness of so many gatherings as this epically bad advice.

The impulse not to make waves is as old as humanity, and formal injunctions against letting controversy into one's gatherings date back at least to 1723. At the time, the Freemasons were a burgeoning secret society, and one of their members, the Reverend James Anderson, drafted the first constitution for the Premier Grand Lodge of England. This document explicitly forbade "doing or saying anything offensive, or that may forbid an easy and free Conversation, for that would blast our Harmony, and defeat our laudable Purposes." The Freemasons had taken up and promoted an idea that would become an erroneous touchstone for gatherers: that the airing of differences can do no good, that harmony is made never to be broken.

More than 150 years later, in 1880, Thomas Edie Hill showed the continued vitality of this thinking with advice printed in his book *Hill's Manual of Social and Business Forms*: "Do not discuss politics or religion in general company. You probably would not convert your opponent, and he will not convert you. To discuss those topics is to arouse feeling without any good result." In 1922, Emily Post, in her book *Etiquette*, gave the advice her own twist, counseling the avoidance of all negativity. "Talk about things which you think will be agreeable to your hearer," she wrote. "Don't dilate on ills, misfortune, or other unpleasant-nesses. The one in greatest danger of making enemies is the man or woman of brilliant wit."

And you wonder why so many gatherings are time-wasting and yawn-inducing.

The advice continues into today, thriving in the media and online people-to-people advice forums. On a Quora thread titled "Why is it considered rude to discuss sex, politics, and religion?" a woman who claims to have read etiquette guides "since age 6" wrote: "The goal of etiquette is to make people feel welcome and comfortable. So why look for fights?" An essay on the career website Glassdoor warns of the politics-sex-religion unholy trinity: "Before you make the potentially career-endangering mistake, here is why you should stay away from all three topics in the workplace."

The funny thing about this advice is that it is followed nowadays even by people who do not think they are following it. Many gatherers obey its spirit even if they do not agree with the letter, making choices that elevate harmony in gathering over controversy. Universities whose founding purpose was dispute and argument now regularly rescind invitations to speakers whom some students deem too controversial and out of line. Condoleezza Rice, who served as secretary of state under George W. Bush, had to withdraw from giving the commencement speech at Rutgers University because of student protest, as did Christine Lagarde, who runs the International Monetary Fund, from an address to Smith College. Michelle Obama, the former first lady, eloquently weighed in and encouraged students to "run to, and not away from, the noise." (Presumably, not the kind of noise that was generated at Middlebury College when the sociologist Charles Murray came to speak and students physically barred him from entering the building to which he had been invited, injuring his host, a female professor, in the process.)

It's not only campuses. Virtually every conference or industry gathering I have attended features panels, and virtually every panel I have ever seen is dull. The people who pick the panel topics pick the blandest ideas they can find—something about collaboration or partnership, prosperity or building bridges, new horizons or growth. In this they follow the Freemasons' mantra of avoiding what would "blast our Harmony." When they select moderators, they seem to pick people trained in the Emily Post tradition of smoothing things over and preventing the eruption of "unpleasantnesses." When was the last time you heard a panel moderator ask a tough question instead of tossing softballs? When was the last time you saw a couple of panelists truly argue about something worth arguing about? The panel, like the university, is a venue that prides itself on being about debate, when in fact it has given in to the dogma that controversy must be avoided at any cost.

When I work with clients, they often tell me they want to do a "town hall" to air opinions and get people to speak their truth. Then the day comes, and if I haven't managed to wrest control over the event, the town hall is used to recirculate the old platitudes, to reassure those in charge about the wisdom of their rule, to keep everything exactly as it is. When I challenge the organizers, they often tell me that it's too risky to introduce controversy in a group setting.

So how do we create gatherings that can hold some heat

without burning up in flames? How do we cause, and have the group benefit from, good controversy?

CAGE MATCHES AREN'T JUST FOR WRESTLERS

Sometimes, the elevation of harmony over everything else merely makes a gathering dull. Often, though, it is worse than that: The goal of harmony burrows its way into the core of the gathering and becomes a kind of pretender purpose, hampering the very thing the gathering was supposed to be about. That was what happened at a very polite architecture firm I worked with.

"Priya, we need more heat," my client whispered nervously in my ear.

He was watching what had been planned and billed as a contentious conversation about the future of his firm slip into a polite, cheerful discussion. I was facilitating a gathering for a team of architects to think about their firm's long-term vision. We had spent the morning imagining radical future scenarios, like a world where no new buildings were needed, or one in which their largest client was the Catholic Church, or one in which they had become a subscription service. These provocative prompts were purposefully designed to create a conversation that got to the heart of the question they were debating: Did they want to remain a bricks-and-mortar architecture firm, or did they want to morph into an experience-design firm?

There was serious disagreement in the room on that question, which is why they asked me to orchestrate the gathering. But as the conversation got under way, you wouldn't know it. Everyone around the table was smiling, friendly, and polite. Each time a partner would go out on a limb and dip a toe into the underlying controversy, she would quickly withdraw.

I tried to redirect the group to what divided rather than united them. "Let's get back to Anne's point," I'd suggest. But they were a sophisticated group and were well practiced at what I realized was one of the firm's dominant norms: avoiding anything that could stir the pot. The emotions I knew to be in the room were not surfacing. I knew that I would soon have to try a new approach, lest the whole meeting come to nothing.

So with the help of my extremely open-minded client, an executive who was not an architect himself but worked for them, we began to scheme at lunch, while everyone was away. In their absence, he and I restructured the room, gathered some towels, and located some *Rocky* music on YouTube. We were preparing for a cage match.

When the architects returned, they found two giant posters. One extolled a character called the Brain, the other a character called the Body. Each poster featured an actual wrestler's body, onto which one of the architects' heads had been hastily photoshopped. We had chosen two architects we knew to be charismatic, playful, and eloquent. Both of them immediately erupted in laughter when they saw what we had put up. We built on their surprise and didn't give them much of a chance to think.

I jumped into the middle of the crowd and announced that there was now going to be a cage match. I laid out the rules: In Round 1, each wrestler would be given three minutes to make the strongest argument for his side. The Body would have to argue why the firm should absolutely remain focused on the physical, on bricks-and-mortar architecture, on building buildings, for the next hundred years. The Brain would have to make the case for becoming a design firm, an increasingly popular if ethereal creature that took on jobs like crafting the signage within a hospital or organizing the flow of processes in an airport but didn't necessarily build things. It was a choice between moving with the times and sticking to their core talent.

I wasn't sure if people would go for it, and I could see the architects trying to figure out whether their colleagues were going to engage or not. I kept my own energy up and my voice confident, trying to push past their hesitancy.

Each "wrestler" was then assigned a coach, who was a member of the organizing team, and given a small white towel. Each coach stood behind his or her player and started massaging shoulders and whispering advice. Both men started rolling their heads around as if they were actually preparing for a fight. Nobody knew yet what exactly we meant by a "cage match." Were they actually going to physically fight? What the hell was going on?

I now told the rest of the group their role. They would have to listen to each fighter's argument and choose the side they were most convinced by. Then I added the most important rule for the audience: They could not stay neutral; they had to pick a wrestler to back. After every round, there would be a five-minute period in which the wrestlers could receive advice on their next round of argument. In Round 2, each wrestler would have another three minutes to make the next iteration of his case.

I egged the crowd on to make some noise—cheering and jeering were encouraged—to help the wrestlers feel the crowd's support. Once Round 2 was complete, the crowd would have the chance to make their final, updated decision on whom to stand behind. Everyone must choose a side, I repeated, because I knew this group had a tendency to blur distinctions. In the end, three independent judges (the executive assistants, who were in the room for administrative support), would make the final call on who won this Rumble in the Architecture Jungle.

Everyone began to talk excitedly among themselves. When we put the *Rocky* song on, people started to laugh, and the Body stood up and started gesticulating toward the Brain, playfully jeering at him. We were off. For the next twenty minutes, thanks to the willingness of the two wrestler-architects, this stuffy, buttoned-up, conservative, genteel group barked, hissed, laughed, taunted, and listened as two architects made two strong, interesting, sharp, and radically different cases for two very different futures. When certain architects were waffling, trying to claim a spot between the two fighters, it was their previously polite peers who called them out: "You have to choose!" The match was confrontational, heated, and argumentative, and it was exactly what we needed.

If you must know, the Body won.

The group was suffering from what many of us suffer from: a well-meaning desire not to offend that devolves into a habit of saying nothing that matters. They were not getting ideas out into the open. Because of this, they couldn't have a rich and honest dialogue, air their very real differences, and make an important decision together that they would stand by. And by avoiding what truly mattered to them in the name of not ruffling feathers, they were evading the questions they most cared about answering. They were kicking down the road the issue of their own future, as individuals and as a firm.

In so many gatherings, we are so afraid of getting burned that we avoid heat altogether. There is always risk inherent in controversy, because things can go very wrong very quickly. But in avoiding it, we waste countless opportunities to truly connect with others about the things they care about. The responsible harnessing of good controversy—handling with structure and care what we normally avoid—is one of the most difficult, complicated, and important duties for a gatherer. When it is done well, it is also one of the most transformative.

GOOD CONTROVERSY DOESN'T JUST HAPPEN

What, you might ask, is "good controversy"?

Good controversy is the kind of contention that helps people look more closely at what they care about, when there is danger but also real benefit in doing so. To embrace good controversy is to embrace the idea that harmony is not necessarily the highest, and certainly not the only, value in a gathering. Good controversy helps us re-examine what we hold dear: our values, priorities, nonnegotiables. Good controversy is generative rather than preservationist. It leads to something better than the status quo. It helps communities move forward in their thinking. It helps us grow. Good controversy can be messy in the midst of the brawling. But when it works, it is clarifying and cleansing—and a forceful antidote to bullshit.

In my experience, though, *good* controversy rarely happens on its own. It needs to be designed for and given structure. Because, almost by definition, controversy arises from what people care enough about to argue over, most gatherings are marred either by unhealthy peace or by unhealthy heat. Either no one is really saying anything that they actually think, or you end up with what I call the "Thanksgiving problem": a total free-for-all of pent-up grievances that often brings out tears and a screaming match, culminating in your cousin's announcement that he will be attending his "Friendsgiving" back home from now on. Good controversy is much more likely to happen when it is invited in but carefully structured.

One way to achieve that structuring at your gathering is to do what we did with the cage match: We moved the controversy from implicit to explicit by ritualizing it. We created a temporary alternative world within the larger gathering, a wrestling match that allowed the controversy to be litigated in a way that was honest and aired feelings without being bridge-burning. We borrowed from an earlier chapter's idea of pop-up rules, and made the whole thing playful. The purpose of a cage match is, after all, to fight. If there was no way they would debate within the context and norms of their everyday collegiality, we had to change that context and those norms temporarily. To do that safely, we turned to ritual.

This is what the organization DoSomething.org does when it hosts its annual Social Good cage fight. (Promotional poster: "Watch industry leaders duke it out on some of the sauciest topics in the nonprofit sector like: One organization can't claim to own an entire movement—Volunteering abroad perpetuates the white savior complex—Social Media campaigns are just another form of slacktivism—'Raising awareness' doesn't do sh*t.") They take topics that are taboo within the "social good" field and move them front and center for the audience (and speakers) to examine openly.

Many societies have their own versions of cage matches, using ritual to carve out a space for conflict and controversy (and therefore removing conflict and controversy from other spaces). Every year in Chumbivilcas Province, Peru, villagers mark Christmas—the birthday of the Prince of Peace—by gathering to beat one another up. In this region, which lacks a reliable judiciary, the fighting has evolved as a way of airing and resolving disputes before the year flickers out. In Chumbivilcas, January must begin with a clean slate. In the South African village of Tshifudi, Venda men gather regularly for a wrestling tradition called musangwe, where they fight in part to sort out and relieve the tension around lingering disputes. Tshilidzi Ndevana, a fifty-six-year-old teacher and father who is also the president of musangwe and goes by the wrestling name Poison, told *The New York Times*: "If there is a problem in the community, if people are fighting, we tell them: 'Wait. Don't quarrel. We will bring it to musangwe and sort it out there.'"

The cult film *Fight Club* captures the generalized feeling among thirtysomething men in America in the late 1990s that they were losing their masculinity. *Fight Club* depicts a Saturday-night ritual: an underground gathering that serves as a release for these men. It's a gathering where they don't have to "be a slave to the IKEA nesting instinct," as one character puts it. *Fight Club* is an embodiment of all that modern men are not supposed to do during their day jobs and home lives: fight, be aggressive, feel pain, cause pain. *Fight Club* borrows from an age-old idea of dealing with the more dangerous aspects of ourselves by separating them from everyday life and creating a space to safely release that darker energy. And in each of these varied forms of fight clubs, there are strict rules and practices and rituals, with a beginning, a middle, and an end. Yes, these are physical fight clubs, but they're doing what our little cage match was trying to do:

bringing conflict out into the open, in a safe, regulated, constructive way.

As you think about your own gatherings, ritualized controversy may sometimes make sense. I will be the first one to tell you it is not for every event. In many cases, doing something out of the ordinary isn't a great idea. Sometimes the key to safely bringing in generous heat is to identify the hot spots in a group and then simply organize the conversation around them, protected by some ground rules. This was my approach to a gathering I facilitated among a dozen or so leaders working on one of the most politically divisive issues of our time.

HEAT MAPS, SAFE SPACES, AND GROUND RULES

I received a phone call out of the blue one day, asking if I would facilitate a meeting in the U.K. that no one wanted to attend. It was a gathering of a dozen major civic leaders in Europe, all of whom worked on the same hot-button issue, but from radically different angles. The leaders were, technically, on the same side of the issue, but they had among themselves a long, complicated history and a lot of internal politics. They were being convened to reflect on a global project they had collaborated on, which was largely seen as a bust. But no one, I was told, was willing to admit it was a bust, at least not to one another. I had three weeks to figure out how to run the meeting.

The organizers were ambivalent as to whether it would be better to be polite and go through the motions of feigning agreement, or whether they should take off the lid and try to sort out some of the deeper contentious issues—both interpersonal and strategic. On the one hand, they figured it might be better to pretend everything is fine to keep the coalition together. On the other hand, they hadn't been particularly successful in achieving their overall mission, and maybe it was time to let things hang out. I was new to this domain and didn't know the players. So I began where I begin any attempt to cause good controversy: I made a heat map.

In almost any group of people—including strangers—certain areas of conversation will generate more heat than others. This heat can arise from conflict, taboos, transgression, power differences, hypocrisy, identity clashes, etc. Part of my job is to figure out the sources of potential heat and then decide what to do with them. In a church, a source of heat may be the issue of gay marriage within the congregation, but it could also be how tithes and collections are spent. In a newsroom, the heat may come from what stories get best placement on the front page and on the paper's website, but it could also be about expected layoffs that have yet to be announced. In a university administration, a source of heat may be the treatment of legacy applicants or the renaming of buildings. Issues have heat when they affect or threaten people's fears, needs, and sense of self. And when they poke at a source of power. Touching on these elements with care can produce transformative gatherings, because you can dig below the typical conversation into the bedrock of values.

To address these areas of heat, you need to know where they are. Thus you make a heat map. You can do this by asking yourself (and others) the following questions: What are people avoiding that they don't think they're avoiding? What are the sacred cows here? What goes unsaid? What are we trying to protect? And why?

In the case of the architecture firm, I had learned through a number of one-on-one interviews and conversations ahead of the gathering that the heat they most needed to face was around their identity: Who did they want to be in the future? In the case of this political meeting, I set out to do the same. What were their hot spots, and which of those were worth broaching? I got to work.

I first interviewed every leader by phone. I tried to build trust and a rapport with each of them, and I dug into their sense of what was not working and what they thought the core issues were. Two ideas emerged: First, a fundamental disagreement about whether the core problem was within the cause itself, among the players who would be at the gathering, or between the cause as a whole and those who opposed the cause. Second, there was a massive power imbalance because of differences in size, resources, and public recognition among the partners' organizations that affected all of their interactions.

Not surprisingly, the organizations with less influence were more upset about how things were going than the organizations with more influence. But almost all this dissatisfaction was coming out in proxy wars: battles over language on pamphlets, over the sharing of data, over who gets to stand on a dais or which country's newspapers to publish in. Yet because each of these seemingly small group decisions symbolized larger issues for many in the group, they mattered.

After these initial phone calls, I created a digital workbook in which I asked questions to continue the process of naming what participants believed were the core issues. I asked them all to fill out the workbook ahead of time and return it to me, and told them that their answers would be read aloud in the room, anonymously. Unlike the phone calls, which were confidential, they were now answering these questions knowing that they would be shared, if untraceably. By making this transition, I introduced the next level of risk into the process. The workbook included prompts about participants' personal history, to get them to connect back to their own core values: "Tell me about a moment in your early life that deeply influenced you and, in some way perhaps, led you to the work you do today." But the majority of the questions encouraged the leaders to speak about what wasn't working: "If you were to say something that was politically incorrect, or taboo, about this process or project, what would it be?" It asked: "What do you think is the most needed conversation for this group to have now?"

They each took the time to fill out the workbook and, fortunately, they were open and honest. I had what I needed to bring their voices and concerns into the room and host a conversation, not a cage match, that I hoped would nurture good controversy.

Me being me, I insisted that we first do a dinner the night before. I didn't want to walk into this meeting and dive into the controversy. I wanted to warm them up. We hosted a 15 Toasts dinner with the leaders and chose the theme of conflict. I wanted to normalize the word and show that there was some light in it. At first, people seemed confused by the theme, but before too long the toasts started rolling in. (A lot of people did not want to sing.) The toasts progressed through the night, and what they began to demonstrate was that there are all kinds of conflicts: within families and between friends, though the one that most resonated with people was of a different kind: inner conflict. A number of toasts exposed sides of these leaders that we hadn't known before. That was a vital lesson. More important for the next day's gathering, it was a reminder that they were complicated, multifaceted people who didn't have everything worked out. And that good conflict could lead them somewhere new.

The day of the gathering, I decided I would frame the entire day as a one-group conversation. It was rare for all these busy leaders to be in the same region, let alone one room, and part of their dynamic was that their most honest conversations as a group tended to be offline or in sidebars. I wanted to see if they could build the muscle to talk openly and rigorously about what was facing them.

To do this, I began the day by setting ground rules. I asked the following questions:

What do you need to feel safe here?

What do you need from this group to be willing to take a risk in this conversation today?

Spending the time asking such questions helps further prime your guests to take chances in the conversation and to listen more deeply than they otherwise might. Getting them to participate in creating the rules, as opposed to just presenting the rules myself, is also a way to begin naming and acknowledging past behaviors at some of their meetings that served to shut people down—behaviors now inspiring the suggestion of new rules to foster new behaviors. It also lends a legitimacy to the rules. It lets the facilitator say: "These are the rules you said you wanted."

After creating those ground rules, I engaged in my second act of naming: I began by reading aloud from the workbooks. I had organized my excerpts by question and theme and anonymized them as thoroughly as I could. I began reading out people's personal stories. As often happens, many of the participants had shared powerful stories from early in their lives that the others had never heard. These stories reminded all of us of the feeling with which we had left the previous night's dinner. It helped draw a thread back to that sensation. Though they had answered a range of questions, I spent a disproportionate amount of time reading their answers on the questions about taboos. I had given each participant a Post-it pad and pen and asked them to capture any words and phrases they heard that struck them. As I spoke, I noticed that people were busy writing as fast as they could. It gave them something to do and would help them remember these phrases.

Once I was done reading, I looked up. The leaders were sitting straight up, paying full attention. A few of them had funny looks on their faces. Without saying anything more, I invited each one to share two phrases they had written down. This was yet more naming. Within twenty minutes, what had never really been said out loud in this community was buzzing in everyone's ears. A number of phrases were repeated by different members, thereby showing resonance within the group. It was the ripping off of a Band-Aid. Rather than trying to get there over the course of a conversation, we began with it all on the table. Only ninety minutes had passed, and there was a palpable sense of both expectation and relief in the room.

The rest of the day was organized around the taboos that most resonated with them. We spent the day getting their assumptions out in front of one another. I used all my tricks to guide their conversation over the next six hours. We'd gather for ninety-minute sessions at a time and then break, gather again and break. We worked through lunch. When some people began to dominate the conversation, I would pause them, pointing to a ground rule if need be, and try to bring in the quieter folks. When tension arose between two participants about a relevant topic, rather than cool it down, if I believed it was relevant to the group, I would have them lean into it. At one point, a specific past incident between two people arose. One of them said something like "It's OK, we can talk about it offline." But another member of the group (not in that pair) pointed out that the incident actually reflected a dynamic that existed among a number of them, and she thought it would be helpful for the group as a whole to discuss. Others agreed, and I facilitated the pair through their issue in front of everyone else.

I repeatedly urged the group to go below the surface, into the assumptions beneath what they were talking about. When things would get heated, I would slow them down and try to help them go "below the iceberg." Rather than looking at the specific incidents and events above the water line, I would ask them how those moments revealed their underlying beliefs, values, and needs. I would try to make what they were saying more hearable to everyone else. So that even if they didn't agree, they understood.

Throughout the day, I was building their muscle as a group to collectively witness one another, not just through being polite but, as in the case with the cage match, through having good controversy. I continued, at various moments, to check in with the group and with individuals to see how they were doing. When they needed a break, we took a break. The day was punctuated with laughter as much as with tension. Often within the same moment. At one point, a newer member of the group expressed worry about the direction of the conversation. She said something like "Why are we spending time looking at all of this negative stuff? I think this is very unproductive." I paused. I didn't defend. I waited. At that moment an older leader looked at her kindly and said something along the lines of "Oh no, this is a breakthrough. In twenty-five years, we have never had this conversation."

By confronting the heat, the participants began to see glimpses of alternative, more productive ways of interacting with one another. They became clearer on where it made sense to collaborate and where it didn't. They also got a lot off their chests.

As the day continued, I noticed a number of participants taking more risks. They would voice to the group what they had written in the workbooks. They would say out loud what they had told me on the phone in confidence. At the end of the day, they agreed as a group to continue to meet to pursue these conversations in greater depth. It was a step forward.

WHAT IS THE GIFT? WHAT IS THE RISK?

Seeking the heat in any gathering is inherently risky. When you can put some process or structure around that heat-seeking, though, there is a chance for real benefit. Still, that doesn't mean heat-seeking should be part of every gathering. I bring good controversy to a gathering only when I believe some good can come out of it—enough good to outweigh the risks and harm. For your gatherings, you should make a similar assessment.

In the course of researching this book, I met a woman named Ida Benedetto who creates secret, underground gatherings that help guests safely take risks they wouldn't normally take. Benedetto and her partner N. D. Austin are self-described "transgression consultants" and cofounders of a design practice called Sextantworks. They were behind gatherings like the Night Heron, a New York speakeasy housed illegally in a water tower. Benedetto and Austin are also the creators of a fake conference called the Timothy Convention, an annual, flash-mob-like gathering at the iconic Waldorf Astoria hotel in New York. At this "convention," one hundred strangers dressed in black tie descend on the hotel and have to complete "harmless transgressive acts," such as "Deliver room service to a hotel guest," "Wear a robe in an unlikely place," "Acquire Waldorf cutlery for your entire team," "Collect two business cards from hotel guests," and take a "team photo in the maid's closet." Benedetto and Austin have been described as "New York's wildest underground event planners," and their events as nights "you'll never forget."

Though these gatherings might appear to be frivolous, Benedetto is driven by something deeper. Before every gathering she creates, she asks herself two questions: What is the gift? And what is the risk? She thinks of each of her gatherings as fulfilling a specific need for a specific group of people. But for that gift to be given, she has learned, there needs to be some amount of risk. "No true gift is free of risk," Benedetto told me. She defines risk as "a threat to one's current state that could destabilize the way things are." The risk is what allows for the possibility of the gift.

In Benedetto's gatherings, the risks are often legal and physical: trespassing and entering abandoned buildings. But they can also be psychological: Each Timothy Convention is designed around breaking a small taboo or social norm. In fact, the entire gathering is designed to help people "cross boundaries" and "transform their relationship to the city" by changing what they assumed to be out of bounds to them.

In the same way, should you decide to bring some good controversy to your next gathering, you can benefit from asking yourself Benedetto's questions: What is the gift in broaching this issue? And what is the risk? Is it worth it? And can we handle it with care?

Eight

Accept That There
Is an End

• • •

B y now it's getting late. Some of your guests could go on all night while others are starting to look sleepy. The last of the graduating class has accepted his diploma onstage. It's the closing session of the conference, and people are fumbling for their bell-desk tags, hoping to retrieve their luggage quickly. It's the final breakfast of the family reunion before everyone takes off. How do you actually close this gathering? How do you end on a high? How do you graciously say goodbye?

I NEED YOU TO BREAK UP WITH ME

Earlier we explored the widespread tendency to open without opening. Instead of drawing us in with a bang and catering, above all, to the human need to be welcomed and entranced, people start with logistics, announcements, housekeeping, and the set-tling of corporate sponsor debts. Now we turn to an equal and opposite problem: a widespread tendency to close without clos-ing. When it comes to our gatherings, far too many of us are that horrible person who never really breaks up with anyone but just stops calling. That person may tell himself that he is being kind or low-key. But guests, like romantic partners, deserve a proper breakup.

Gatherers don't skip the closing because they are bad people. They tend to skip it because they assume that, like other elements of gathering, it will happen on its own. They treat the closing like sunset. But as I learned when a gathering of mine wound down in Minneapolis, the closing isn't like sunset at all. If it was, it would have arrived.

I was cofacilitating a two-day workshop in that city, hosted by a foundation. Our task was to help change the way its external evaluators measured the impact of the work the foundation funded. This might sound dry, but in the nonprofit world it is a vital and controversial subject. Changing what evaluators mea-sure, and how they measure it, changes the results of their studies. It changes which kinds of help are found to be effective and which are not. Such adjustments could, in turn, alter what the founda-tion funded. They were ready to open up their assumptions of what actually works, which in the long run might mean ending relationships with certain NGOs or beginning new streams of giving. This tweak in evaluations would ultimately affect their identity and role as a funder in the larger ecosystem of American philanthropy.

Over the course of the two days, our job was to take what these evaluators had been trained to value and shift it. We had been hired less to teach them the new approach than to get them to buy into it and even believe in it.

We facilitators spent all our preparation time on the content of the sessions. We designed role plays. We staged complicated conversations. We figured out ways to host technical conversations on subjects we didn't fully understand. Everything—every session, every transition, every break—was tightly designed, down to the minute. Everything except for the final ten minutes of the conference. Like sunset, we assumed it would come.

Before we knew it, the two days had whizzed by, and now we were in the final session. We had seven minutes left on the clock until the event was officially over. The three of us hadn't explicitly talked about how we would close the workshop. The lead facilitator stepped up to the podium, looked at her watch, and made a few announcements about shared rides to the airport. The audience turned toward her, looking up attentively, waiting for more. There was a sense of expectation in the room. She looked out at them, presumably thinking it was obvious that we were done, but they kept staring at her, waiting for more. "OK, thank you!" she said. Everyone kept staring. She tried again: "We're done here! It's over!" Finally, after another awkward pause, realizing there really wasn't anything more, the attendees broke into conversation, grabbed their bags, and left.

We closed without closing. We didn't take stock of what they had absorbed over the two days. We didn't gauge their buy-in. We didn't talk about how they would carry what we had done together into their daily lives—for example, by retraining their researchers in the new approach. Most basically, though, we allowed the clock—and only the clock—to demarcate our ending. In one of the two most vital moments in any gathering, we offered only a gaping void. Even when our guests seemed to challenge this void, begging with their facial expressions for more, we refused to close meaningfully.

And the only consolation in telling you this story is that I know I am not alone. It's the party that is hurriedly evacuated at 10 p.m., just because it said so on the invitation. It's the conference that fizzles out after the last session ends at 3:30 p.m., because there is nothing else listed on the agenda. It's the school homeroom that ends at 8:32 a.m., because of the bell. More often than not at our gatherings, hosts passively allow their events to flicker out instead of claiming a specific concluding moment—a real send-off. Too many of our gatherings don't end. They simply stop.

WHY CLOSINGS MATTER

I once had an improv teacher, Dave Sawyer, who told us that you can tell the difference between good actors and great ones not by how they enter a stage, which every actor thinks about and plans for, but how they exit. Good actors enter dramatically and in character, say their lines, and when they're done, assuming their job has finished, scuttle off the stage. Great actors spend as much time thinking about the parting. Great hosts, too. Because great hosts, like great actors, understand that how you end things, like how you begin them, shapes people's experience, sense of meaning, and memory.

Remember what Neo Muyanga, who could tell whether he was going to like an opera within the first sixteen bars, said about closings? The second-most-important part of the opera is the "final four pages of the score." He explained: "This is where the composer must have, once and for all, justified the first notes sung and played by the ensemble and where the conductor needs to push the entire alternate universe—the one that has recently been magically conjured up—over the edge of the abyss, leaving the listener to fall back into their own skin."

That sounds like a lot, right? But it's not as unreasonable a standard as it may sound. As with the operas Muyanga listens to, you, too, have hopefully created a temporary alternative world in your gathering, and it is your job to help your guests close that world, decide what of the experience they want to carry with them, and reenter all that from which they came.

So, you might ask, how do you actually do that? It can be as simple as a professor's surprise tequila party.

Michael J. Smith is a professor at the University of Virginia, and he knows how to close. He runs the Political and Social Thought program at the university, an intensive, two-year-long seminar that takes each class of twenty students through a rigorous study of political philosophy. The culminating moment of the program is the submission of a final thesis. Students work on the thesis for more than a year. The final weeks tend to be grueling, filled with all-nighters. It is generally the most intensively any of the students have ever worked thus far.

Every year, Professor Smith tells his flock to bring the final thesis, every "i" dotted and every "t" crossed, to his office at 5 p.m. on the second Friday of April. For most professors, that would mean leaving a box outside their office door for the students to place their bound theses and walk out. But at the appointed time,

Professor Smith, to the surprise and delight of his students, stands inside his office, waiting for them with a platter of tequila shots. You walk down the hall toward his office, with two printed copies of your thesis ready to submit. And rather than slipping it through a mail slot, you are welcomed by Professor Smith to a surprise party and inducted into post-thesis life. With that simple act of turning an ending into a closing, he transforms the act of submitting a thesis and creates a moment that students never forget (including this one, from the Class of 2004).

JUST ACCEPT IT

The first step to closing a gathering well is less practical than it is spiritual or metaphysical: You must, before anything, accept that there is an end. You must accept your gathering's mortality.

This may sound like a bizarre instruction, or utterly obvious. Who doesn't accept that their gathering has an end? People come and they go; hosts say goodbye. Who's not accepting the end?

Look a little closer. In so many gatherings, somewhere during the inevitable wind-down, there comes a moment when the host or the guests or some combination make a faint, usually futile bid to prolong it. We often take these bids to be charming, and sometimes indeed they are. But they are also symptoms of gatherings that lack a clear closing. We force wedding bands to play that One Last Song three different times, so that the third- or fourth-to-last song has the kaboom of a send-off and the remaining songs have the quality of a balloon slowly letting out its air. We keep dinner guests at our table for as long as the person who least wants to go home wishes to stay, even if one or two people have started to fall asleep. We create WhatsApp chat groups after conferences, promising to "keep the spirit alive." We promise to sustain what is better surrendered.

Accepting the impermanence of a gathering is part of the art. When we vaguely try to extend our gatherings, we are not only living in denial, we are also depriving our gathering of the kind of closing that gives it the chance of enduring in people's hearts.

I once went to see a couple of Zen Buddhist monks with a strange idea. I wondered if the two of them, who had made a specialty of helping people face their resistance and avoidance of endings, had something to teach the everyday gatherer.

Zen teachers Robert Chodo Campbell and Koshin Paley Ellison founded and are the guiding teachers of the New York Zen Center for Contemplative Care, which has gained attention for its innovative and thoughtful approaches to helping people deal with death, direct case, and Zen training. I know what you're thinking: Who said anything about death? I'm just trying to have a better picnic. But I have found, again and again, that the failure to close well is rooted in the avoidance of an end. And the people most thoughtful about why we avoid endings, and how we might accept them, are people who spend a lot of time thinking about death.

The Zen Center for Contemplative Care has a variety of offerings, from meditation courses to student training in contemplative care for those facing illness and grief and hospice care. But a thread that runs through its work is an effort to push back against a culture that the monks see as ducking the reality of death and endings in general. In the United States, for example, there has been an increase in the number of people wanting to treat funerals as celebrations rather than sad or mournful occasions. In a 2010 survey, 48 percent of people said they preferred a "celebration of life" compared with 11 percent who wanted a "traditional funeral." One-third of all respondents said they wanted no funeral at all. This idea of celebration may seem evolved and selfless at first, but the monks believe it deprives people of the experience of processing a death for what it is. In their center, they pursue the opposite philosophy, doing everything they can to make people confront the end for what it is. For example, when a person dies in their community, the monks encourage, when appropriate, family members to wash and shroud the body themselves, and to carry it down the stairs rather than taking the elevator. They encourage people to turn toward the fact of the death rather than away from it. And they show people that they can, in fact, handle death.

Among the Zen Center's offerings is a nine-month training called Foundations in Contemplative Care. It aims to teach each cohort of thirty to forty students how to provide a "compassionate approach to life transitions." Which is why it's funny that some of these students, signing up for this program and learning to grow more comfortable with the End, avoid the last class. Every year, the monks told me, there tends to be regular attendance throughout the program. And then, on the last day of class, a handful of students will routinely fail to show—year after year, and only ever for that last class. "People get sick. They have urgent knitting to do! It's really amazing. Suddenly things will come up," said Koshin, as he is known to his students. "There are always three or four people that have to be at their child's ball game, and they've been otherwise present."

Students often approach the teachers seeking a prolonging. "Almost every group, every time, during the last week, there has been a group discussion asking me if we can extend the group by two weeks. And I always say, 'No, it's done. You signed up for nine months; it's nine months.' But every group does it," Koshin said. The monks never grant these requests "because life is not about extensions. It's finite. There's a beginning, a middle, and an end. And that's the same in a group. Once you've gone through that process, what are we doing now? We're rehashing. What is it in you that doesn't want this group to end?" he asked.

Understanding this tendency in students, Koshin and Chodo try to prepare them for the end of their gathering as a class. Midway through their nine months together, they talk to the students about their "mid-life" as a group. "Look around again, see how it feels, how your relationships have changed," they might say. "We're at our mid-life, and in four and a half months this group will die. So what do you need to do in the next four months in these relationships? What are your patterns of leaving? What are your habits?" They use the group itself and the experience of being part of a group to help them look at their own "habits of how they end things."

Why do they do this? "Because everything ends," Chodo said. "There's nothing that doesn't end. On some level, what we do in our work is hold that truth. This is going to end, whether you like it or not. Whether it's meeting your ninety-eight-year-old grandma in this hospice bed; whether it's a week long or a day long, it's going to end. No question. We don't hold magical thinking for anyone," he says. They will do sixty-minute lectures with a thousand doctors in the room and have them turn to the person next to them, try to connect briefly and deeply by looking into their eyes in silence, and then do a guided visualization imagining that other person getting old and frail and weak. And then the monks will ask,

"What does that do to your awareness and your relationship to this person you have just met?" Koshin said. "People are weeping. It's incredible." The crux of what they teach health-care professionals and laypeople is, as one of the monks put it, "How do you allow them to welcome everything and push away nothing?"

It was interesting that the monks found in the banal sphere of class attendance the same resistance to the end that people feel about death itself. Listening to them, I realized that the task they have set themselves in closing their training programs is the task of every gatherer who must close any kind of event: to help people fight their urge to turn away from the finitude. It is your job as a gatherer to create an intentional closing that helps people face, rather than avoid, the end.

LAST CALL

When done well, openings and closings often mirror one another. Just as before your opening there should be a period of ushering, so with closings there is a need to prepare people for the end. This is not ushering so much as last call.

In drinking establishments around the world, bartenders loudly announce last call. Why? To prepare you for the end of your time in that place. To allow you to resolve whatever unfinished business you may have at that bar—be that settling the tab or ordering a final drink or asking that man for his number. The announcement of last call unites the gathering of the bar around the knowledge of the night's finitude. I believe many gatherings—in homes and workplaces and beyond—could benefit from adopting the idea behind issuing the last call.

If last calls would make our dinner parties and conferences and work meetings better, why don't we issue them? One reason is that, in a bar, the closing time is an unavoidable legal reality that applies equally. In other gatherings, people are having different experiences side by side, and gatherers are often reluctant to impose a universal closing.

Perceptive hosts notice when an event is waning. Perhaps a few guests are rubbing their eyes, or they start shifting in their seats, or no one is asking questions of the panelists. The trouble for the host is that, for every person who is tired or checking out, there are presumably others who look as if they could keep going for hours. One of the most interesting—and divisive—dilemmas in hosting is what to do in this situation. Do you relieve the entire group at the first sign of a significant minority being done? Do you quit while the party is ahead? Or do you let the guests be your guide?

I live in a house divided, because my husband is staunchly in favor of letting people linger as long as they want, and I strongly favor ending an event preemptively so as to give guests an escape. To Anand's horror, when we were first married, I would close many dinners by suddenly blurting out, "Thank you all so much for coming!" In my mind, I was emancipating my guests; in his, I was kicking them out. He comes from a family culture where you always wait for the guests to signal that they're leaving, and I come from one where you don't leave until your hosts, in effect, dismiss you.

So we came to our own version of a last call. Once I can see the conversation petering out after dessert, I pause, thank everyone for a beautiful evening, then suggest we move to the living room to have a nightcap. I give the guests who are tired the opportunity to leave, but both my husband and I emphasize that we'd rather everyone stay. That invitation to the living room is a soft close; in a sense, it's the equivalent of the last call. You can ask for the check, so to speak, or you can order another round. Those who are tired can leave without appearing rude, and those who want to stay can stay. The party, relocated and trimmed, resumes.

A last call is not a closing; it's the beginning of an outbound ushering. A last call can be verbal, as at our dinner parties. But it doesn't have to be. Dario Cecchini, at the end of the long beefy dinners he presides over, rings a cowbell to signal the night is winding down. I know some managers who purposefully have their assistants knock on the conference room door five minutes before the end of the meeting to signal to them (and everyone else there) that the meeting is finite. This knock is not the closing but a signal to people to wind down.

WHEN AND WHO?

Maybe you are like my husband and are hesitant to give people any kind of signal to leave. But if I have even slightly convinced you about issuing a last call, the question of timing arises. When the law doesn't mandate a last call, when should it be declared?

This question of timing is particularly complicated in informal gatherings without an agenda. On the one hand, you don't want to kill the vibe and seem like a party pooper. On the other hand, you shouldn't wait until everyone is dead.

Lady Elizabeth Anson, Queen Elizabeth's party planner for more than half a century, suggests ending a party while there are at least twenty people on the dance floor. She is speaking, of

course, of one particular kind of gathering, but there is a principle behind the number. If you wait too long, it can seem that you
are being led by events instead of leading them. "If you let it peter
out, it's death," she once told *The New York Times*. Her greatest
regret involved asking a band, at the behest of certain guests, to
play a last song after their actual last song. "I made one mistake
in the whole of my career, which was being persuaded to restart
the band," she said. "It was a flop."

So ask yourself: What is your equivalent of the twenty-people-
left-on-the-dance-floor moment? When, by transitioning into that
last call, are you still in charge of events instead of being carried
by them? When are you still quitting while you are ahead? When
are you allowing things to go on long enough to feel satisfied with
the event—but not so long as to feel the energy draining from the
room?

And who should make this decision to issue the last call?

On the night before my wedding, we hosted an evening talent
show in which many of our guests performed, borrowing from
and adapting the Indian tradition of the *sangeet*, which usually
features choreographed dances by friends and relatives. After all
our friends' performances, with the mood lively and festive, the
whole thing turned into a dance party. Well into the dancing, a
few friends requested that we show a video that a friend had
made for us and that had been played at a smaller rehearsal dinner the night before. I looked out at the dance floor and people
seemed to be having a great time dancing. But here were some
guests who really wanted to have this video shown then. We
hadn't planned on showing it again, but I agreed, thinking, "If
it's what people want . . ." We turned down the music and watched
the film. I had thought it would be fun, and a short break before

resuming the dancing. But by the end of the fifteen-minute film, guests had cooled down and were ready to turn in. The night was over. I had ceded my own ending by giving someone else a chance to issue a kind of unintended last call.

On the other hand, sometimes the right decision may be to let the guests choose their own ending. I have facilitated many dinners with teams that go late into the night and take on a life of their own. I once facilitated a dinner in Singapore with a team that was trying to unearth some deeper conflict. Perhaps it was because of the late hour, or the wine, or the exhaustion, but at 11:30 p.m. the guests finally began to speak truth, just as I was preparing to close down the evening. I had started my last call, which in this case was a "checkout" process, asking each person to say just one word about how they were feeling. One of the participants interrupted me, saying: "I think we're finally getting somewhere. If we go to sleep, and we wake up and are fresh and showered and back in that conference room, anything that is getting opened up here is going to disappear. I'd like to request that we continue this conversation and don't close right now." There were a number of nods around the table, so I intentionally ceded the closing to the group. We reopened and continued to share for ninety more minutes, ending the session at 1:30 a.m., exhausted, but having had an emotional breakthrough as a group.

THE ANATOMY OF A CLOSING

So you've issued your last call, people have been primed to think about the end, and the event is winding down. How do you actually close?

A strong closing has two phases, corresponding to two distinct needs among your guests: looking inward and turning outward. Looking inward is about taking a moment to understand, remember, acknowledge, and reflect on what just transpired—and to bond as a group one last time. Turning outward is about preparing to part from one another and retake your place in the world.

Looking inward: meaning-making and connecting one last time

Many, though not all, gatherings will benefit from a pause to reflect on what happened here. A gathering is a moment of time that has the potential to alter many other moments of time. And for it to have the best chance of doing so, engaging in some meaning-making at the end is crucial. What transpired here? And why does that matter?

Whether or not a gathering creates space for meaning-making, it is something that individual guests will do on their own. What did I think of that? How am I going to talk about it with others? A great gatherer doesn't necessarily leave this process to unfold only within individuals. Rather, the gatherer might find a way of guiding guests toward some kind of collective exercise of stock-taking.

For example, the organizers of the TED conference often ask a comedian to close a days-long conference with a fifteen-minute wrap. (Our master opener Baratunde Thurston, being a great closer as well, has done the wrap in the past.) The comedian's assignment is not easy. He or she must listen deeply throughout the week and then stand before hundreds of people who have been through the same experience and, with humor and insight, juice meaning from that multitude of moments. When a mother asks her children every night at dinner not just what happened today, but for their "rose" and "thorn" (the best and worst parts of their day), she is helping them make meaning. When a group comes back onstage at the end of a Battle of the Bands to play a mash-up of the songs the audience has already heard, the band members are helping us process the journey as a whole.

Looking back, though, is just one aspect of turning inward. Another is connecting the tribe one last time. To have an affirming moment of recalling not what we did here but who we were here.

A gathering that does this kind of final connecting well is Renaissance Weekend. The event's origins trace back to 1981, when a couple named Philip and Linda Lader threw a house party to which they invited some of the most interesting thinkers they knew. The Laders felt more and more siloed in their work. They wanted to do something different for New Year's Eve, so they invited sixty families, made up of friends and acquaintances from diverse fields across the country, down to Hilton Head, South Carolina, for a weekend together. They asked each friend to prepare something to share with the group. They continued doing the same year after year, though with considerably less obscurity once two of their longtime participants, Bill and Hillary Clinton, came into the national spotlight. Twenty-five years later, the weekend has grown into an organization and a series of events, with an executive director and five annual weekends that occur around the country. The number of attendees at their New Year's gathering, which has since moved to Charleston, South Carolina, is now approaching one thousand.

The organizers' declared purpose is to build bridges across the customary divides of race, religion, age, profession, and politics, to encourage people to come together to agree and disagree with respect. They are adamant about gathering people as equals, and they embed that value into the structure of their gathering by requiring that every participant over the age of six (yes, six!) participate in at least one panel and by doing away with keynote speeches. The entire agenda is built from scratch each time, based on participants' interests that particular weekend. "If we see that three people raise llamas, we'll have a conversation about that," Alison Gelles, Renaissance's executive director, told me.

Over the four and a half days of the festival, a certain intimacy forms. That is because people show up as families, and because every family member is treated as a contributor to the program, and because people are encouraged to show different sides of themselves. When you ask a national security expert not to talk about national security but rather what he's learned from love, Gelles tells me, something interesting happens, both for those speaking and those listening.

So after going to these lengths to create that intimacy and exploration, what does Renaissance do to tie the collective experience together? How does it connect the tribe and affirm this new sense of belonging one last time?

The answer is a special closing session called "If These Were My Last Remarks." The session features approximately twenty participants, each of whom is given two minutes to tell the group what they would say if this were the end of their life. People read poems, share stories about their faith, confess doubts, recall tragedies large and small. "It's motivating, it's touching, it's tragic, and it kind of seals the bond," Gelles said. Notably, by asking the participants to contemplate their actual, physical mortality, the group is subtly reminded to confront its metaphorical mortality. Most important, though, the group is being shown itself in dramatic fashion before it disperses. *This is who we were here*— open, vulnerable, thoughtful, funny, complicated. Tribe-making is vital to meaning-making.

Turning outward: separation and reentry

Once a group has been invited to take stock and connect one last time, it is ready for the second phase of the closing, which concerns itself with the transition back to the world from which the gathered came. This second phase is defined by the question: What of this world do I want to bring back to my other worlds?

The more different from the real world your gathering was, the more important it is to create a strong, clear ending to prepare your guests for reentry into the real world. The more tightly bonded your gathering is, the more it forms a tribe, the more important it is to prepare your guests for the dissolution of that tribe and for the opportunity to join and rejoin other tribes.

Consider the example of Seeds of Peace, a summer camp that tries to reduce conflict and suffering in the Middle East and beyond. Every July since 1993, several dozen teenagers from specific conflict regions, including Israel, Palestine, Egypt, and Jordan, as well as India and Pakistan, gather in Otisfield, Maine. They gather to see if, over the course of three weeks, under carefully designed rules of engagement, they can create an alternative world with the very people they are supposed to distrust, even hate.

At Seeds of Peace, the hosts are the camp counselors, many of whom are Seeds of Peace alumni themselves. As at many summer camps, there's a lake and canoeing and arts and soccer. But every day also features 110 minutes of intense, facilitated small-group conversations in which teenagers from different sides of conflict come together to engage more deeply.

Over the course of the camp, these teenagers, many of whom are meeting "the Other" for the first time, begin to change their perceptions. By the end of the three weeks, when campers are boarding buses to return home, many have gone from theoretical enemies to flesh-and-blood friends. But the counselors also have a big responsibility to give the students the skills to reenter their very different realities back home.

Reentry, as the term is used in conflict resolution, refers to helping someone who has gone through an intense experience within the bubble of a dialogue return to their original context. The term is also used for circumstances such as soldiers returning from war or prisoners finishing their sentences. Yet even the most ordinary comings-together of people have an element of reentry. As a host, you can help your guests think about what they would like to take with them as they go back into the world, given what they have experienced with you. In the case of Seeds of Peace, now that they're a "seed," how will they plant themselves in the hostile, messy soil beyond?

At Seeds of Peace, they start reentry a full three nights before the last day of camp. At the end of their evening talent show, the director of the camp, Leslie Lewin, walks onto the stage in the Big Hall to make her closing remarks. Midway through, the lights suddenly go out. It seems like it's just a technical glitch, but all of a sudden a Metallica song, "Enter Sandman," starts to play. In the dark, dozens of counselors come running into the room with blue and green glow sticks wrapped around their heads and arms. They dance like crazy, and then they run out to the back of the Big Hall toward the lake. At that moment, two other lead directors jump onstage and explain to the disoriented campers what is about to happen. One of the camp directors will then say something like "Welcome to Color Games. The next few days are going to be a series of events that will push you. You will soon be divided into two teams, but you will still be upholding and building on the values that we have been holding onto as a community. As you join these two teams—Green and Blue—it's an opportunity to try new things and to step outside of ourselves." Unbeknownst to the campers, the process of reentry into the outside world has begun.

Over the next two days, the campers are involved in a series of competitive activities, from rock climbing to canoe racing, from a variety show to an activity race they call the Hajime. During the two days of the Color Games, a new (arbitrary) identity, Blue or Green, is purposefully forged within each Seed. "Years later, when you talk to alumni, they will often cite the Color Games as the most transformative experience. And they will absolutely know if they were Blue or Green and whether they lost or won," Kyle Gibson, one of the camp directors, told me.

The Color Games culminate in an awards presentation. Everyone gathers on the lake to find out the winner. The winning team gets to run into the lake first, after which everyone joins them. Then, soaking wet, they will all run back to their bunks, take off their colors (and Color Game identities) for the last time, and change back into their original dark green Seeds of Peace T-shirts.

Each step of the Color Games is designed to help them with reentering their home lives. In addition to being fun and competitive, the games give them an experience in which they can put on and take off an identity as easily as switching T-shirts.

That evening, the campers gather again in those matching Seeds of Peace T-shirts and "equality descends again." A counselor discusses for the first time explicitly the identity-formation that they just went through by partaking in the Color Games. They say something like this:

> Look at how quickly your identity has formed, a group of people who maybe two days ago you didn't talk to, but now they are forever in your memory of this team of yours. Look at how you were fighting till the end two days ago, and now there's no more Green team. There's this construction of a team and a cause that was valuable and supporting, but also look at how quickly we can coalesce around this constructed identity.

The counselor then relates it back to society: "People think in groups. It can be a force for good, in the case of the Blue and the Green, or it can also be a force of evil, and quickly coalesce around hatred or mistrust." They use the Color Games to remind the campers of one of the core insights they learn at this summer camp: how identity is created.

The final session on the last night of camp is called "Life as Seeds." The counselors talk about going home and how challenging it can be. Second-year campers, having gone through the reentry process before, guide the discussion in small groups, helping Seeds reflect on questions like these:

> What does it mean to go home?
> How are you feeling?
> What is making you anxious?
> What are you excited about?
> What are some of the issues you think you might face?

During that session, the Seeds think back on the last few weeks of the gathering and begin to integrate what they experienced with the world they are returning to. The next morning, as the buses pull up, the campers get into their final "Line Up," which they have been doing three times a day for three and a half weeks. The reality of the departure has set in. People speak, second-year students share poems, and then they finally close. For several years, the camp director read aloud a poem that is painted on the back of the shower house at the camp:

> I met a stranger in the night whose light had ceased to shine. I
> paused and let him light his lamp from mine.
> A tempest sprang up later on and shook the world about. When
> the storm was over, my lamp was out.
> But back to me the stranger came his lamp was glowing fine.
> He held to me his precious flame and thus rekindled mine.

At that point, the students are dismissed and begin to board the buses to head to the airport. Many are crying as they hug one another and say their goodbyes. They know that they will be meeting other Seeds again in about a month, which can help give them strength to hold on to this identity when they are back home. As the buses pull out of camp, the camp bell is rung one last time.

FINDING THE THREAD

Seeds of Peace might sound beautiful but ultimately remote from your garden-variety gatherings. What if you're gathering not Israelis and Arabs but just some of your friends?

The dynamics of extreme cases are not all that different from the dynamics of ordinary events. The advantage of the extreme is that the dynamics are easier to see. No matter how ordinary your gathering, if you have forged a group and created something of a temporary alternative world, then you should also think about helping those you gathered "take the set down" and walk back into their other worlds. Whether implicitly or explicitly, you should help them answer these questions: We've collectively experienced something here together, so how do we want to behave outside of this context? If we see people again, what are our agreements about what and how we'll talk about what occurred here? What of this experience do I want to bring with me?

At a company retreat, when only one slice of an organization has been convened, how do you prepare employees to return to the company, where they will be back in the mix with VPs, assistants, research fellows, and interns?

After a family reunion, when you've bonded with your cousins in a way that is harder to do when your spouses are around, how do you interact the next time you are all together, spouses and all?

Part of preparing guests for reentry is helping them find a thread to connect the world of the gathering to the world outside. That thread could come in the form of a verbal or written pledge, as some conferences have begun to do in their closing sessions. They give guests an opportunity to make public pledges to the group of what they will do differently moving forward, and often have a physical wall that people can write the pledges on. A thread could be a letter that each guest can write to their future self on a self-addressed postcard, to be mailed out by the organizer a month later. A thread can also be a physical symbol that helps connect the two worlds in some way, as my own mother did with a gathering she called Circle of Friends.

When I was fifteen, she offered to host a weekly gathering in our basement, with me and eleven other girls from my high school, to help us think about our identity and transformation as women. She wanted to bring her own experience as an anthropologist to help us with the fraught transitions we found ourselves in.

My mother could have said what she wanted to say just to me, but she realized that there was something powerful about doing it in a group. She was aware that the group saw one another every day in school, a context very different from the twelve pillows she set up in her basement. Over those six weeks, the twelve of us had bonded, shared secrets and insecurities, and learned breathing techniques and other physical practices that could help us stand our ground in school. At the last meeting, my mother gave each of us little multicolored spiral bracelets. I didn't think much of it at the time; we simply slipped them around our wrists.

The next morning, though, I wore my bracelet to school. As I ran into the other girls in the group, I saw that many of them were wearing theirs, too. It gave me an added confidence that I was not alone, and reminded me to practice some of the things we had learned together. That bracelet became a bridge from those special evenings into real life.

Two decades later, one of my friends from that group, Jenna Pirog, reflected on the impact the gathering had on her. While the gathering was made up of many elements, there was a component of meditation each time. For Pirog, that part stuck:

As a 35-year-old woman, I can make sense of the social dynamics that governed my Northern Virginia high school. Now, they seem tame compared to what I encountered in college or later at work.

But as a 15-year-old teenager lying on floor pillows in Deepa's basement, this was all I knew, and my young mind was awash with anxiety about where I fit in. The meditation group spanned the social spectrum of our grade. One of the girls was perhaps one of the most popular and well-liked in our school. I remember how desperately I wanted to be friends with her. Another got such good grades that I was too shy to speak to her for fear she would be bored by me. Others seemed adept at the art of flirting with boys, or knew what they wanted to be when they grew up.

But lying on the floor, then eating crackers afterwards in Deepa's kitchen, we were all the same, we were all calm, and we were all there for the same purpose: to learn how to meditate. It gave us something to talk about, something to share and something interesting that we had in common.

What happened in Circle of Friends didn't stay in Circle of Friends. Doing these strange activities together in the temporary alternative world of my mother's basement allowed for new con-nections back at school, because the two worlds were connected by a thread of reentry.

Party favors are a common, if mundane, version of the bridge, though because they have become part of "what you do," they often don't have the same effect. They represent, therefore, a ripe opportunity for rethinking and refreshing. The next time you have the chance to distribute party favors, whether for a child's birthday or something more unusual, like a work event, ask your-self: How can I use this gift to turn an impermanent moment into a permanent memory? I once had a client give me a piece of a re-cycled shipping container after a particularly intense meeting I facilitated for her in Detroit. The meeting had been about her dream of starting a hotel in a deserted part of town to attract in-vestment and reanimate the area, while highlighting the stories of the people who grew up in Detroit. The scrap sat on my desk for many years as a reminder of the hope for rebuilding a city.

AND NOW, THE END IS NEAR

So you have made your last call, and you've created a moment for a closing. You've helped your guests face inward, and you've prepared them to turn outward again. Your time together is al-most over. You're approaching the last few minutes of the gather-ing. What do you do? How do you close with a bang?

Let's talk first about what you *don't* do. I know how hard it was to quit the habit of opening with logistics, housekeeping, and thank-yous. But now the end is near, and all those thanks and logistics might be pent-up, and you might be tempted to stick them at the end instead.

Don't even think about it.

Just as you don't open a gathering with logistics, you should never end a gathering with logistics, and that includes thank-yous. I was once asked to officiate the wedding of two close friends. We were at the wedding rehearsal, standing in the living room of the bride's home with her parents, her in-laws, and her husband-to-be, running through the ceremony we designed to-gether. We came to the final few minutes, and I happened to no-tice in their notes the word "Announcement." I asked them about it. The groom said something like, "Well, after all of this, we'd love to say, Now please come join us in the hall for food!"

I was horrified.

In the groom's mind, he was ending on a tone both of gra-ciousness (we will now feed you!) and of practicality (that's where to find the food). Like openings, though, closings are a moment of power and memory formation. Ending well is a crucial way to cement the feelings and ideas you want your guests to take with them.

I tried to convince my friends that the guests would see where the food was once they exited the ceremony (it was in the next room). They saw the logic in what I said and we decided to end with a kiss, the presentation of the newlyweds to the community, and their dramatic exit to song, followed by their parents, and then the remaining guests. Years later, the husband said to me: "I now never end anything on logistics. I don't even have a 'thank you' slide in my presentations!" I was, of course, thrilled.

I am not suggesting that you cannot thank people. I simply

mean that you shouldn't thank them as the last thing you do when gathering. Here's a simple solution: do it as the second-to-last thing.

My son's music teacher, Jesse Goldman, is an aficionado of second-to-last-thing logistics. He hosts half a dozen music classes every week for toddlers. Goldman is a much-beloved teacher and singer-songwriter. His classes are forty-five minutes long, and to close them he strums the first note of the final song, his version of the last call, triggering the expectation of a closing in the kids, and then he pauses and makes announcements while still holding the note: Please turn in your check to me if you haven't already. No class next week. Someone left their jacket. He technically does these logistics between the first and second note of the final song. Once he's finished with the logistics, he resumes the good-bye song. It's subtle but quietly brilliant.

The last call, the logistics, and the dramatic close. We could all come up with our own adaptations of Goldman's habit of striking that note, then exploiting the space between that note and the second one.

And one further point: Once you figure out an appropriate place to tuck any thank-yous, try to avoid making them actual, literal thank-yous. Try honoring instead.

In far too many of our gatherings, the cue to guests that we are closing comes through people standing up and spewing a stream of thank-yous. The problem with that is that people's eyes glaze over, particularly when they follow a script. This doesn't mean that you don't publicly thank anyone at your gathering, just that you need to think about how to do so, in addition to when.

Don't use your thanking time to describe people's jobs and areas of responsibility. That is better confined to LinkedIn: "To

our production team, led by Rachel, for keeping the trains running; to Scott in AV; to Sarah for logistics." Nobody in the audience cares about the org chart of your gathering. Rather, find a
way to honor that person instead of their job description. This
will make your thank-yous meaningful—both to those thanked
and to your guests.

When I attended a gathering called Daybreaker, a morning
dance party that occurs in dozens of cities around the world, I
witnessed a fantastic thank-you toward the end of the event.
Hundreds of people meet at 6 a.m. and, completely sober, participate in a rave before going to work. Most Daybreaker gatherings
happen in secret locations, and the one I attended was in the
basement of the iconic Macy's department store in Herald Square.

After the three-hour party, complete with a visit from Santa
and Mrs. Claus, a New Orleans brass band, break-dancers, illu-
minated sweaters, and one person dressed up as a giant blue
dreidel, one of the organizers, Radha Agrawal, grabbed a microphone and asked everyone to sit down. She thanked the members
of the Macy's team by name, and made us realize what a risk
Macy's took to do something so wild: Many of the organizers
hadn't slept the night before so that they could clear the floor.
They took a huge leap of faith in admitting three hundred strangers and trusting them not to steal anything. Agrawal reminded us
that people have to take chances to do something extraordinary,
which was a lesson she wanted us to take back to our real lives.

So she made the thank-yous meaningful, honoring what was
least rather than most obvious about what people did in the
run-up to the event. And she massaged those thank-yous into a
lesson for the rest of us, so that it didn't feel like housekeeping.
She didn't let those thanks, elevated though they were, mark the

ending. Instead, she closed by handing out copies of a poem that Daybreaker events routinely end on. She understood how vital it is to end freshly and well.

MY OWN LAST CALL

We are approaching the end of this book, and I would not want to end on thank-yous after telling you not to do so. And so I'd like to pause before we end and honor the people who have helped me create *this* gathering.

Zoë Pagnamenta, my agent, who believed in me and this book from the very beginning. Jake Morrissey, my indefatigable editor, who helped me through multiple rounds of this manuscript until it settled into its skin. Jane Fransson, my chief organizer, cheerleader, and first line of defense. My writing group—Ann Burack-Weiss, Mindy Fullilove, Maura Spiegel, Jack Saul, Kelli Harding, Jim Gilbert, and Simon Fortin—for reminding me on those Friday mornings to preserve the spirit of "the mess of groups." My dear friends and family—Rukmini Giridharadas, Tom Ferguson, Mo Mullen, Kate Krontiris, and Luis Araújo—for your close reads of the manuscript. The good folks at Wet Dog Farm for helping me see what this book could be. The entire team at Riverhead—especially Katie Freeman, Jynne Dilling Martin, Lydia Hirt, and Kevin Murphy—whose enthusiasm, creativity, and championing of authors show in everything you do; I am so grateful to be in your orbit. My professional community, especially Amy Fox and Mobius Executive Leadership, for keeping me both sharp and open, and for embodying power and love. My six parents, for always cheering me on. My husband, Anand Giridharadas, for being by my side with this book from the time of the seed to the time of the harvest. I could not have done this without you. And the late Harold "Hal" Saunders, who taught me, and many others on many continents, that when you gather differently, everything can change.

RECALL YOUR PURPOSE

As you close, there may be a brief moment to hark back to the place this book began—to your purpose for gathering. There is often a subtle way to remind people of why what is now ending was initiated in the first place.

My friend Emily told me a story about a trip she made to Jamaica to volunteer for an NGO. One day she was cohosting a pool party for kids from the countryside. The end approached, and there wasn't necessarily a plan for a "closing." This concerned Emily, because not long before her trip, I had lectured her about closings. And it concerned her, moreover, because it had been a powerful day, more powerful than your usual pool party. Many of the children there had never swum before, despite being from an island nation—a legacy that dates back to colonial laws in the Caribbean forbidding slaves from swimming, out of fear that they would escape. Emily and the other volunteers and the children themselves had been visibly moved by the day, and now it was over. But there was nothing to mark the end.

There was a school bus waiting outside. Emily knew that, within minutes, the kids would have to file out for a bumpy four-hour bus ride back home. So she grabbed as many volunteers as she could and lined them up in the front hallway to wait for the kids to file through. As the first kids started to come in, the volunteers started clapping and cheering and high-fiving and hugging the kids as they walked down the hall.

"The children looked overwhelmed and bewildered, but also utterly thrilled to be celebrated like that by these people they had only just met but already formed close bonds with," Emily told me. It was a closing that embodied the gathering's purpose: communicating to a group of kids that they matter.

My father-in-law, without any pressure from me, ends a course he teaches by recalling his purpose in his own compelling way. He is a professor at the George Washington University School of Business, in Washington, D.C. At the end of every semester, he has three slides ready for the students. One is titled "Work-life balance," one is titled "Meaning," and the third has a poem he reads aloud. He begins that final class not by reviewing lessons from the course (which is on management consulting), but by warning about the seductions of the consulting field and the dangers of not pursuing meaning and balance from the beginning.

"I advise them not to wait till it becomes a crisis before committing to living a balanced life," he told me. "Recognizing that you cannot balance your life at every moment, I urge them to think of immediate priorities so that over an arc of eighteen to twenty-four months, their life seems to be balanced and under control," he said. He then performs a card trick, and at the end of the trick he says to his students that while it looks like magic, it is just technique, and that he hopes for them to master the techniques in his course until they look like magic. Then he reads a poem by the Irish poet John O'Donohue, "For a New Beginning," urging his students to "Unfurl yourself into the grace of beginning." Finally, he ends the way the class began, by asking the students to close in a minute of silence.

All this for a consulting class? I had heard from him that, year after year, the students are really moved, with the class often ending in tears. (He also regularly wins teaching awards.) I asked him why he spent his final class in this way. He said the send-off was not only to remind his students of their purpose together in the class, but to remind himself of his own purpose as a teacher as well. He teaches, he said, because he likes the idea of investing in "citizens of character that I am unleashing into the world." The content of his course is incidental to that larger purpose. And so after a semester of delving into the specifics of consulting, he wants to remind his students why he is in the classroom and why they are, too.

Those closing moments can also be a time to connect your specific gathering to the universal. When Amy Cunningham, a funeral director in New York, ends a service, she purposefully tries to connect the grief of the family with that of mourners everywhere. She told me that she often ends her service by saying, "May the source of peace grant you peace, and grant peace to all who mourn." She connects this individual suffering to the larger existence of suffering in the world, thereby making it both smaller and bigger.

THE EXIT LINE

You may remember the idea of the threshold from the chapter on openings. You draw a line and you help your guests walk over it. There is an analogous concept to employ when closing.

With your guests now leaving the world of your gathering, it is time to draw another line, the line of exit, and help them cross this, too. The last moments of a well-run gathering are, subtly or explicitly, a crossing of that line, a signal that it is over. The closing's closing, so to speak, should represent a marking and an emotional release. It can take many forms.

The exit line can be physical and symbolic. On Commencement Day, Princeton University students walk through the Fitz-Randolph Gate at the end of the ceremony, a gate they have been warned never to pass through until that day for fear of not graduating. The sustaining of that myth of not graduating, and then the crossing of the line on the appointed day, makes it clear that this day is unlike the other days, and that this time is over.

In certain parts of Colombia, villagers still bid goodbye to the year gone by making an "Año Viejo," or Old Year, a human-shaped effigy, sometimes stuffed with hay and fireworks, that represents a negative theme of the past year that they wish to burn. They dress it up, give it a funny name, and on New Year's Eve burn it. With or without their effigy, the year would end. But the exit line underlines that ending and converts it into a proper closing.

The exit line can also, or instead, be drawn through language. In my own Labs, as the very last act, I often have everyone stand in a circle. Then I mirror my opening, in which I had read aloud excerpts from what people told me in interviews or workbooks ahead of time. The grist for the closing version of this exercise is not what people sent in beforehand but rather what occurred during the Lab. All day long, I have been taking notes on what people say and jotting down specific phrases, confessions, epiphanies, jokes, and one-liners that I think capture an important moment. Then, in my closing, after all the other participants have shared, I have them stand up, look at one another, and listen. I read aloud bits and phrases that people have said over the preceding day. In hearing their own voices, presented in the order of the day's events, they are reminded of all we did together. I am also showing them how deeply they were listened to, and signaling to them that what they said was remembered. Finally, I come to my last quote. (Often it is something that was said by another participant in their closing comments just a few minutes prior to me speaking.) I close my iPad or the notebook from which I'm reading. I pause. I look up. I let the moment hang. And then I say some version of "I pronounce this Lab . . ."—then I clap: an exit line—"closed." I mark it. I end it. And they are released. And usually everyone starts clapping. It's over. (Don't worry. I don't do this at parties.)

Whatever your final moment is, it should be authentic and make sense in your context.

When Amy Cunningham first began work at a funeral home, she struggled with how to help people exit a funeral. It is a hard and awkward moment, and most people aren't sure what to do. Do you just walk away? Do you wait? Do you say a round of goodbyes, or is that better for Super Bowl parties? What order should people exit?

Cunningham derived inspiration from studying the funeral rituals of various cultures. And she ended up adopting one from the Jewish tradition. In it, the person presiding over the funeral asks everyone except for the immediate family to form two lines facing each other, making a kind of human hallway from the gravesite to the cars. Then the rabbi asks the immediate family to turn away from the grave and walk down that makeshift aisle, and as they do so, to look into the eyes of their friends, who "are now like pillars of constancy and love." Cunningham described it as "a way to usher them into the next part of their journey, and the next stage of their grieving." As the family walks by, the people at the farthest-back part of the line fold in and follow them, and then the rest, slowly, join a kind of procession out of the cemetery. It is a simple structural process that helps organize a group and facilitate a graceful exit. Yet it does so in a purposeful way that supports the people who most need it, connects them to the people still present, and gives everyone a way to move forward together.

A good and meaningful closing doesn't conform to any particular rules or form. It's something you have to build yourself, in keeping with the spirit of your gathering, in proportion to how big a deal you want to make of it. Just because it's a regular weekly sales meeting doesn't mean that a closing is too fancy or strange. A huddle and group chant of "Front line matters!" before the meeting ends might quickly but meaningfully remind people why they choose to do what they do. Just because it's a casual dinner with friends doesn't mean it shouldn't have a closing. A simple, subtle one, like a goodbye chocolate as they walk out the door, can make a difference. Even a minimalist closing can manage to acknowledge what transpired and offer a release.

There are masterful closers everywhere, finding small but powerful ways to metaphorically wrap their gatherings in a bow and thereby distinguish them. It's the yoga classes that end in a collective "Om" versus those that don't. It's teachers who end class on a story versus those who end with an assignment. It's walking your guests to the door to say goodbye versus having them let themselves out. Sometimes it can be just a pause, a moment, a tight squeeze, to acknowledge what has happened.

As with every rule, there are exceptions. I know of a wonderful gathering of friends who decided to do their partings in defiance of everything I have preached. They decided that they don't much like goodbyes. And so when they gather and the night is approaching its end, without any coordination or warning or ceremony, each person just leaves whenever he or she feels like it. It is an evening that ends with a collective ghosting. This breaks many of my minor rules, but it aces one of my transcendent principles. The friends found a way to say, "This gathering was different from all the others."

Notes

Introduction

x **"With the occasional exception"** Duncan Green, "Conference Rage: 'How Did Awful Panel Discussions Become the Default Format?'" *Guardian*, June 2, 2016, https://www.theguardian.com/global-development-professionals -network/2016/jun/02/conference-rage-how-did-awful-panel-discussions -become-the-default-format.

x **"wasteful meetings"** Harris Poll, *The State of Enterprise Work* (Lehi, UT: Workfront, 2015), accessed October 10, 2017, https://resources.workfront .com/ebooks-whitepapers/the-state-of-enterprise-work.

x **75 percent of respondents were unsatisfied** Tim Walker and Alia McKee, *The State of Friendship in America 2013: A Crisis of Confidence* (Brooklyn: LifeBoat, 2013), accessed October 10, 2017, https://static1.squarespace .com/static/5560cec6e4b0cc18bc63ed3c/t/55625cabe4b0077f89b718ec /1432509611410/lifeboat-report.pdf.

x **"As traditional religion struggles"** Angie Thurston and Casper ter Kuile, *How We Gather* (Cambridge: Crestwood Foundation, 2015), accessed May 15, 2015, https://caspertk.files.wordpress.com/2015/04/how-we-gather .pdf.

Chapter 1: Decide Why You're Really Gathering

2 **In college, we stare** Digital learning organizations such as the Khan Academy have popularized the "flipped classroom" model where students learn material from online videos and teachers become facilitators of learning rather than imparters of knowledge.

2 **not wanting any funeral** Alan D. Wolfelt, *Creating Meaningful Funeral Ceremonies* (Fort Collins, CO: Companion Press), 1. According to a 2010

survey conducted by Funeralwise.com, 31 percent of people want no funeral at all. Wolfelt runs the Center for Loss and Life Transition based in Fort Collins, Colorado. He writes extensively about the purpose of authentic funeral ceremonies. He believes we have forgotten the many purposes of a funeral and worries about a growing trend of people who want "celebrations of life" rather than "traditional" funerals. "We have confused honoring with celebration and celebration with partying. And regretfully, we've transferred this idea onto funerals," he writes.

4 **Its founders** The Justice Center was formed as a partnership between the New York State Unified Court System and the Center for Court Innovation, a nonprofit that works to reform the justice system throughout New York City and the world.

4 **"It was either prosecute or dismiss"** "Alex Calabrese, Judge, Red Hook Community Justice Center: Interview," accessed October 17, 2017, https://www.courtinnovation.org/publications/alex-calabrese-judge-red-hook-community-justice-center-0.

4 **"We give them every reasonable chance"** Jim Dwyer, "A Court Keeps People Out of Rikers While Remaining Tough," *The New York Times*, June 11, 2015, https://www.nytimes.com/2015/06/12/nyregion/a-court-keeps-people-out-of-rikers-while-remaining-tough.html?_r=0.

6 **"Obviously, this is a good result"** Alex Calabrese in *Red Hook Justice,* 5:16.

7 **According to independent evaluators** Cynthia G. Lee, Fred L. Cheesman II, David Rottman, Rachel Swaner, Suvi Hynynen Lambson, Michael Rempel, and Ric Curtis, *A Community Court Grows in Brooklyn: A Comprehensive Evaluation of the Red Hook Community Justice Center.* (Williamsburg, VA: National Center for State Courts, 2013), accessed November 15, 2017, https://www.courtinnovation.org/sites/default/files/documents/RH%20Evaluation%20Final%20Report.pdf.

7 **"I have been in the justice system"** Alex Calabrese in *Red Hook Justice,* 7:18.

10 **many no longer want** See, for example, Mitali Saran, "I Take This Man/Woman with a Pinch of Salt," *Business Standard*, December 6, 2014, http://www.business-standard.com/article/opinion/mitali-saran-i-take-this-man-woman-with-a-pinch-of-salt-114120600014_1.html; Sejal Kapadia Pocha, "From Sexist Traditions to Mammoth Costs, Why It's Time We Modernised Asian Wedding Ceremonies," Stylist.co.uk, June 23, 2015, https://www.stylist.co.uk/life/bride-groom-cost-traditions-why-it-s-time-asian-indian-weddings-changed-modernised/60667; Jui Mukherjee, "Mom and Dad, You're Not Invited to My Wedding," *India Opines,* November 13, 2014, http://indiaopines.com/sexist-indian-wedding-rituals/.

11 **First conceived in 1946** Kyle Massey, "The Old Page 1 Meeting, R.I.P.: Updating a Times Tradition for the Digital Age," *The New York Times*, May 12, 2015, https://www.nytimes.com/times-insider/2015/05/12/the-old-page-1-meeting-r-i-p-updating-a-times-tradition-for-the-digital-age/?_r=1.

12 **"only a third of our readers"** A. G. Sulzberger, *The Innovation Report* (New York: *The New York Times,* March 2014), http://www.niemanlab.org

/2014/05/the-leaked-new-york-times-innovation-report-is-one-of-the
-key-documents-of-this-media-age/.

14 **In an email to his staff** Massey, "The Old Page 1 Meeting."

Chapter 2: Close Doors

38 **"If everyone is family, no one is family"** Barack Obama, *Dreams from My
Father* (New York: Crown, 2004), 337.

46 **In 2010, what was then your standard-issue retirement community decided
to try an experiment** Heather Hansman, "College Students Are Living Rent-
Free in a Cleveland Retirement Home," Smithsonian.com, October 16, 2015,
https://www.smithsonianmag.com/innovation/college-students-are-living
-rent-free-in-cleveland-retirement-home-180956930/.

47 **The idea was rooted in studies** Hansman, "College Students."

47 **in the Netherlands to much fanfare** Carey Reed, "Dutch Nursing Home Offers Rent-Free Housing to Students," *PBS News Hour,* April 5, 2015, https://
www.pbs.org/newshour/world/dutch-retirement-home-offers-rent
-free-housing-students-one-condition.

47 **"What is the match?"** "Music Students Living at Cleveland Retirement
Home," YouTube video, 3:09, posted by "The National," November 9, 2015,
https://www.youtube.com/watch?v=hW2KNGgRNX8.

48 **"That's where life is"** "Music Students Living at Cleveland Retirement
Home," YouTube video.

48 **"It's crazy to think"** Daniel Parvin in "Music Students Living at Cleveland
Retirement Home," YouTube video.

54 **"The room is doing 80 percent of the job"** Colin Cowherd, *The Thundering
Herd with Colin Cowherd,* Podcast audio, June 4, 2015, 25:08, bit.ly/
1IgyxQf.

59 **more than $20 billion** Nikhil Deogun, Dennis K. Berman, and Kevin De-
laney, "Alcatel Nears Deal to Acquire Lucent for About $23.5 Billion in
Stock," *Wall Street Journal,* May 29, 2001, https://www.wsj.com/articles
/SB991078731679373566.

60 **"In Alcatel's failed effort"** Eric Pfanner and *International Herald Tribune,*
"Failure of Alcatel-Lucent Merger Talks Is Laid to National Sensitivity in
the U.S.: Of Pride and Prejudices," *New York Times,* May 31, 2001, http://
www.nytimes.com/2001/05/31/news/failure-of-alcatellucent-merger
-talks-is-laid-to-national-sensitivity.html.

60 **"Lucent officials are reported"** "Alcatel-Lucent Merger Is Off," *BBC News,*
May 30, 2001, http://news.bbc.co.uk/2/hi/business/1358535.stm.

61 **merger between Lucent and Alcatel** Vikas Bajaj, "Merger Deal Is Reached
with Lucent and Alcatel," *New York Times,* April 3, 2006, http://www.ny
times.com/2006/04/03/business/merger-deal-is-reached-with-lucent-and
-alcatel.html.

62 **"gazed with surprise"** Patrick Leigh Fermor, *Mani: Travels in the Southern
Peloponnese* (New York: NYRB Classics, 1958), 31.

62 **Fermor's *New York Times* obituary** Richard B. Woodward, "Patrick Leigh Fermor, Travel Writer, Dies at 96," *New York Times,* June 11, 2011, http://www.nytimes.com/2011/06/11/books/patrick-leigh-fermor-travel-writer-dies-at-96.html.

67 **occurs in a different space** "Ed Cooke—Memory Techniques for Learning," *The Conference,* August 19, 2014, http://videos.theconference.se/ed-cooke-memory-techniques-for-learning.

69 **"square feet of your party space"** Maxwell Ryan, "Party Architecture: #1—Density," *Apartment Therapy,* December 15, 2008, https://www.apartment therapy.com/party-architecture-density-how-to-plan-a-party-5359.

Chapter 3: Don't Be a Chill Host

73 **spice up the night** Werewolf, also called Mafia, is a psychological group game created by a teacher, Dmitry Davidoff, in the psychology department of Moscow State University during the Cold War that has spread across Europe and to the United States, where it has become popular at late-night technology conferences. See, for example, Margaret Robertson, "Werewolf: How a Parlour Game Became a Tech Phenomenon," *Wired UK,* February 4, 2010, http://www.wired.co.uk/article/werewolf.

73 **Alana Massey's essay "Against Chill"** Alana Massey, "Against Chill," *Medium,* April 1, 2015, https://medium.com/matter/against-chill-930dfb60a577.

82 **cut off much of his tie** Chris Anderson, *TED Talks: The Official TED Guide to Public Speaking* (New York: Houghton Mifflin Harcourt, 2016), 190.

82 **"On the corner of"** Jessica P. Ogilvie, "Amy Schumer's Irvine Set Disrupted by Lady Heckler," *Los Angeles Magazine,* October 12, 2015, http://www.lamag.com/culturefiles/amy-schumers-irvine-set-disrupted-by-lady-heckler/.

84 **"I've texted in all"** Alamo Drafthouse, "Don't Talk PSA," YouTube video, 1:46, posted June 2011, https://www.youtube.com/watch?v=1L3eeC2lJZs.

84 **"When you are in a cinema"** Tim League, "Alamo Drafthouse: Them's the Rules," CNN.com, June 10, 2011, http://www.cnn.com/2011/SHOWBIZ/Movies/06/10/alamo.drafthouse.league/index.html.

88 **"At public ceremonies"** Lucia Stanton, *Spring Dinner at Monticello, April 13, 1986, in Memory of Thomas Jefferson* (Charlottesville, VA: Thomas Jefferson Memorial Foundation), 1–9.

88 **"The ensuing social tempest"** Stanton, *Spring Dinner at Monticello.*

89 **Whether addressing students at Benedict College** "Text from President's speech, Q&A at Benedict College," WYFF4.COM, March 6, 2015, http://www.wyff4.com/article/text-from-president-s-speech-q-a-at-benedict-college/7013346.

89 **public question-and-answer** "Remarks by the President at a Town Hall on Manufacturing," Office of the Press Secretary, the White House, published October 3, 2014, https://obamawhitehouse.archives.gov/the-press-office/2014/10/03/remarks-president-town-hall-manufacturing.

89 **his own press corps** At his annual year-end conference in 2014, Obama took it even further by only answering questions from female journalists. See Kathleen Hennessey, "Obama Takes Questions Only from Women, Apparently a White House First," *Los Angeles Times,* December 19, 2014, http://beta.latimes.com/nation/politics/politicsnow/la-pn-obama-reporters-women-20141219-story.html.

91 **"There was something radically democratic"** Deborah Davis, *Party of the Century. The Fabulous Story of Truman Capote and His Black and White Ball* (New York: Wiley, 2006).

91–92 **He even had thirty-nine-cent masks** Guy Trebay, "50 Years Ago, Truman Capote Hosted the Best Party Ever," *The New York Times,* November 21, 2016, https://www.nytimes.com/2016/11/21/fashion/black-and-white-ball-anniversary-truman-capote.html.

Chapter 4: Create a Temporary Alternative World

111 **From SheKnows.com** Kat Trofimova, "Ways to Spice Up Your Next Dinner Party," SheKnows.com, December 2, 2013, http://www.sheknows.com/food-and-recipes/articles/1064647/ways-to-spice-up-a-dinner-party.

111–12 **From the online-invitation company Evite** "5 Ways to Spice Up Your Office Party," Evite.com, retrieved August 26, 2017, https://webcache.google-usercontent.com/search?q=cache:4Z5QBG-pOjcJ:https://ideas.evite.com/planning/5-ways-to-spice-up-your-office-party/+&cd=1&hl=en&ct=clnk&gl=us&client=safari.

112 **From Wisdump** Sophia Lucero, "Holding a Conference? Spice It Up with These Geeky Ideas," Wisdump.com, January 21, 2011, https://www.wisdump.com/web-experience/geeky-conference-ideas/.

112 **From the Catholic Youth Ministry Hub** Eric Gallagher, "Twelve Ways to Spice Up Your Next Youth Group Breakfast," *Catholic Youth Ministry Hub,* March 23, 2011, https://cymhub.com/twelve-ways-to-spice-up-your-next-youth-group-breakfast/.

113 **so-called Jeffersonian Dinner** "How to Plan a Jeffersonian Dinner," The Generosity Network, accessed August 25, 2017, http://www.thegenerositynetwork.com/resources/jeffersonian-dinners.

115 **"a three year curriculum"** "Junior Cotillion: 5th–8th Grade," National League of Junior Cotillions, accessed August 30, 2017, http://nljc.com/programs/junior-cotillion-5th-8th-grade/.

118 **"You have acquired knowledge"** Philip Dormer Stanhope, *Letters to His Son on the Fine Art of Becoming a Man of the World and a Gentleman* (Toronto: M. W. Dunne, 1901), 302.

119 **"We truly believe manners"** "History," National League of Junior Cotillions, accessed August 30, 2017, http://nljc.com/about/history/.

120 **"among the most successful"** "History," National League of Junior Cotillions.

123 **flash mob of a dinner party** Technically, it's been pointed out to me that Dîner en Blanc is not a traditional "flash mob" per se, as every organizer is required to obtain local permits.

123 **women sit on one side** This rule has been a hotly contested one, and in Tokyo, they chose not to observe it. "In Tokyo, for example, where the pair is of the same sex (not necessarily because they are gay or lesbian but simply because they are more comfortable attending parties with friends of the same sex), this rule is not observed," Kumi Ishihara, the organizer and licensee of Dîner en Blanc Tokyo, told me.

124 **"Over the past three and a half years"** Dîner en Blanc, "Dîner en Blanc 2015 Official Video," YouTube video, posted on October 15, 2015, https://www .youtube.com/watch?v=x4Er5bWJeY8.

126 **male side and a female side** This gendered rule is one of the organizers' more controversial rules. Ishihara and the Japanese organizers, for cultural reasons, received permission not to follow this rule, and guests could bring a guest of either gender along with them.

128 **Singaporean food was "formal" enough** Walter Lim, "The Dîner en Blanc Debacle," *Cooler Insights*, August 25, 2012, http://coolerinsights.com /2012/08/the-diner-en-blanc-debacle/.

128 **"ancient colonial master mindset"** Rendall, August 25, 2012, comment on "SINGAPORE TAU HUAY TOO LOW CLASS FOR FRENCH UPSCALE EVENT DINER EN BLANC?!" *Moonberry Blog*, August 24, 2012, http: // blog.moonberry.com/singapore-tau-huay-too-low-class-for-french -upscale-event/.

128 **"Um, so if I'm part of a same-sex couple"** Allison Baker, "Why I'm Not Going to Dîner en Blanc," *Nuts to Soup* (blog), July 28, 2012, https://nutsto soup.wordpress.com/2012/07/28/why-im-not-going-to-diner-en-blanc/.

128 **"No event has ever"** Maura Judkis, "Why Do People Hate Dîner en Blanc? The Word 'Pretentious' Keeps Coming Up," *The Washington Post*, August 26, 2016, https://www.washingtonpost.com/lifestyle/food/why-do-people -hate-diner-en-blanc-the-word-pretentious-keeps-coming-up/2016/08/24 /3639f2c6-6629-11e6-be4e-23fc4d4d12b4_story.html?utm_term= .458b82f6d226.

128 **"This whole thing makes me feel"** Kevin Allman, "Le Dîner en Blanc: *The Great Doucheby*," *Gambit*, April 4, 2013, https://www.bestofneworleans .com/blogofneworleans/archives/2013/04/04/le-diner-en-blanc-the -great-doucheby.

128 **"snobbish"** Sabrina Maddeaux, "Toronto's Most Stupidly Snobbish Food-Meets-Fashion Event Returns," *Now Toronto*, August 5, 2015, https://now toronto.com/lifestyle/t/.

129 **"ad hoc, barely-even-organized, family-friendly"** Alexandra Gill, "Dîner en Blanc Is Overrated. Try Ce Soir Noir, Vancouver's Playful Alternative," *Globe and Mail*, August 26, 2016, https://www.theglobeandmail.com /news/british-columbia/ce-soir-noir-vancouvers-playful-subsitute-for -diner-en-blanc/article31585611/.

129 **"The beautiful thing about this event"** Jennifer Picht, "This Is What Happens When You Go to Dîner en Blanc in NYC," *Time Out,* September 16, 2016, https://www.timeout.com/newyork/blog/this-is-what-happens-when -you-go-to-diner-en-blanc-in-nyc-091616.

129 **"We may have been all dressed in white"** Shane Harris, "D.C.'s Snobbery-Free 'Diner en Blanc' Showed Washington at Its Partying Best," *Daily Beast,* August 31, 2015, https://www.thedailybeast.com/dcs-snobbery-free-diner en blanc-showed-washington-at-its-partying-best.

132 **average of 150 times a day** "2017 Global Mobile Consumer Survey: US Edition," Deloitte Development LLC. https://www2.deloitte.com/content/dam /Deloitte/us/Documents/technology-media-telecommunications/us -tmt-2017-global-mobile-consumer-survey-executive-summary.pdf.

132 **"Never before in history"** Bianca Bosker, "The Binge Breaker," *Atlantic,* November 2016, https://www.theatlantic.com/magazine/archive/2016/11/the -binge-breaker/501122/?utm_source=atltw.

142 **Law of Two Feet** "A Brief User's Guide to Open Space Technology," Open Space World, accessed November 30, 2017, http://www.openspaceworld .com/users_guide.htm.

142 **"merely to eliminate all the guilt"** "Opening Space for Emerging Order," Open Space World, accessed November 30, 2017, http://www.openspace world.com/brief_history.htm.

Chapter 5: Never Start a Funeral with Logistics

146 **"Party-Planning Guide"** "Party-Planning Guide," Martha Stewart.com, accessed August 30, 2017, https://www.marthastewart.com/275412/party -planning-guide.

147 **She breaks creating a gathering** Rashelle Isip, "The 10 Lists You Need to Make to Plan a Great Party or Event," Lifehack, accessed August 30, 2017, http://www.lifehack.org/articles/lifestyle/the-10-lists-you-need-make -plan-great-party-event.html.

147 **"It was blissful torture"** David Colman, "Mystery Worker," *New York Times,* April 29, 2011, http://www.nytimes.com/2011/05/01/fashion/01 POSSESSED.html.

160 **"parking for your Landspeeder"** Brooks Barnes, "'*Star Wars: The Force Awakens'* Has World Premiere, No Expense Spared," *New York Times,* December 15, 2015, https://www.nytimes.com/2015/12/16/business/media/star -wars-the-force-awakens-premiere.html?_r=0.

162 **"All of us have anti-bucket lists"** Sarah Lyall, "Starring Me! A Surreal Dive into Immersive Theater," *New York Times,* January 7, 2016, https://www .nytimes.com/2016/01/08/theater/starring-me-a-surreal-dive-into-immersive -theater.html.

165 **"the artist's medium is the body"** "Conceptual Art," *MoMA Learning,* accessed September 12, 2017, https://www.moma.org/learn/moma_learning /themes/conceptual-art/performance-into-art.

166 **"hypnotic wonderment"** Jacob Slattery, "Hypnotic Wonderment: Marina Abramović and Igor Levit's *Goldberg Variations* at Park Avenue Armory," *Bachtrack,* December 10, 2015, https://bachtrack.com/review-goldberg -variations-abramovic-levit-park-avenue-armory-new-york-december-2015.

173 **Studies show that audiences disproportionately remember** Neal Hartmann, "Community Strategy and Structure; Persuasion and Ethics," MIT Sloan School of Management, September 10, 2013. See also Daniel Kahneman studies.

175 **"we want to take you into a future"** Micah Sifry, "[#PDF15 Theme] Imagine All the People: The Future of Civic Tech," *techPresident,* March 17, 2015, http://techpresident.com/news/25488/pdf15-theme-imagine-all-people -future-civic-tech.

182 **Tough Mudder Pledge** "Tough Mudder Facts & Trivia," Tough Mudder, accessed November 27, 2017, https://mudder-guide.com/guide/tough -mudder-facts-and-trivia/#pledge.

182 **"Tough Mudder was built"** Dan Schawbel, "Will Dean: How to Build a Tribe Around Your Business," Forbes.com, September 12, 2017, https:// www.forbes.com/sites/danschawbel/2017/09/12/will-dean-how-to-build-a -tribe-around-your-business/#1e9757224005.

184 **"People get up on the box"** Chris Gardner, "'I Love Dick' Cast Inherits 'Transparent's' Emotional Exercise," *Hollywood Reporter,* May 4, 2017, https://www.hollywoodreporter.com/rambling-reporter/i-love-dick-cast -inherits-transparents-emotional-exercise-997344.

184 **"Things get purged"** Gardner, "'I Love Dick' Cast."

184 **"This woman got up there"** Gardner, "'I Love Dick' Cast."

184 **"cry when they leave our set"** Kelly Schremph, "The Unexpected Way 'Transparent' and Jill Soloway Are Changing How Great TV Is Made," Bustle.com, September 23, 2016, https://www.bustle.com/articles/184353 -the-unexpected-way-transparent-jill-soloway-are-changing-how-great -tv-is-made.

185 **"It turns into this collective moment"** Schremph, "The Unexpected Way."

185 **"We get to play"** Jason McBride, "Jill Soloway's New Family," Vulture.com, July 25, 2016, http://www.vulture.com/2016/07/jill-soloway-i-love-dick-c-v-r .html.

187 **fell by 35 percent** "Atul Guwande's 'Checklist' for Surgery Success," Steve Inskeep, *Morning Edition,* National Public Radio, accessed November 2017 https://www.npr.org/templates/story/story.php?storyId=122226184.

187 **"conferences can be re-imagined"** "How Spark Camp Came About," Spark Camp, accessed August 30, 2017, http://sparkcamp.com/about/.

Chapter 6: Keep Your Best Self Out of My Gathering

194 **"provide innovative thinking"** "1,500 World Leaders, Pioneers and Experts Volunteer to Tackle Global Challenges," World Economic Forum,

accessed September 25, 2017, https://www.weforum.org/press/2014/09/1500
-world-leaders-pioneers-and-experts-volunteer-to-tackle-global
-challenges/.

195 **"profound shift in the context"** Lynda Gratton, "Global Agenda Council on
New Models of Leadership," World Economic Forum, 2012, http://reports
.weforum.org/global-agenda-council-on-new-models-of-leadership/.

207 **Scholars like Brené Brown** Brené Brown, *Daring Greatly: How the Courage
to Be Vulnerable Transforms the Way We Live, Love, Parent, and Lead*
(New York: Gotham Books, 2012), 2.

208 **Crucible moments** Bill George, "Coping with Crucibles," *Huffington Post*,
September 1, 2015, https://www.huffingtonpost.com/bill-george/coping
-with-crucibles_b_8071678.html.

216 **He issued a public invitation** "Party Puts Conversation on the Menu,"
BBC, August 22, 2009, http://news.bbc.co.uk/2/hi/uk_news/england/lon
don/8215738.stm.

Chapter 7: Cause Good Controversy

226 **"doing or saying anything offensive"** James Anderson and Benjamin Frank-
lin, "The Constitutions of the Free-Masons (1734): An Online Electronic
Edition," edited by Paul Royster, Faculty Publications, University of
Nebraska—Lincoln Libraries, 25, http://digitalcommons.unl.edu/cgi/view
content.cgi?article=1028&context=libraryscience.

226 **"Do not discuss politics"** Thomas Edie Hill, *Hill's Manual of Social and
Business Forms: A Guide to Correct Writing,* (Chicago: Standard Book Co.,
1883), 153.

226–27 **"Talk about things"** Emily Post, *Etiquette: In Society, in Business, in
Politics and at Home* (New York: Funk & Wagnalls Company, 1922), 55.

227 **"The goal of etiquette"** Anne Brown, August 11, 2015, answer on the question, "Why is it considered rude to discuss sex, politics, and religion?,"
Quora, https://www.quora.com/Why-is-it-considered-rude-to-discuss-sex
-politics-and-religion?share=1.

227 **commencement speech at Rutgers University** Kelly Heyboer, "Condoleezza
Rice Pulls Out of Giving Rutgers Commencement Speech," NJ.com, May 3,
2014, http://www.nj.com/education/2014/05/condoleezza_rice_pulls_out_of
_giving_rutgers_commencement_speech.html.

227 **address to Smith College** Alexandra Sifferlin, "IMF Chief Withdraws as
Commencement Speaker," Time.com, May 12, 2014, http://time.com
/96501/imf-chief-withdraws-as-smith-college-commencement-speaker/.

227 **"run to, and not away from, the noise"** White House Remarks by the First
Lady at Oberlin College Commencement Address, 2015, accessed November 30, 2017, available at https://obamawhitehouse.archives.gov/the-press-
office/2015/05/25/remarks-first-lady-oberlin-college-commencement
-address.

227–28 **noise that was generated at Middlebury College** Peter Beinart, "A Violent Attack on Free Speech at Middlebury," *Atlantic,* March 6, 2017, https://www.theatlantic.com/politics/archive/2017/03/middlebury-free-speech-violence/518667/.

234 **"Watch industry leaders duke it out"** "You're Invited to DOSOMETHING .ORG's 2016 Annual Meeting," www.dosomething.org, accessed September 20, 2017, https://dsannualmeeting2016.splashthat.com.

235 **beat one another up** Thomas Morton, "Takanakuy," *Vice,* March 12, 2012, https://www.vice.com/sv/article/avnexa/takanakuy-part-1.

235 **"'sort it out there'"** Ben C. Solomon, "Musangwe Fight Club: A Vicious Venda Tradition," *The New York Times,* February 26, 2016, https://www.nytimes.com/2016/02/27/sports/musangwe-fight-club-a-vicious-venda-tradition.html.

Chapter 8: Accept That There Is an End

248 **experience, sense of meaning, and memory** The behavioral psychologist Daniel Kahneman writes and speaks extensively about what he calls our "remembering self" and our "experiencing self," and how they differ. In his 2010 TED Talk, he describes the difference between two patients who undergo a colonoscopy treatment, and how the patient with the longer treatment (and therefore who experiences a longer period of pain) reports a better experience than Patient A (with the shorter treatment) because he experienced a better ending. "What defines a story are changes, significant moments, and endings. Endings are very, very important," he says. See https://www.ted.com/talks/daniel_kahneman_the_riddle_of_experience_vs_memory?language=de#t-383109. See also his original study on this work: Daniel Kahneman, Barbara L. Fredrickson, Charles A. Schreiber, and Donald A. Redelmeier, "When More Pain Is Preferred to Less: Adding a Better End," *Psychological Science* 4, no. 6 (November 1993): 401–5.

252 **"traditional funeral"** "New Funeralwise.com Survey Shows Contrasting Funeral Choices," Funeralwise, December 8, 2010, https://www.funeralwise.com/about/press-releases/funeral-choices-survey/.

257 **"If you let it peter out, it's death"** Courtney Rubin, "Queen Elizabeth's Party Planner Is Proud to Wear $35 Shoes," *The New York Times,* April 23, 2016, https://www.nytimes.com/2016/04/24/style/queen-party-planner-lady-elizabeth-anson.html.

262 **supposed to distrust, even hate** Seeds of Peace, like many programs, has evolved over time to also include teenagers from the United States and the United Kingdom. It also runs a two-and-a-half week summer program for teenagers from the United States alone, as well as educators from the communities of campers to engage in adult dialogue. For more information, see https://www.seedsofpeace.org.

Index